BECOMING DELINQUENT:
BRITISH AND EUROPEAN YOUTH, 1650-

Advances In Criminology
Series Editor: David Nelken

Titles in the Series

Governable Places
Readings on governmentality and crime control
Edited by Russell Smandych

Engendering Resistance: Agency and Power in Women's Prisons
Mary Bosworth

Blood in the Bank
Social and legal aspects of death at work
Gary Slapper

Integrating a Victim Perspective within Criminal Justice
International debates
Edited by Adam Crawford and Jo Goodey

Contrasting Criminal Justice
Getting from here to there
Edited by David Nelken

Critique and Radical Discourses on Crime
George Pavlich

Migration Culture, Conflict and Crime
Edited by Joshua D. Freilich, Graeme Newman, S. Giora Shoham and Moshe Addad

Items
Stories of product counterfeiting
Jon Vagg and Justine Harris

Informal Criminal Justice
Edited by Dermot Feenan

In Search of Transnational Policing
James Sheptycki

Becoming Delinquent: British and European Youth, 1650-1950

Edited by
PAMELA COX
Department of Sociology, University of Essex

HEATHER SHORE
School of Social and Historical Studies, University of Portsmouth

Routledge
Taylor & Francis Group

LONDON AND NEW YORK

First published 2002 by Ashgate Publishing

Reissued 2018 by Routledge
2 Park Square, Milton Park, Abingdon, Oxon OX14 4RN
711 Third Avenue, New York, NY 10017, USA

Routledge is an imprint of the Taylor & Francis Group, an informa business

Publisher's Note
The publisher has gone to great lengths to ensure the quality of this reprint but
points out that some imperfections in the original copies may be apparent.

Disclaimer
The publisher has made every effort to trace copyright holders and welcomes
correspondence from those they have been unable to contact.

A Library of Congress record exists under LC control number: 2001099637

ISBN 13: 978-1-138-74045-7 (hbk)
ISBN 13: 978-1-138-74042-6 (pbk)
ISBN 13: 978-1-315-18349-7 (ebk)

Contents

Acknowledgements

We would like to thank all those who took part in the international conference, 'Becoming Delinquent: European Youth, 1650-1950' held at the University of Cambridge in 1999. The stimulating debates initiated and invaluable networks forged there made this collaborative book possible.

Particular thanks to Andrew Davies, Peter King and Deborah Thom for their help in organising that event and for sharing their ideas on delinquency with us over the years. Thanks, too, to all the contributors for their patience and co-operation. Finally, huge thanks to Bill Hayton for helping two hard-pressed academics to transform the manuscript into camera-ready copy.

Pamela Cox and Heather Shore

Contributors

Astri Andresen is associate professor at the Department of History, University of Bergen, Norway. She has published on urban history, social history, Saami history and Norwegian-Russian relations. Her current research and teaching focuses on the history of childhood, delinquency and welfare in the nineteenth and twentieth centuries.

Jenneke Christiaens is a lecturer in criminology at the Vrije Universiteit in Brussels, Belgium. She teaches research methodologies and researches across the history of social and penal policy, the history of crime and punishment, and criminology. She is the author of *De geboorte van de jeugddelinquent, Belgie 1830-1930* [The birth of the juvenile delinquent Belgium 1830-1930] (VUB Press, 1999).

Pamela Cox is a lecturer in the Department of Sociology at the University of Essex, England where she teaches the history of criminal justice and public policy. She is the author of *Bad Girls: Gender, Justice and Welfare in Britain, 1900-1950* (Palgrave, forthcoming) and one of the co-authors of *Crime in Modern Britain* (Oxford University Press, 2002) and *The Criminological Imagination* (Routledge, forthcoming).

Sarah Fishman is an associate professor of history at the University of Houston in Texas, USA. Her research focuses on the social impact of World War II in France, and her publications on this area include, *We Will Wait: Wives of French Prisoners of War 1940-1945* (Yale, 1992), *France at War: Vichy and the Historians* (co-edited, Berg, 2000) and *The Battle for Children: World War II, Youth Crime and Juvenile Justice in Twentieth-Century France* (forthcoming). She teaches European history and modern French history.

Paul Griffiths teaches early modern English social and cultural history at Iowa State University. He is the author of *Youth and Authority: Formative Experiences in England, 1560-1640* (Oxford, 1996), and editor (with Adam Fox and Steve Hindle) of *The Experience of Authority in Early Modern England* (Basingstoke, 1996), and (with Mark Jenner), *Londinopolis: Essays in the Cultural and Social History of Early Modern London* (Manchester University Press, 2001). He is currently completing a book on crime and policing in London c.1545-1660.

Chris Leonards is assistant professor of history at the Universiteit Maastricht in the Netherlands. He is currently researching Congress Culture in Europe, 1800-2000. His publications on delinquency include, *De ontdekking van het onschuldige criminele kind; bestraffing en opvoeding van criminele kinderen in jeugdgevangenis en opvoedingsgesticht, 1833-1886* [The Discovery of the Innocent Criminal Child; Punishment and Education of Criminal Children in Youth Prison and Reformatory, 1833-1886] (Verloren, 1995).

Cat Nilan is now an independent scholar living and working in Seattle, Washington. Her ongoing projects include designing and developing a website dedicated to English translations of nineteenth-century French poetry and preparing her manuscript, *Precocious Perversity: Childhood, Crime, and the Prison in July Monarchy France*, for eventual publication.

Benjamin Roberts teaches the history of education at the Free University of Amsterdam in the Netherlands. He recently published *Through the keyhole. Dutch child-rearing practices in the seventeenth and eighteenth century* (Verloren, 1998), and is currently writing a book about Dutch youth culture in the seventeenth century.

Heather Shore is a lecturer in social and cultural history at the University of Portsmouth and former research fellow at the University of Cambridge, England. Her publications include *Artful Dodgers: Youth and Crime in Early Nineteenth Century England* (Boydell, 1999), *The Streets of London* (edited with Tim Hitchcock, Rivers Oram, 2002) and several other chapters and articles on crime, delinquency and London life. She is currently completing a new book, *London Underworlds: Crime, Criminal Networks and Law Enforcement, 1725-1968* (London Books, forthcoming).

Valentina K. Tikoff is assistant professor of history at DePaul University in Chicago, USA where she teaches European history. Her research focuses on the history of the family and charity. She is currently completing a book about young people in the orphanages of Seville between the late seventeenth and early nineteenth centuries.

Series Editor's Preface

It is a pleasure to present this exceptionally interesting and well organised collection of essays on modernity and the making of juvenile delinquency. This contribution to the *Advances in Criminology* series amply fulfils its declared promise to show how the study of crime and crime control can benefit from a critical dialogue between history and criminology. We are shown the series of practices and interventions which helped to define the category of youth crime as it emerged from early modernity and special emphasis is given to exploring the tension of showing continuity in the handling of disorderly youth whilst avoiding teleological assumptions about an inevitable progress towards our current ideas about delinquency. Careful attention is dedicated to the problem of explaining change against a background of wider socio-economic political and cultural developments. The editors argue that delinquency should not be viewed as the history of an autonomous individual but as the history of a series of relational categories. The history of 'delinquency', they rightly suggest, cannot be separated out from the history of families, institutions and legal processes, nor from the history of youth culture, consumption, and gender. But they also recognise the relative autonomy of specialised knowledge, classificatory categories and social narratives about youth and crime, and consider the extent to which the 'causes' of social change work through their capacity to be transformed into narratives.

In addition to their relevance to and for historical debates the wide ranging chapters in this volume reveal similarities and differences in the emergence of modern ways of dealing with delinquency in England and Wales, Holland, Spain, France Belgium, and Norway. These clearly demonstrate the importance of comparative work in this and other fields of criminal justice. The authors rightly balance respect for the specificities of given national political and legal cultures with a recognition of the importance of those factors which can and must be identified at a level that is both wider and more local than nation states.

Much of what we learn about past ways of constructing the problem of delinquency shows a strong resemblance with the present. The range of those involved are more or less the same: the family, local government, the church, philanthropists and the voluntary sector, judicial and welfare institutions. Modern dilemmas, whether and when to separate the deprived from the depraved, or how to ensure that institutional care serves as a refuge and not a source of harm, come with a long history. Likewise, ambivalent attitudes to childhood, concerns about leisure, the dangers of consumption and urban pleasures, and the way 'respectable fears' about delinquency are linked to broader generalised fears about social crisis, social breakdown or social collapse. Other matters, especially those from less recent periods, are less familiar: for example the use of institutions by well off families as a form of social control of their children or the extreme differences in gender expectations. Some of what was taken as 'knowledge' of delinquency is no longer current, though there is little new about the way different (scientific and moral) explanatory discourses can clash. But what the contributors to this volume call modernity is itself no more than a stage. Remarkably, (and worryingly?) some of the developments in crime control associated with the period of 'high modernity', at least in English speaking societies, seem to have more in common with the early modern period: responsibility for youthful misbehaviour is being moved back from welfare professionals to parents and the community, the age of adult responsibility begins to be lowered again and - in the USA - serious consideration is being given to abolishing the juvenile court.

DAVID NELKEN
Series Editor

Introduction

Re-inventing the Juvenile Delinquent in Britain and Europe 1650-1950

Heather Shore (with Pamela Cox)

Forasmuch as the Lord's day is very much pphaned [profaned] by a disorderly sort of idle children in unlawfull Exercises and pastimes in the greate church yarde, and the streets, and divers other places within this citty, It is therefore ordained and established by the Assemble, that the Parents of such children doe for the tyme to come take care that their sayd children doe not offend herin, upon paine of Two Shillings for evry tyme that they shall neglect the same...
(Winchester, 1656)

[Wilhelm P.]...belongs to the club 'The Wild Boys' where he sees and hears nothing but bad things; what goes on in the club is nothing but thefts and pranks...The club consists of groups of youths which have been forming recently in all the districts; they adorn themselves with coloured school caps and with trousers and waistcoats covered with pearl buttons.
(Hamburg Juvenile Court Assistance Report, 1928)[1]

European youth have been 'becoming delinquent' throughout the three centuries dividing these two comments. What forms did this process take? What responses did it draw, and how far was it constituted by these responses? How did all these things vary between and within states and across different periods of time? This collection aims to address these questions and to begin to synthesise and evaluate the growing body of work on the history of juvenile delinquency in Britain and Europe. The expansion of criminology as a discipline has been accompanied by an expansion in studies of youth crime and child welfare. These studies are often comparative, but they are very rarely historical. If they do address historical developments, they tend to do so via a short survey of key developments within twentieth century (and often post-second world war) statutory infrastructures set up to deal with delinquency (such as juvenile-specific legislation, institutions and protection mechanisms). Considerations of longer historical processes are very rare. This collection aims to redress this by analysing definitions of, and responses to, disorderly European youth across time (from the mid-seventeenth to the mid-twentieth centuries) *and* across space (covering developments across Western Europe). This comparative approach fruitfully challenges conventional criminological chronologies by showing how certain themes have dominated European discourses of delinquency across this period, not least panics about urban culture, poor parenting, dangerous pleasures, family breakdown, national fitness and future social stability. It also shows how these various threats have been countered by recurring strategies, most notably by repeated attempts to deter delinquency, repeated attempts to divide responsibility between the state, civil society and the family, and finally repeated attempts to find a 'proper' balance between moral reform and physical punishment, between care and control. To this end, the chapters in this collection explore a number of key issues: attitudes to delinquent youth from the mid-seventeenth to the mid-twentieth centuries; the development of juvenile justice practices over time; the inter-relation of punishment, reformation and welfare; delinquency and constructions of national and ethnic identity; violent children; vulnerable children; war; youth subcultures; absent fathers; single mothers; and resistance.

The period covered by these chapters was shaped by a number of key social, economic, demographic, political and cultural processes: industrialisation, urbanisation, population growth, nation-state formation and consolidation, revolution and war. Whilst it is certainly not easy to generalise about these processes (indeed many historians have pointed to the difficulties of doing so), they are not easily ignored in a collection of this kind. Attitudes to children and youth were shaped by, and themselves helped to shape, these processes in a number of ways. How should family life be organised? How and where should children work? Where and how should they spend their leisure? Which children should inherit property? Where should they live, if not with their families? When and with whom should they be allowed to begin sexual relationships? What kind of values, skills and morals should they be taught? How, why and when should they be chastised, disciplined and punished? What kind of threats, hopes and fears did they seem to embody? What kinds of mothers, fathers and workers would they make? What kind of future nation, race or citizenry would they go on to create? All these questions and more were debated across Europe in the period considered in these chapters: they were certainly not simply 'modern' questions in the conventional sense. Moreover, they were debated across the social spectrum, from ordinary families to statutory legislatures. As the chapters here show, efforts to stop children becoming delinquent were clearly made by a whole range of agents in the name of a whole range of causes.

This collection does not set out to argue that there was a uniquely European construction or response to juvenile delinquency. To do so would be to ignore vital differences within and between the six states featured here: Belgium, Britain, France, the Netherlands, Norway and Spain; and to overlook vital developments in other parts of the world, not least southern, central and eastern Europe, North America and European colonial societies.[2] However, the collection does seek to show that there were many important parallels in different European communities' attempts to frame and to solve the question of delinquency. Each of the examples studied here can be read as evidence of similar concerns and processes which might be broadly summarised as follows: a gradual centralisation of local judicial and welfare procedures; a gradual separation of children and young people from adults within emerging judicial and welfare systems; an overwhelming concern to publicly (rather than privately) police boys and young men rather than girls and young women; a drawing of distinctions between the reform of boys and girls, between older and younger children, between innocent and depraved children, and often between children of different religious faiths; a belief in the desirability of removing vulnerable children from bad families and a continual search for a workable and often institutional substitute for those families; a need to combine private (notably familial and philanthropic) ways of dealing with delinquency with public (notably statutory educational, medical and penal) ways of so doing; a tendency to explain delinquency in terms of a familiar and contradictory cluster of causes, notably dangerous urban pleasures, poverty, precocity, bad parenting and more general breakdowns in traditions of authority.

Such comparative historical claims have been rightly complicated by recent critiques of the use of the nation-state as a unit of comparison and by a questioning of the notion of grand social processes (such as industrialisation, urbanisation, judicial formation and so on) and, by extension, of the salience of the grand narratives that help to sustain them.[3] It is certainly true that this collection, like other comparative projects, runs the risk of emphasising similarities over differences, of placing very varied practices in an overly artificial framework. However, it has been compiled in the belief that the benefits of a trans-European approach make these risks worth taking. Reading these varied chapters as a single body of work suggests a number of fruitful approaches to the history of crime and to the history of youth. It suggests that tentative conclusions, as outlined above, can be drawn as to the kinds of social concerns and social processes that shaped trans-European approaches to delinquency; that assumptions about the timing and characteristics of 'modernity' should be much more rigorously investigated; that histories of crime can usefully combine the cultural, representational and sensational with the penal, legal and institutional.

In a modest but important way, the collection also suggests some new ways of doing critical comparative history. In stressing the benefits of an analysis of delinquency that moves beyond the historically and nationally specific to consider developments across time and space, it allows a new look at the old idea of the *long durée*. The patterns of similar concerns and processes explored here clearly cannot be explained in terms of an older grand narrative of economic change and capital (re)formation. Yet they might be explained in terms of a broader raft of powerful and enduring narratives, in which the economic is located alongside the familial, the life cyclical, the religious, the moral, the shameful, the patriarchal, the scientific and so on. The fact, that, for example, the leisure pursuits of youths in the early modern Dutch Republic, nineteenth century France and mid-twentieth century Britain could generate very similar outrage; that the search for institutional solutions to delinquency should prove so enduring; that 1950s anxieties around the sexual propriety of girls was expressed in ways that echoed those of the 1750s or even the 1550s, should convince us of the value of a long comparative analysis and of the need to revitalise, but not simply to return to, old languages of hegemony, structure and tradition.

New Directions

The collection aims to contribute to a growing body of valuable comparative work on the history of European delinquency[4] and to make connections with work on the history of European childhood and youth[5], crime[6] and welfare.[7] It sets out to begin to blur boundaries that seem to have become overly fixed in much writing on disorderly youth, juvenile delinquents and children in need.[8] These boundaries are marked by binaries between, for example, delinquency and youth culture; the state and charities; experts and amateurs; science and religion; punishment and welfare; the modern and the early modern. This collection begins to ask what happens if these boundaries are shown to be more fluid. Taken individually, each chapter seeks to take the study of delinquency in a new direction. Obviously, readers will respond to particular chapters in their own ways, but may find it helpful to consider the treatment of six themes across the collection: youth culture and consumption, gender, knowledges, violence, crises and voices.

The study of delinquency is not easily separated from the study of youth cultures. Many writers have, of course, examined the connections between the two, but most of them have treated youth culture as a modern phenomenon.[9] In this collection, Paul Griffiths, Valentina Tikoff and Benjamin Roberts examine elements of early modern male youth cultures in Britain, Spain and the Netherlands respectively. Roberts, in particular, shows how early modern concerns about (male) delinquency were linked to concerns about consumption and the perceived dangers of commercial urban pleasures.

Studies of delinquency have also, in recent years, paid much attention to gender. In this collection, chapters by Astri Andresen and Pamela Cox on early twentieth century Norway and Britain respectively represent what might be seen as two key strands in this kind of work. Andresen shows how girls and boys were treated in very distinct ways in the Norwegian after-care system, while Cox shows how divisions were drawn *between* wayward girls by examining the question of delinquency and difference through the inter-relation of ideas of gender and ideas of race. Both approaches are valuable as, together, they show firstly, how definitions of, and responses to, delinquency were clearly gendered and, in the case of girls, sexualised; but, secondly, how gender differences were always constituted through other observed differences. Other chapters also offer crucial new insights into young masculinities. Tikoff, in particular, shows how the sexual behaviour of young Spanish men was policed and punished, while Roberts reveals the lengths to which Dutch parents went to stop their sons from becoming delinquent and shaming their family.[10]

The history of delinquency is, to a large degree, a history of competing knowledges of delinquency. Chris Leonards shows how these knowledges were firmly internationalised in the nineteenth century through a series of European penal congresses. Yet he also details recurring contests between different kinds of experts, notably between philanthropists and state employees. Similarly, Cat Nilan shows how scientific, moralistic and romantic discourses clashed in their efforts to explain violent children in post-Revolutionary France.

Child violence has received much academic and media attention in recent years, not least because of a number of highly publicised killings of children by other children.[11] Again, though, the longer history of this phenomenon has tended to be overlooked. Nilan examines the cases of a number of French juveniles who killed, or tried to seriously harm, other children in the early nineteenth century. She shows that, although rare, these cases forced a searching debate about the very nature of society just as they have done in Europe since the 1990s.[12]

Nilan's work points to a very clear link between delinquency and crisis. Indeed, it could be argued that, to quote Pearson's classic study, 'respectable fears' about delinquency are very often linked to broader generalised fears about social crisis, social breakdown or social collapse.[13] However, this view can lead to a conflation of what are actually very different kinds of crises. As Sarah Fishman shows, the second world war constituted a European crisis of major and immediate proportions which shaped discourses of delinquency in very particular ways. Focusing on Vichy France, she shows how the war-related absence of fathers took on a new significance.

Finally, the collection seeks to explore something of what it actually meant to be a juvenile delinquent or a child in trouble. While it is, of course, crucial to acknowledge the difficulties of using what feminist historian Joan Scott has called 'the evidence of experience', it is surely also crucial to seek out that evidence wherever possible.[14] The voices of delinquents (as well as their families and those involved in policing, punishing and protecting them) offer particular perspectives within the history of delinquency, not least because they are generally unpublished and tell stories that can very easily slip from the academic record. Obviously they are constructed voices but arguably all the more significant for that because they can help to show how discourses of delinquency were produced, internalised and resisted. In this collection, Jenneke Christiaens' work stands out in this respect. Using unpublished disciplinary records, she explores the complex relationships between boys and their gaolers in a Belgian boys' prison at the turn of the twentieth century.[15]

However, arguably all nine chapters employ a broadly similar method. They are all based on close readings of often very fragmentary textual sources identified through protracted and detailed archival work: in this sense they could be said to epitomise historians' very particular contribution to the study of crime and control. The narratives of delinquency found in court depositions, case files, probation reports, magistrates' minutes, institutional records, commission evidence, conference proceedings, newspapers, specialist journals, personal letters and so on play a vital part in aiding the understanding of the many processes by which European youth continue(d) to 'become delinquent'.

Re-inventing the Delinquent

Of all the new directions suggested by the researchers within this collection, perhaps the most significant is that historians and criminologists should look again at the 'invention' of delinquency.[16] Read individually, the chapters show how the phenomenon of delinquency was framed as 'new' in different ways at different times in different settings. However, read across each other, they demonstrate the need to engage with the vexed question of continuity and change at a more macro level.

The flood of recent historical work has made it clear that simple teleological approaches to the history of juvenile delinquency will no longer suffice. Geoffrey Pearson's classic text on hooliganism identified a series of 'moral panics' about youth and violence. Pearson argued that successive generations of Britons voiced similar fears about social breakdown and moral degeneration, their fearful rhetoric embodied in the form of the hooligan, the garrotter, and the juvenile delinquent.[17] His account, however, does not reach very far beyond the nineteenth century. An aim of this collection is to further question that apparently specific moment of modernity - the early nineteenth century 'age of reform' - and to place Pearson's argument in a broader geographical context.

Perhaps it would be more fitting to search for a series of 'moments' when delinquency was (re)created, (re)discovered and (re)invented. The final sections of this chapter seek to begin this search by examining a further three recurring themes within the history of north-western European delinquency: legal processes, institutions and families. It is possible to argue that juvenile delinquency emerged as a distinct social problem once it came to be named in new ways through juvenile-specific legislation; once it came to be managed in new ways within juvenile-specific institutions by specialised staff; and once the families of deprived and disorderly children came to be subject to new forms of external intervention and regulation. These processes can be read as intrinsically modern in the sense that all three 'belong' to the nineteenth century and that all three signified the rise of new forms of social management which required a wider re-organisation of the relationships between the state, civil institutions and citizens. Persuasive as this chronology might be, however, it is necessarily complicated by the fact that the very same three developments can be identified in the two centuries prior to the nineteenth. Early modern European societies legislated for deprived and disorderly youths, set up institutions to reform them and tried to enforce parental responsibility for them. How might criminologists and modern historians of crime deal with these earlier organised efforts to discipline disorderly youth?

Legal Processes and Language

Legal distinctions between adults and children can be identified in many forms of historical social legislation. Thus acts and statutes defining inheritance, apprenticeship, and parental responsibility can be traced throughout the early modern period. Likewise, it would be unwise to overlook the power of early modern orders and proclamations, many of which stipulated restrictions or regulation of delinquent youth. The connections between these measures and what Natalie Zemon Davis has identified as 'an international movement for welfare reform in Europe in the decades after 1520' could be usefully investigated further.[18] Joel Harrington has highlighted the progressive legislation passed in sixteenth century Nuremburg, in particular the child begging laws which were a response to a continuing concern about poor children.[19] In 1580 Orders were enacted by the City of London Council to bar delinquent children from inheriting, and earlier in the thirteenth century there was a considerable body of law in the City regulating apprenticeship, with specific inclusions for disorderly apprentices.[20] Similar concerns about the control of poor children can also be identified in seventeenth century Stockholm when, in 1682, the Governor appointed guards to prevent street children from entering the church during sermons.[21]

Age-related definitions of young offenders have long been part of European legal systems, although they have also always been subject to discretion and negotiation. In early modern Spain the age of criminal responsibility was set at 14, although the age at which females could be accused of sexual misconduct was 12. In old regime France a distinction was made between *infantia* (from birth to seven), *pueritia* (from seven to 12 for girls, from seven to 14 for boys), and *adolescentia* (from 12 to adulthood).[22] In Britain the formulation of *Doli Incapax*, allowed that children between the ages of seven and 14[23] were presumed to be incapable of criminal intent; the prosecution task was to undermine this presumption.[24] In France, Belgium, and several other continental states under the Napoleonic Code (1810), minors found guilty aged under 16 had to have been found to have *discernment*, thus to have knowledge and understanding of their wrong-doing.[25] In addition, European legal systems developed more specific legislations to deal with criminal children from the late eighteenth century onwards. In the Netherlands, in 1809, the Crimineel Wetboek voor het Koningrijk Holland was introduced which contained separate articles on children. Under this Act, children aged under 12 were not punished, since they were always supposed to have acted without discernment; those aged between 12 and 15 could be imprisoned for two months without verdict or given 'childish punishment', while those between 15 and 18 were also given lesser punishments.[26] This was replaced in 1811 by the Napoleonic Code. In France, the Penal Codes of 1791 and 1810 had made the 'minority plea' a formal element of French law. Articles 66 and 67 of the 1810 code regulated discernment. Thus for all children under the age of 16, discernment was to be investigated. Moreover, juveniles (under 16) 'were exempt from the death penalty and other harsh or degrading punishments'.[27] What is remarkable here is a certain continuity in the range of formal measures to deal with social, and particularly youthful, disorder. While no-one can deny the rush of legislative response to juvenile crime that was a feature of the later nineteenth and the twentieth centuries, these acts might be more usefully regarded as a progression from such earlier measures. As Paul Griffiths remarks in this collection, 'The coining of juvenile delinquency after 1800, then, was not a sudden or neat break with the past'.

In many ways the acts of the nineteenth and early twentieth centuries formalised (and very often nationalised) processes which had been in place for centuries. As we have seen, social welfare legislation of the early modern period was often concerned with poor and disorderly children. However, there is little doubt that from the nineteenth century onwards the use of a specific terminological category, 'the juvenile delinquent', became more pronounced. The Juvenile Offenders Act of 1847 in Britain, the 1896 Child Welfare Act (vergeradsloven) in Norway, the 1902 Swedish Reformatory Acts, the 1912 Act establishing the Tribunaux Pour Enfants et Adolescents in France, and the Belgium Child Protection Act of 1912 all explicitly described this new legal subject and defined clear processes of reform.[28] These acts, perhaps for the first time, adopted the 'new' vocabulary of juvenile delinquency. A stronger linguistic delineation of juvenile delinquency thus aided the move from a more informal system to a more formal system of regulation, in which, for the first time, state responses dominated. However, this shift should not be over-stated. Public and private sector measures co-existed in different ways across the period covered by this collection; that the state and philanthropic measures were not mutually exclusive can be seen in the case of institutional provision. The British Industrial and Reformatory School Acts of the 1850s and 60s; the French Law of 1850 which proposed 'reformation of juvenile offenders by agricultural labour', and the Dutch Wetboek Van Srafrecht of 1886, were all, to an extent extending standardising state regulation to a philanthropic sector which was already well established.[29]

In most European countries the establishment of a separate juvenile justice system did not occur until the twentieth century. In France, for example, the 1912 law establishing separate juvenile courts and a probation system (or 'liberté surveillée') was followed by a 1935 law which decriminalised vagrant minors, and a 1945 law that further reformed juvenile justice. This law established penal irresponsibility for all minors under 16; judges were instructed to base their decisions on the concept of 'protection'. The law also created the Children's Judge, still a key figure in the French justice system, empowered to make decisions specifically about minors.[30] In Germany, youth welfare became increasingly significant after the First World War. Upon their post-war advent to power, the Social Democrats adopted a much more proactive attitude towards juvenile justice. *Verwahrlosung* (delinquency) was often seen as an illness; the Social Democrats' bureaucratic prescriptions for youth delinquency were accompanied by the growing impact of behavioural explanations for deviance. Thus, the National Youth Welfare Law of 1924 was strongly informed by the idea that German youth had become both physically and morally damaged by the war. A Juvenile Courts law was also passed in 1923.[31] By the mid-twentieth century then, most European countries had some form of similar separate juvenile justice system in place, governing both court procedures and the application of punishment or/and welfare.

As the chapters by Griffiths, Roberts and Tikoff in this collection show, there are significant continuities with the early modern period; it is also clear that, in the move towards a separate juvenile justice system, wheels turned exceedingly slowly. This raises a number of questions. Should the rise of separate juvenile justice systems be necessarily read as a sign of progress? Did the decline of older institutions like apprenticeship undermine existing forms of social support for adolescent youths? How far did a changing vocabulary promote a separate discourse, and thereby engender this judicial separation? In this collection, Paul Griffiths sees the emergence of new terminologies as key to understanding continuities and discontinuities. As he points out, nineteenth century discourses of delinquency can seem very familiar to a historian of 'disorderly youth', 'idle apprentices', and 'saucie wenches' in the earlier period. Such historians can cite William Fleetwood, Recorder of London in the late sixteenth century, and his descriptions of young boys, who, having learnt to 'cut purses' were judged 'judicial nypper[s]', or an ordinance from the Reformed Palatinate of 1563, bemoaning irresponsible parents who, 'paid less attention to their children than cows, letting them do whatever they want'.[32] Yet even early modern commentaries have been largely located in a similarly teleological account of juvenile crime. The historian of medieval youth, Barbara Hanawalt, has problematised what she calls the 'question of naming'.[33] The same issues that have shaped the history of juvenile delinquency are discussed by Hanawalt in her consideration of adolescence in history. The issue of language is central to her analysis:

> For medievalists the question of naming has always had a special fascination...Does giving the life stage a name - 'adolescence' - make it real and therefore a phenomenon that is historical and can be dealt with, or should we assume that because it has no medieval name it was not real, because to have no name means it has no existence?[34]

In her investigation of linguistic constructions of the child criminal in late eighteenth and early nineteenth-century France, Cat Nilan argues that the romantic view of childhood was fundamentally ambivalent and led to a stronger re-configuration of the child as 'other'. Thus to some extent whilst Rousseau exalted the innocence of the child, children who failed to conform to the romantic model became perhaps more inexplicably deviant than previously. According to Nilan, the model of innocent childhood promulgated in romantic-era France re-emphasised the abnormality of the criminal child in opposition to the normal child.[35] What this suggests is that the coincidence of new legal structures that enabled developments in legislation, a reformulation of youth and childhood, and a move towards the sometimes punitive reformatory systems to be found in many European countries during the nineteenth century may have broader significance. Thus powerful dichotomies were increasingly shaping the treatment of the juvenile offender. These dichotomies were increasingly class-based. The difference between the hardened and corrupted working class child, and the innocent and pure middle class child found its echo in the language of penality. Certain disruptive boys in Belgian reform institutions in the later nineteenth century, for example, were labelled as 'incorrigibles'. Jenneke Christiaens argues here that this labelling represented a move away from a classic penal logic (founded on responsibility or guilt) towards a new social logic (based on individual abnormality or dangerousness). Consequently, 'incorrigible boys' who did not respond to standard reform efforts could be removed to a special disciplinary section of an adult prison and thereby pushed to the margins of the emerging juvenile justice system, having doubly compromised their status as 'innocent' children. This marginalisation was symptomatic of further trans-European development: the late nineteenth century pathologisation and scientifically-supported othering of the (juvenile) deviant.

In the twentieth century the language of delinquency again arguably shifted to reflect a new language of welfare which, however, also has certain interesting early modern echoes. In Britain, for example, the more specific 'juvenile delinquent' was to some extent, replaced by the more generic 'neglected child'. Whilst 'care and protection' had been implicit in previous legislation, the 1908 Children Act (and its successors in 1933 and 1948) took major steps to protect vulnerable children. This Act both extended the range of reasons for which a child (under 14) could be brought to court, and also blurred the distinction between the 'incorrigible' child and the child 'in danger'. Although this neo-welfarism had its earlier antecedents and its clear punitive sides, especially perhaps for girls, it does seem to have marked a broadening of the category 'juvenile delinquent' to the point where the category began to lose something of the specificity which it had begun to carry since the mid-nineteenth century.[36]

In summary, there is a clear divide here between historians of the pre-nineteenth century who tend to focus on 'disorderly youths', and historians of the post-nineteenth century who tend to focus on 'juvenile delinquents'. This divide is not based simply on the preferences of different scholarly camps, but, to a large extent, on the distinct (legal) languages used by contemporaries in each period and by the fact that the legal treatment of *all* children, as opposed to disorderly children, was fundamentally altered by far-reaching legal reforms of the early nineteenth century. That said, there is room for new research on at least three fronts: the judicial treatment of young offenders (as opposed to disorderly youths) in the early modern period; the more general policing of disorderly youth cultures (as opposed to juvenile delinquents) in the modern period; and the relationship between these two.

Institutions

The emergence of child specific institutions has been seen as one of the key features of the nineteenth century development of juvenile justice. By the twentieth century, as we have already seen, most European countries had some form of state reformatory programme made up of a range of institutions. However, European institutional initiatives to deal with the disorderly young date back at least to the fifteenth century. Criminal children, paupers, orphans and foundlings were catered for by a variety of local initiatives, mostly managed by religious charities or more secular civic agencies. The Spanish humanist Juan Luis Vives recommended a division of pauper boys between seminaries and workshops in his *De Subventione Pauperum* written in 1520.[37] In 1677, the London philanthropist Thomas Firmin established a spinning school for delinquent poor children, recommending that, 'every Parish that abounds with Poor People' should 'set up a School in the nature of a Workhouse, to teach their poor Children to work in, who for want thereof, now wander up and down the Parish and parts adjacent' who 'between Begging and Stealing, get a sorry living; but never bring any thing to their poor Parents, nor earn one Farthing towards their own maintenance, or the good of the Nation'.[38] In this collection Benjamin Roberts identifies similar institutional impulses in seventeenth century Dutch urban society, citing the example of the Rasphuis (Saw house) in Amsterdam.[39] And in eighteenth-century Paris, the Hôpital Général had designated areas for juvenile delinquents.[40] The key aim of such correctional homes and orphanages was to keep pauper children off the streets. However, institutions such as the Rasphuis, along with Seville's Toribios (established in the late eighteenth century and discussed by Valentina Tikoff here) had more than a street-cleansing function. They also provided a place of regulation and correction of supposedly delinquent children, to which 'respectable' families and guardians had resort. In urban European societies that were becoming increasingly characterised by a commercial and consumptionist culture, the 'street' was an increasingly significant and visible site of social interaction.[41] 'Public' bad behaviour by the children of the poor was a nuisance to be removed, but public bad behaviour by the children of the respectable was a threat to a family's status and reputation which, in an age where much was traded, literally, on 'good name', also had to be regulated. This, perhaps, was Habermas' 'bourgeois public sphere' in the making.

Nevertheless, despite clear evidence for institutional provision in the early modern period, and particularly in eighteenth century European urban centres, the phase of institutional building associated with the early nineteenth century is still considered by many to be a watershed in the management of delinquency.[42] Hugh

Cunningham, for example, sees that from the 1830s, 'there was an intensified phase of institution-building, catering for children of all kinds thought to be in need'.[43] The early nineteenth century seems to be distinct in two major respects: in terms of the growth of a wider public debate about juveniles and the purpose of juvenile institutions, and in terms of the new ability and willingness of increasingly consolidated nation states to become involved in such projects. The result was a comprehensive programme of building and redevelopment.

Certainly, the innovative nature of these 'new' institutions can be overstated, given that they often incorporated early modern elements. Many, if not most, retained charitable management, large amounts of charitable funding and old-style discretionary admissions policies. Many, too, looked back to an idealised rural past and in this sense consciously saw themselves as stemming a 'modern' urban industrial tide. Pioneering projects such as the Mettray agricultural colony in France and the Rauhe Haus near Hamburg, and their British successors, the Philanthropic Society school in Redhill, Surrey, and the Hackney Wick Academy on the borders of London, tried to evoke an old rural society that, contemporaries felt, was increasingly under attack.[44] This model proved highly influential and continued to shape European juvenile institutions, at least for boys, well into the twentieth century.

If, as the previous section suggested, European courts' treatment of juveniles narrowed somewhat in the early nineteenth century, European institutions' treatment of juveniles arguably widened. Increasingly, children deemed to be 'at risk', as well as those who had already committed crimes, were incorporated within the expanding welfare-punishment nexus. In the Netherlands, a specialised juvenile prison was opened in Rotterdam under article 66 of the Code Pénal. Subsequently, from 1857, special reformatories (verbeterhuizen) were opened for children who had not actually been convicted but who were felt to be in need of moral reformation (the equivalent of the British industrial schools). Thus the Huis van Verbetering en Opvoeding was opened for boys in Alkmaar, and in 1859 a similar institution for girls was opened in Montfoort.[45] In Belgium, as Jenneke Christiaens shows in this collection, an institution which had been founded in the 1840s as a 'maison pénitentiaire pour jeunes délinquants' (a penitentiary house for young delinquents), had, by the 1890s, been renamed and become an 'école de bienfaisance' (a welfare school). In Britain, the incorporation of 'at risk' children into the state system was formalised in legislation. An Industrial Schools Amending Act of 1861 redefined the 'vagrant child' as 'almost any child under 14 found begging, receiving alms, of no settled abode or means of subsistence or one who frequented criminal company'.[46] A further Consolidating Act of 1866 widened the net even further by including orphans, children of criminal parents, and children whose parents were undergoing penal servitude. By the 1860s, delinquent, semi-delinquent and non-delinquent children were admitted to the industrial schools without previous imprisonment.[47] This broadening of definitions of delinquency was neither smooth nor seamless, however. It was the subject of much debate among many agencies in many arenas across Europe, from institutional superintendents to elected representatives to, as Chris Leonards shows here, delegates at European penal congresses. The questions at hand were as difficult then as they are today: should children who had actually committed crimes be treated in the same ways as that of those who might go on to commit crimes? Was there any meaningful difference between the 'experienced' and the 'innocent', between children in trouble and children in need?

If nineteenth century reformers sought to transform traditional charitable juvenile institutions by standardising their organisation and broadening their admissions, twentieth century reforms sought to transform them further by keeping broad admission criteria but by using them much more as a last resort. In the early twentieth century, these institutions came under considerable attack across Europe. Spaces that had been seen as safe for children were now widely cast as placing children in danger. In Germany, institutions established under the Kaiser were implicated in a series of scandals involving maltreatment in the late 1920s. A reformatory run by the public youth welfare authorities in Berlin was the focus of much controversy when one of the boys died of injuries received from other inmates in 1931.[48] In Britain, a 1913 government committee produced a damning report on industrial and reformatory schools, complaining of treatment that was harsh, old fashioned and unproductive. Critical voices had been raised prior to this, but were particularly galvanized during the First World War in opposition both to the hard-line regimes of the juvenile institutions and to the hard-line taken by magistrates against young offenders whose actions seemed to be more harshly punished because they were committed during a national crisis.[49] They also drew strength from, and in turn helped to strengthen, broader penal reforms of the time, which, for example, aimed to alter the purpose and composition of many European and North American prisons.[50] Critics of institutionalisation in Britain and elsewhere in Europe were increasingly turning to more community-based responses to juvenile delinquency and child neglect. Probation schemes, after-care schemes, and family visiting schemes, which had all been present in many European states in various philanthropic forms prior to this, began to be increasingly state sponsored. In Norway, for example, the 1915 Child Welfare Committee (*barnevernskomiteen*) recommended that a more formal statutory after-care system be established to monitor the progress of those discharged from reformatories. In Britain, probation schemes sanctioned by the 1907 Probation Act were gradually extended and urban local authorities began to appoint salaried child welfare workers.

Yet although these developments were significant, they should not be taken to represent a more general move towards decarceration. Despite the criticism of 'old-style' institutions, significant numbers of delinquent and neglected children across Europe continued to be sent to 'new-style' juvenile justice custodial facilities and to a whole range of both private and public children's homes. Institutions were renamed, rebranded, in some cases reformed (but in few cases actually rebuilt) across the interwar period and beyond. British industrial and reformatory schools, for example, became 'approved schools' in the 1930s and 'community homes with education' in the 1960s. Together with other locked residential institutions (notably borstals, remand homes and, later, secure units) they arguably formed part of a new 'incarceral archipelago'. Instead of prompting simple decarceration, then, early twentieth century criticisms of old institutions helped to lay the foundations of new kinds of dispersed regulation which was both community-based and custodial.[51] As Astri Andresen notes in her discussion of the reformed Norwegian after-care system, child welfare officers wielded enormous power over young people, some by then in their twenties, who had already spent several years being 'reformed'. In this sense, the early twentieth century does seem to occupy a particular place in the history of European states' ever-proliferating efforts to discipline, punish and care for their young citizens. Of course, those young citizens and their families played a key role in this broad history of governmentality themselves, and certainly not just as 'docile bodies', which, as the final section shows, should not be overlooked.

Families

Home environments and family relationships were, and remain, central to discourses of juvenile delinquency. The proper upbringing of children and the proper duties of parents were common subjects in medieval and early modern advice books, catechism and tracts.[52] Parents' anxieties about the behaviour of their disorderly and potentially disorderly children were as much a feature of early modern as of late modern European life. Moreover, concerns then and now seem very similar: schooling, play, peers and work all exercised the minds of worried parents. Obviously, these concerns had many aspects, yet at least one theme does seem to stand out here. The idea that children were moving beyond authority and stability, variously defined, was common to many of these fears. On the one hand, the (continual) rise of 'new' urban commercial pleasures, from coffee houses to video arcades, have been repeatedly identified as a recurring source of young people's rejection of established social order, although, on the other, the (continual) disempowering of 'old' authorities, from apprentice masters to priests to teachers to parents, have been too. As Paul Griffiths notes in this volume, much of the 'invention' debate has rested on the behaviour of a new generation of 'masterless' youths apparently created by the decline of apprenticeship and increase in urban migration in large areas of Europe in the late eighteenth and early nineteenth centuries. A long literature on European age-relations has argued that these developments caused very significant changes to the life-cycle experience of youths and their families, some of which resulted in both an actual and a feared increase in delinquency.[53] It would be interesting, however, to look also at the ways in which later 'macro' European social changes, such as the decline of child labour, the rise of compulsory schooling or the experience of mass war-time evacuation and displacement, affected later discourses of delinquency and later claims that young people's behaviour was becoming steadily 'worse'.

Another fear expressed across discussions of delinquency in different periods is that of systematic generational decline. In short, many feared that the delinquent children of that particular day would be the terrible parents of that particular tomorrow. In mid-nineteenth century Britain, reformer Mary Carpenter wrote of both the short and long-term costs of delinquency: 'These young beings continue to herd in their dens of iniquity, to swarm in our streets, to levy a costly maintenance on the honest and industrious, to rise up to be the parents of a degraded progeny of pauper children'.[54] A century later, similar frenzied concerns continued to be raised about delinquent and neglected children in general, and perhaps in particular about 'mixed race' and black migrant children. As Pamela Cox argues in this volume, the 'social time-bomb' which both 'miscegenation' and migration were thought to herald hinged to a large extent on fears about black children's expected failings as future parents. An earlier investigation into Liverpool's 'colour problem' in the 1930s suggested that the fact that the 'majority of Anglo-Negroid girls seem to drift inevitably into undesirable surroundings' and that it was 'impossible for them to secure work either in domestic service or in factories' would undoubtedly increase 'the number of prostitutes and the number of illegitimate children, born with a definitely bad heredity, and exposed to a definitely bad environment'.[55] The terminology may have changed since Carpenter's day, heightened by variants of social Darwinism, but the sentiment was clearly recognisable.

Parents themselves, though, were also blamed for causing their children's delinquency across the periods covered here. In 1530, Luther wrote that if parents failed to properly discipline their children then children would 'cease to belong to their parents and fall to the care of God and community'.[56] In 1816, the *Report of the committee for investigating the alarming increase of juvenile delinquency in the Metropolis*, named 'The improper conduct of parents' as one of the principal causes of juvenile crime in London.[57] Again in England, in 1834 Thomas Jevons wrote in his *Remarks on Criminal Law*, of the inadequacies of parents when it came to their delinquent children, 'If the neglect of a parent occasions his child to commit a crime, such parent is in fact the author of that crime, and ought to be made accountable to the state'.[58] Jevons' suggestion was realised to a degree with the institution of parental prosecutions for neglect towards the end of century. Further, the removal of certain delinquent and neglected children to state sponsored juvenile institutions across Europe was certainly intended to protect them from bad home environments but also to remind their parents and guardians of their duties both to their child and their nation. With the expansion of more diffused and community-based child welfare programmes in the early twentieth century, as outlined above, the potential for public regulation of private homes increased dramatically. Jenneke Christiaens' conclusions from her earlier study of the Belgian Child Protection Act of 1912 - that to broaden the scope of the juvenile courts was to broaden the possibilities of intervening in family life - could be applied more generally to many European states, as could Sarah Fishman's conclusions here that 'broken' families, variously defined, were the object of particular investigations.[59] To cite Donzelot, the policing of children and youths was very much part of a wider 'policing of families'.[60]

A further important and controversial claim by made Donzelot is that some families colluded with external authorities in this process, that they 'invited' experts into their homes. Certainly, chapters in this collection and other historical research bear this out. Valentina Tikoff shows how both plebian and elite parents used Seville's Toribios as a disciplinary device. English sources from the early modern period also show how many 'ordinary' parents were prepared to place their wayward children in the bridewell, house of correction or in similar institutions.[61] Parents in early nineteenth century London used a variety of means to keep their delinquent children out of trouble. One 13 year old boy named Samuel Holmes told his interviewer, W.A. Miles, how his 'father tried to keep me at home - has stripped me, taken away my clothes and tied me to a bed post - because the boys used to come round the house at night and whistle and entice me to go out thieving again with them'.[62] Astri Andresen shows how parents in inter-war Norway were often those who alerted child welfare officers to their own children's misbehaviour. Pamela Cox has shown how the committal of many children to British juvenile institutions in the first half of the twentieth century was presaged by conflicts within their own (extended) families: mothers-in-law reported daughters-in-law to the authorities for alleged neglect; stepmothers reported stepdaughters for being wayward; estranged sisters reported their brothers for being bad fathers, and so on.[63] Here, Cox shows briefly how child welfare mechanisms were put to further 'strategic' use by some young white women who did not want to keep their accidentally conceived 'mixed race' children and by some black migrant families seeking 'white care' for their own children.

Assumptions about good and bad family life therefore did a great deal to shape reformatory strategies. Those children removed from their own families, for whatever reason, and placed in nineteenth century juvenile institutions were being consciously placed in alternative 'families'. These institutions were commonly designed to emulate, and improve upon, the supposed security, stability and order of an ideal family home. At Mettray in the 1840s, boys were divided into 'families', 'Each family resides in a distinct house...The boy feels that his master is not a mere officer to watch him and enforce discipline, or a mere instructor to teach him, but is a relation, - a friend - to sympathize with him and assist him'. Two boys, known as 'frères aînés' (older brothers) were elected on a monthly basis to assist with the regulation of the each group.[64] Again, however, 'family' style institutions like Mettray and many others were subject to much debate in the nineteenth and twentieth centuries. And again, much of the debate dwelt on the nature of the children admitted and, by extension, the primary purpose of the institution. Were children sent to such places to be punished, or to be protected? If they were sent to be punished, was the family model 'too lenient'? If they were sent to be protected, was it still 'too harsh'? The search for the 'ideal' juvenile institution, like that for the 'ideal' family, continues in many parts of Europe today.

The importance of the family, broadly conceived, in very many debates about delinquency across the times and spaces covered here gives further weight to the argument that history of 'the juvenile delinquent' should not be viewed as the history of an autonomous individual but as the history of a series of relational categories. As this collection hopes to show, the history of 'delinquency' cannot be separated out from the history of families, institutions and legal processes, nor from the history of youth culture, consumption, gender, knowledges, violence, crises and marginal voices.

Investigations of all these issues over a wide time-span show how conventional criminological and historical chronologies can be usefully challenged and how the conventional boundaries of 'modernity' can be usefully questioned. However, we are not likely to achieve (nor should we expect) any absolute consensus between early modern and modern historians or between historians and criminologists more broadly defined as to the wider implications of this challenge. Some will continue to argue that the nineteenth century represents a watershed in the definition and management of social disorder, while at the same time acknowledging crucial early modern and medieval antecedents. Others will continue to argue that early modern developments should be treated in their own terms and not as 'antecedents' within some broader teleological framework. Still others will argue that the whole question of a periodisation which insists on any kind of 'break' between early modern and modern history should be thrown wide open. As the chapters in this collection show, however, all these are creative points of tension to be encouraged rather than glossed over. These chapters are therefore presented in the hope that they will encourage similarly broad comparative work, and in the belief that understandings of crime and crime control can only benefit from a critical dialogue between history and criminology.

Endnotes

1   C. Bailey, *Transcripts from the Municipal Archives of Winchester, and Other Documents, Elucidating the Government, Manners, and Customs of the Same City, from the Thirteenth Century to the Present Period* (Winchester, 1856), pp. 72-3, cited in W.B. Sanders, *Juvenile Offenders for a Thousand Years: Selected Readings from Anglo-Saxon Times to 1900* (Chapel Hill, 1970), pp. 10, 17; Cited in E. Harvey, *Youth and the Welfare State in Weimar Germany* (Oxford, 1995), pp. 196-7.

2   Other European and Russian studies include, J. Neuberger *Hooliganism: Crime, Culture, and Power in St. Petersburg, 1900-1914* (Berkeley, 1993); S. Vidali, 'Youth Deviance and Social

Exclusion in Greece', in V. Ruggiero, N. South and I. Taylor eds., *The New European Criminology: Crime and Social Order in Europe* (London, 1998) pp. 339-49; M. Gibson, 'Criminal Anthropology and Juvenile Delinquency in Liberal and Fascist Italy' unpub. paper presented at the 'Becoming Delinquent' conference, University of Cambridge, 1999. African and Latin American studies include, J.A. Carreras, 'Los Reformatories De Menores', *Santiago* [Cuba], 41 (1981), pp. 148-66; S. Heap, "Jaguda Boys': Pickpocketing in Ibadan, 1930-60', *Urban History*, 24/3 (1997), pp. 324-43. Classic US studies include, A.M. Platt *The Child Savers: The Invention of Delinquency* (Chicago, 1969); J. Sutton, *Stubborn Children: Controlling Delinquency in the United States, 1640-1981* (Berkeley, 1988). Australian studies include, P. Buddee, *The Fate of the Artful Dodger* (Perth, 1984); A. Gill, *Forced Labour for the West: Parkhurst Convicts 'Apprenticed' in Western Australia, 1842-1851* (Perth, 1997); K. Humphery, 'Objects of Compassion: Young Male Convicts in Van Diemen's Land, 1834-1850', *Australian Historical Studies*, 98 (1992), pp. 13-33.

3   See, for example, K. Jenkins, *Re-thinking History* (London, 1991); A. Munslow, *Deconstructing History* (London, 1997).

4   For comparative historical studies, see A.G. Hess and P.F. Clement eds., *History of Juvenile Delinquency: A Collection of Essays on Crime Committed by Young Offenders, in History in Selected Countries* (Aalen, 1990); T.J. Bernard, *The Cycle of Juvenile Justice* (Oxford and New York, 1992). For comparative criminological studies, see L. Walgrave and J. Mehlbye eds., *Confronting Youth in Europe: Juvenile Crime and Juvenile Justice* (Denmark, 1998); F. Bailleau, 'A Crisis of Youth or of Juridical Response?', in Ruggiero, South and Taylor, pp. 95-103; F. Heidensohn and M. Farrell eds., *Crime in Europe* (London, 1990).

5   See, for example P. Ariès, *Centuries of Childhood* (Harmondsworth, 1960); H. Cunningham, *The Children of the Poor: Representations of Childhood Since the Seventeenth Century* (Oxford, 1991); Idem., *Children and Childhood in Western Society Since 1500* (London, 1995); L. De Mause, *The History of Childhood* (New York, 1974); J. Gillis, *Youth and History: Tradition and Change in European Age Relations* (London, 1974); G. Levi and J.C. Schmitt eds., *A History of Young People in the West* (Cambridge, Mass., 1997); M. Mitterauer, *A History of Youth*, trans. G. Dunphy (Oxford, 1992); S. Shahar, *Childhood in the Middle Ages* (London, 1990). For comparative sociological studies, see L. Chisholm ed., *Growing Up in Europe: Contemporary Horizons in Childhood and Youth Studies* (Berlin, New York, 1995); K. Pringle ed., *Children and Social Welfare in Europe* (Buckingham, 1998).

6   See, for example M. Arnot and C. Usborne eds., *Gender and Crime in Modern Europe* (London, 1999); V.A.C. Gatrell, B. Lenman, and G. Parker eds., *Crime and the Law: The Social History of Crime in Western Europe since 1500* (London, 1980); P. Spierenburg, *The Prison Experience: Disciplinary Institutions and their Inmates in Early Modern Europe* (New Brunswick, 1991); M.R. Weisser, *Crime and Punishment in Early Modern Europe* (Hassocks, 1979).

7   See, for example G. Bock and P. Thane eds., *Maternity and Gender Policies: Women and the Rise of the European Welfare States, 1880s-1950s* (London, 1991); A. De Swaan, *In Care of the State: Health Care, Education and Welfare in Europe and the USA in the Modern Era* (Cambridge, 1990); A. Gueslin and D. Kalifa eds., *Les Exclus en Europe 1830-1930* (Paris, 1999); J. Lewis ed., *Women and Social Policies in Europe: Work, Family and the State*

(Aldershot, 1993); S. Woolf, *The Poor in Western Europe in the Eighteenth and Nineteenth Centuries* (London, 1986); J. Henderson and R. Wall eds., *Poor Women and Children in the European Past* (London, 1994).

[8] See key comparative historical studies, endnote 4. For fuller listing and discussion of different national historical studies, see endnotes of individual chapters.

[9] Key exceptions here are G. Pearson, *Hooligan: A History of Respectable Fears* (Basingstoke, 1983); J. Springhall, *Youth, Popular Culture and Moral Panics: Penny Gaffs to Gangsta-Rap, 1830-1996* (Basingstoke, 1998).

[10] On gender and delinquency, see B. Koeppel, *Marguerite B. Une jeune fille en maison de correction* (Paris, 1987); M. Sundkvist, *De vanartade barnen. Mötet mellan barn, föräldrar och Norrköpings barnavårdsnämnd 1903-1925* (Linköping, 1994); L. Mahood, *Policing Gender, Class and Family, Britain*, 1850-1940 (London, 1995); H. Schmidt, 'Risky Girls and Girls at Risk: Correctional Education and Girls in Imperial Germany', unpub. paper presented at the 'Becoming Delinquent' conference, University of Cambridge, 1999; H. Shore, 'The Trouble with Boys: Gender and the "Invention" of the Juvenile Offender in the Early Nineteenth Century', in Arnot and Usborne, pp. 75-92. P. Cox, *Bad Girls: Gender, Justice and Welfare in Britain, 1900-1950* (forthcoming). For an overview of more recent trans-European research, see M. Cain ed., *Growing up Good: Policing the Behaviour of Girls in Europe* (London, 1989).

[11] P. Cavadino ed., *Children Who Kill: An Examination of the Treatment of Juveniles Who Kill in Different European Countries* (Winchester, 1996); K.M. Heide, *Young Killers: The Challenge of Juvenile Homicide* (California, London, 1999); G. Sereny, *Cries Unheard: Why Children Kill: The Story of Mary Bell* (London, 2000); D.J. Smith, *The Sleep of Reason: The James Bulger Case* (London, 1994); L.J. Woodhouse, *Shooter in the Sky: The Inner World of Children Who Kill* (Mount Pleasant, SC, 2001).

[12] See also, A. Davies, 'Youth Gangs, Masculinity and Violence in Late Victorian Manchester and Salford', *Social History*, 32/2 (1998), pp. 349-69; Idem., 'Youth Gangs, Gender and Violence, 1870-1900', in S. D'Cruz ed., *Everyday Violence in Britain, 1850-1950* (Harlow, Essex, 2000), pp. 70-85; H. Shore, *Artful Dodgers: Youth and Crime in Early Nineteenth Century London* (Woodbridge, 1999), pp. 64-9.

[13] Pearson, *Hooligan*.

[14] J. Scott, 'The Evidence of Experience', *Critical Inquiry* 17 (1991), pp. 773-97.

[15] On (constructed) delinquent voices, J. Bennett, *Oral History and Delinquency: The Rhetoric of Criminology* (Chicago, 1981); T. Hitchcock, P. King, and P. Sharpe eds., *Chronicling Poverty: the Voices and Strategies of the English Poor, 1640-1840* (Basingstoke, 1997); P. Cox, 'Récits d'exclues en Angleterre (vers 1900)' in Gueslin and Kalifa, pp38-48; Idem., *Bad Girls*, chapter 5.

[16] The notion of an early nineteenth century 'invention' has been most strongly developed in British writings on delinquency. See, for example, P. King and J. Noel, 'The Origins of 'The Problem of Juvenile Delinquency': The Growth of Juvenile Prosecutions in London in the Late Eighteenth and Early Nineteenth Century', *Criminal Justice History*, 15 (1993), pp. 17-41; P. King, "The Rise of Juvenile Delinquency in England, 1780-1840: Changing Patterns of Perception and Prosecution', *Past and Present*, 160 (1998), pp. 116-66; Shore, *Artful Dodgers*; S. Magarey, 'The Invention of Juvenile Delinquency in Early Nineteenth-Century

England', *Labour History* [Canberra] (1978), pp. 11-27; M. May, 'Innocence and Experience: The Evolution of the Concept of Juvenile Delinquency in the Mid-Nineteenth Century', *Victorian Studies*, Sept (1973), pp. 7-29; L. Radzinowicz and R. Hood, *A History of English Criminal Law and its Administration from 1750, V: the Emergence of Penal Policy* (Oxford, 1990), esp. part three; P. Rush, 'The Government of a Generation: The Subject of Juvenile Delinquency', *Liverpool Law Review*, 15 (1992), pp. 3-43.

[17] Pearson, *Hooligan*. See also J. Davis, 'The London Garrotting Panic of 1862', in Gatrell et al, p. 191.

[18] N. Zemon Davis, *Society and Culture in Early Modern France* (Cambridge, 1987), p. 24.

[19] J. Harrington, 'Bad Parents, the State, and the Early Modern Civilizing Process', *German History*, 16/1 (1998), pp. 16-28, particularly 25-7.

[20] Sanders, pp. 3-7, 8-10.

[21] B. Sandin, 'Education, Popular Culture, and the Surveillance of the Population in Stockholm between 1600 and the 1840s', *Continuity and Change*, 3 (1988), pp. 370-1.

[22] C. Nilan, *Precocious Perversity: Childhood, Crime and the Prison in July Monarchy France* (forthcoming).

[23] The specific age boundaries of *Doli Incapax* did vary over time, for example the age was amended to eight in 1933 and ten in 1963. L. Gelsthorpe and A. Morris, 'Juvenile Justice 1945-1992', in M. Maguire, R. Morgan and R. Reiner eds., *The Oxford Handbook of Criminology* (Oxford, 1994), pp. 949-93, The literal translation of *Doli Capax* is 'capable of being sorry', or aware of wrongdoing.

[24] An early seventeenth century English text held that, 'An infant of eight yeares of age, or above, may commit homicide, and shall be hanged for it, viz. If it may appeare (by hyding of the person slaine, by excusing it, or by any other act) that he had knowledge of good and evill, and of the perill and danger of that offence...But an infant of such tender yeares, as that he hath no discretion or intelligence, if he kill a man, this is no felonie in him', M. Dalton, *The Countrey Justice, Conteyning the Practise of the Justices of the Peace out of their Sessions...* (1st ed., London, 1618), pp. 204-6, quoted in Sanders, p. 11. See also A.W.G. Kean, 'The History of the Criminal Liability of Children', *Law Quarterly Review*, 53 (1937), pp. 364-70.

[25] J. Christiaens, 'A History of Belgium's Child Protection Act of 1912: The Redefinition of the Juvenile Offender and his Punishment', *European Journal of Crime, Criminal Law and Criminal Justice*, 7/1 (1999), pp. 5-21, particularly p. 10. See also C. Nilan, 'Hapless Innocence and Precocious Perversity: Constructions of the Child Criminal in Late Eighteenth and Early Nineteenth Century France', *Proceedings of the Annual Meeting of the Western Society for French History*, 24 (1997), pp. 81-91, p. 81.

[26] Crimineel Wetboek, art 21 and 48. Y.G.I. Baaijens-van Geloven et al, *Strafwetgeving in de Negentiende eeuw* (Tilburg, 1985), part 11, pp. 130, 134.

[27] Nilan, 'Hapless Innocence', p. 82; L. Berlanstein, 'Vagrants, Beggars, and Thieves: Delinquent Boys in Mid-Nineteenth Century Paris', *Journal of Social History*, 12 (1979), pp. 531-52, esp. p. 532.

[28] Christiaens; M. Kumlien, 'Uppfostran och Straff: Studier Kring 1902 ors Lagstiftning om Reaktioner mot Ungdomsbrott', (Upbringing and Punishment: Studies on the 1902 Swedish Reformatory Acts), (Dissertation, Uppsala Univ., Sweden, 1994). See also K. Alaimo, 'Shaping Adolescence in the Popular Milieu: Social Policy, Reformers, and French Youth,

1870-1920', *Journal of Family History*, 17/4 (1992), pp. 419-38.

29 Radzinowicz and Hood, p. 159; Berlanstein, p. 531.

30 S. Fishman, *The Battle for Children: World War II, Delinquency and Juvenile Justice in Twentieth Century France* (forthcoming).

31 Harvey, pp. 158-9, 176-80.

32 C.M. Clode, *The Early History of the Guild of Merchant Taylors of...London* (1888), Part II, p. 294, cited Sanders, pp. 10, 17; 1563 *Ehegerichtsordnung*, in J.F.G. Goeters ed., *Die Evangelischen Kirchenordnungen des XIV Jahrhunderts*, vol. XIV (Kurpfalz) (Tübingen, 1969), p. 294, cited in Harrington, pp, 16-28.

33 B.A. Hanawalt, 'Historical Descriptions and Prescriptions for Adolescence', *Journal of Family History*, 17/4 (1992), pp. 341-51.

34 Ibid., p. 342.

35 Nilan, 'Hapless Innocence', pp. 83-4.

36 See H. Hendrick, *Child Welfare, England, 1872-1989* (London, 1994), p. 124; Bailey, *Delinquency and Citizenship*; D. Thom, 'Wishes, anxieties, play and gestures: child guidance in interwar England' in R. Cooter ed. *In the Name of the Child: Health and Welfare 1880-1940* (London, 1992); S. Schafer, *Children in Moral Danger and the Problem of Government in Third Republic France* (New Jersey, 1997); On the punitive elements of twentieth judicial welfarism, especially for girls, see Cox, *Bad Girls*.

37 Cunningham, *Children and Childhood*, pp. 114-6, 146.

38 T. Firmin, *Some Proposals for the Employment of the Poor* (2nd ed., London, 1681), cited in Sanders, p. 18.

39 Spierenburg, *The Prison Experience*; J. Innes, 'Prisons for the Poor: English Bridewells, 1555-1800', in F. Snyder and D. Hay eds., *Labour, Law and Crime: A Historical Perspective* (Oxford, 1987), pp. 42-122.

40 M. Capul, *Abandon et Marginalité: Les Enfants Placés sous L'Ancien Régime* (Toulouse, 1989), 114. See also B. Garnot, 'La Délinquance en Anjou au XVIIIe Siècle', *Revue Historique*, 273/2 (1985), pp. 305-15.

41 See J. Habermas, *The Structural Transformation of the Public Sphere: An Inquiry into a Category of Bourgeois Society* (Cambridge, orig. pub. Germany, 1962).

42 For example see S. Cavallo, *Charity and Power in Early Modern Italy: Benefactors and their Motives in Turin, 1541-1789* (Cambridge, 1989); A. Farge, *Fragile Lives: Violence, Power, and Solidarity in Eighteenth Century Paris* (Cambridge, 1993, orig. pub. France, 1986), pp. 68-71; Radzinowicz and Hood, pp. 133-5.

43 Cunningham, *Children and Childhood*, pp. 146-7.

44 For Mettray, see I. Jablonka, 'Philanthropic Discourse in Nineteenth Century France: The Rehabilitation of Juvenile Delinquents in Agricultural Reformatories', *Revue D'Histoire Moderne Et Contemporaine*, 47/1 (2000), pp. 131-47; F. Driver, 'Discipline Without Frontiers? Representations of the Mettray Reformatory Colony in Britain, 1840-80', *Journal of Historical Sociology* [Great Britain], 3 (1990), pp. 272-93; Radzinowicz, pp. 155-61; J. Dekker, 'Punir, Sauver et Eduquer: La Colonie Agricole 'Nederlandsch Mettray' et la Reeducation Residentielle aux Pays-Bas, En France, En Allegmagne et en Angleterre Entre 1814 et 1914', *Mouvement Social*, 153 (1990), pp. 63-90. For the Hackney Wick Academy see C. Forss, *Practical Remarks upon the Education of the Working Classes: with an*

Account of the Plan pursued under the superintendence of the Children's Friend Society at the Brenton Asylum, Hackney Wick (London, 1835).

[45] C. Leonards, 'From a Marginal Institution to Institutionalised Marginalisation: Developments in the Treatment of 'Criminal' Children in the Dutch Prison System, 1833-84', *Paedagogia Historica* [Belgium], 26/2 (1990), pp. 147-59, esp p. 150.

[46] J. Springhall, *Coming of Age: Adolescence in Britain, 1860-1960* (Dublin, 1986) p. 167; J. Stack, 'Reformatory and industrial schools and the decline of child imprisonment in mid-Victorian England and Wales', *History of Education,* 23/1 (1994), pp. 59-73.

[47] Stack, pp. 64-5.

[48] Harvey, pp. 235-41; also, E.R. Dickenson, *The Politics of German Child Welfare from the Empire to the Federal Republic* (Cambridge, Mass., 1996).

[49] D. Smith, 'Juvenile Delinquency in Britain in the First World War', in *Criminal Justice History,* 11 (1990), pp. 126-7; V. Bailey, *Delinquency and Citizenship: Reclaiming the Young Offender, 1914-48* (Oxford, 1987), pp. 47-57.

[50] See Morris and Rothman; and M. Wiener, *Reconstructing the Criminal: Culture, Law and Policy in England, 1830-1914* (Cambridge, 1990).

[51] See S. Cohen, *Visions of Social Control* (Cambridge, 1985) for a classic statement of this diversification of regulation. See also D. Garland, *Punishment and Modern Society* (Oxford, 1990) and N. Rose, *Powers of Freedom. Reframing Political Thought* (Cambridge, 1999). All three, are, of course, drawing on the work on Foucault in this respect.

[52] Cunningham, *Children and Childhood,* pp. 41-78.

[53] King, 'The Rise of Juvenile Delinquency', pp. 137-51; Mitterauer, pp. 1-34; Springhall, *Coming of Age,* p. 13.

[54] M. Carpenter, *Reformatory Schools for the Children of the Perishing and Dangerous Classes and for Juvenile Offenders* (1851, London, 1968), p. 2.

[55] Discussion of the research of Muriel Fletcher in C. King and H. King, *'The Two Nations': The Life and Work of Liverpool University Settlement and its Associated Institutions, 1906-37* (Liverpool, 1938) pp. 128-9.

[56] G. Strauss, *Luther's House of Learning: Indoctrination of the Young in the German Reformation* (London, 1978), cited Cunningham, Children and Childhood, p. 118.

[57] *Report of the committee for investigating the alarming increase of juvenile delinquency in the Metropolis* (London, 1816), pp. 10-11.

[58] T. Jevons, *Remarks on Criminal Law; with a Plan for an Improved System, and Observations on the Prevention of Crime* (London, 1834), cited in Sanders, p. 153.

[59] Christiaens, pp. 17-19.

[60] J. Donzelot, *The Policing of Families* (London, 1980).

[61] For instance, Shore, *Artful Dodgers,* pp. 10-11, 31-3; Innes, p. 47. See the table of entrants to the Bridewell in *Report from the Select Committee on the State of the Police of the Metropolis,* Parliamentary Papers, 1817, VII, pp. 153-4.

[62] H. Shore, 'Home, Play and Street Life: Causes of, and Explanations for, Juvenile Crime in the Early Nineteenth Century', in A. Fletcher and S. Hussey eds., *Childhood in Question: Children, Parents and the State* (Manchester, 1999), pp. 96-114, esp p. 102.

[63] Cox, *Bad Girls,* chapters 2 and 5.

[64] Carpenter, pp. 326-7.

Chapter 1

Juvenile Delinquency in Time

Paul Griffiths*

Delinquent Juveniles

Can something exist without the power of prior definition? Historians of the sixteenth and seventeenth centuries describe an aspect of youth that they call juvenile delinquency (apparently unaware of its precise chronology and political electricity of two centuries later), yet vocabularies of crime did not feature this phrase at that time. In so doing, they can draw support from two sources. First, the broad palette of behaviour recognised by modern-day senses of juvenile delinquency upset authority structures in early modern society too. Apart from the new possibilities raised by proliferating new technologies, the anti-social behaviour stigmatised as juvenile delinquency - violence, for instance, vandalism, scoffing, or theft - have troubled governors in nearly all historical situations.[1] And, second, juvenile delinquency was not a free-standing late point in discourses about youth and crime, it was instead a sequential stage in social commentaries on youth that evolved over time, though not in any inevitable way, and that simultaneously revealed and reshaped perceptions of day-to-day experiences.

The coining of the term juvenile delinquency after 1800, then, was not a sudden or neat break with the past. Delinquent behaviour by juveniles had a long and chequered history. Yet whether they are fishing for its origins, tracking its rise, shadowing its evolution, or trumpeting its invention, historians of juvenile delinquency usually stick closely to this side of the last five centuries. In their time travels they rarely scale the high fences that they construct between 1750 and 1800. On one side is the dim and distant early modern past with its peculiar social organisations and experiences. On the other side, however, is a modern pulse: steeply rising wage-labour, sweeping urban growth, and creeping industrialisation with its new class formations. One offspring of these new and unsteady circumstances, it is said, was juvenile delinquency.

This narrative of juvenile delinquency is tinged with shades of modernity. It sparkles with fresh claims and one of its crunch-words is 'new'. Jurgen Habermas tells us that one badge of work inspired by modernity is 'the new'.[2] Particular problems raised by the young accelerated quickly after 1800, it seems, and apparently sped out of control thereafter. So it is that Peter King can write that 'contemporary commentators rarely regarded young offenders as a separate distinct problem' before 1750.[3] Debates heated up thereafter. So much so, that not long after the end of the Napoleonic Wars, juvenile delinquency first emerged as a discrete idea and threat, challenging contemporaries to propose new conceptualisations of age-related tensions and new solutions to still these troubled waters.

The understanding of juvenile delinquency in time cannot be imagined apart from historiographical impressions of the nature of childhood or youth at any particular point in time. Early path-breaking work on juvenile delinquency was conceived two or three decades ago when evaluations of the nature of experiences of early modern youth that today seem thin and threadbare were near orthodoxies. Influential, in this respect, was the claim that a 'new world of children' had emerged suddenly in the eighteenth century once the restrictive rules and other debris of the Tudor and Stuart centuries finally disappeared.[4] Thus it has been incorrectly said that 'a more child-centred approach' recast childhood as a 'special' 'separate' stage of life towards the close of the eighteenth century, and that these developing senses of childhood are among the conceptual roots of juvenile delinquency.[5]

Wordsworth once rhymed that it was absolute bliss to be young in the hurricane rush of the French Revolution when nothing ever seemed still. But it was surely dreary and dull to be young before the so-called 'long' eighteenth century if a highly influential historiographical line understands the earlier actions and sentiments of young people correctly. The sources of satisfaction, exhilaration, and comfort said to be missing or at best infrequent and highly circumscribed in youthful experiences before 1700 have included formative experiences, free-time, masturbation, penetrative sex, or sensitive parenting.[6] It was once thought that before the liberating rays of the eighteenth century youth was little more than a drab house-bound, service-framed, and master-led existence, and that this enclosure of youth stifled most independent thought or action. Little by little, however, as time passed, these shackles loosened. Creative energy, for so long dammed-up, at long last burst free. So it is that Mitterauer treats the last five centuries of youth as a protracted struggle for emancipation, a passage in the inevitable rush to modernity, and a voyage of self-discovery from darkness into the light. He concludes that 'formative experiences [of youth] were minimal' in what he calls 'old European society'.[7]

Time after time, early modern youth has been a casualty of twentieth-century historiographies. Its historical agency has been sapped in much historical work, its creative vigour is a pinprick, and its cultural freedoms have been made to seem few and far between. This impression was produced by contemporaries (and later historians) who presented an optimistic picture of the potential of service to shackle youth; by early modern historians who too frequently worked without the archival sources where experiences of youth were more profusely and colourfully recorded, or who confined bursts of youth disorder to apprentice culture or the legitimising cloak of misrule; and by those historians who, gripped by modernisation theories, believe that the roots of present-day experiences are only to be uncovered in the last two or three centuries. More recent work, however, has turned these once powerful interpretations almost upside down. We now know that sections of early modern youth were culturally dynamic, to the extent that they were able to challenge or even modify authority structures.[8] Arguably, our history of juvenile delinquency in the long run over the last five centuries has yet to fully assimilate these latest turns in historical research.

Emphasis must be placed, however, on alterations and modifications over time. Experiences of youth were always changing. To reiterate, however, youth culture or formative experiences of youth did not emerge from a cultural vacuum in the eighteenth century or after, encouraged by changes in the workplace or schooling, for example, or the seemingly limitless possibilities offered by the fast-growing, sprawling cities. More apparent are modifications in the ideas through which 'problems' of youth (and youth itself) were imagined and stigmatised. Youthful delinquency, then, was always being reconfigured over time, in part as the result of changes in perceptions, cultures, and ideologies (the status and politics of the family in the wake of the Reformation is one such case), and in part as the result of changes in material conditions.

The biggest changes over time in responses to delinquent youth, it seems to me, were legal, legislative, and linguistic in nature. At its conception juvenile delinquency was first and foremost a regulatory discourse, and a pliable label through which to pin down undesirable youth and to cut them off from their 'respectable' peers. Scholars refer to the 'subjectification' or construction of juvenile delinquency by legislators, magistrates, and police.[9] In this respect, then, juvenile delinquency is as much an index of perceptions as a catalogue of behaviours. Today as always, after all, most people sail through their youth and rarely cross swords with governors, picking up no 'grave cultural damage' in the words of Bennett Berger.[10] Juvenile delinquency and youth are not synonymous, however much they cannot be interpreted apart from each other.

Nevertheless, it is arguable that a more balanced and nuanced account of the 'rise of juvenile delinquency' is now long overdue. A more context-secure and source-sensitive narrative would reach back to the sixteenth century (and before) and trace ideas about generational disorders to unpick the roots of later semantic twists in discourses about young offenders. It is most certainly the case that a few recent writers on these matters now imagine a nineteenth-century 'rise' or 'evolution' of juvenile delinquency in a far longer time-span than ever before, though their formulations of order and senses of development through time are on occasion fuzzy.[11] John Gillis puts the point neatly: 'concern with juvenile delinquency', he notes, 'has been a recurring problem since at least the sixteenth century'. Hugh Cunningham comments that street children are 'a centuries old problem'. While Martin Neumeyer writes that 'juvenile delinquency is an old problem'.[12] It is frequently felt, however, that this generational threat was much more menacing, long-lasting, and far-reaching after 1800, though it is questionable whether the right sort of work has been completed on the patchier sources of the sixteenth and seventeenth centuries to allow us to pass emphatic generalisations of this sort with confidence.

'Youth were never more sawcie', Thomas Barnes moaned in 1624, 'yea never more savagely saucie, the ancient are scorned, the honourable are contemned, the magistrate is not dreaded'. Several decades earlier, the professional complainer Philip Stubbes asked his readers to consider whether there was 'ever seen less obedience in youth of all sorts, both mankind and womankind, towards their superiours, parents, masters and governors'.[13] These generational blasts are staple propaganda wars in most societies, but though apparently timeless and routine calls to order, their particular preoccupations differed in both time and place. Early modern social commentaries certainly articulated 'problems' of youth in broad brush-strokes, referring in the most general and unspecific terms to a threatening or lost generation that let loose a galaxy of disorders. It was the young who stretched the patience and exercised the policy think tanks of magistrates and moralists more than any other social group. They swelled the ranks of rootless vagrants,[14] raised fevered concern in towns about pockets of criminal youth,[15] contested or flouted moralities articulated by the church courts in the largest numbers,[16] provided the biggest number of thieves prosecuted before the courts,[17] and they were also arguably the major target of the recurring struggles to reform manners in early modern society.[18] Contemporary social commentaries were also perfectly capable, however, of locating particular 'problem' groups like single women who flocked to the trouble-torn towns with their poisoned chalice of opportunities in rising numbers towards 1700, or a vagrant flock of young street-Arabs.[19]

Above all, however, and by way of contrast to nineteenth-century descriptions of 'problems' of youth, early modern anxieties about youth were in large part shaped by the politics and pressures of service. So much so, that waves of panic about the perceived crimes of servants could sweep through elites, and understandings of the lack of participation implicit in conceptions of marginality were frequently focused upon service and the household. Thus when Lawrence Johnson was spotted on the streets late at night by the watch in 1635 and it emerged that he was 'in noe service nor is anie housekeeper', the clerk of London Bridewell reported that he 'therefore is thought to be a vagrant'.[20] This was to some extent a question of numbers and characteristic experiences; the great majority of people of the lower classes spent most of their youth in service or apprenticeship with a master.[21] This situation gave rise to the development of particular age-specific (or age-related) offences, penalties, and policing measures. Being 'masterless', for example, 'out of service', or 'out of place', and a clutch of domestic disorders, derived directly from the principles that underpinned the social discipline of service.

In some places particular processes were developed within the system of courts to settle domestic disputes where servants locked horns with their masters. In London, many such squabbles were quickly referred to the Chamberlain's Court. There and elsewhere, interventions in disordered households were a substantial portion of court business.[22] The potential also existed within early modern systems of regulation to design penalties to punish and reform the disorderly young. In a society in which the most familiar understanding of the formation of criminal character was in some respects rooted in the life-cycle, where the fall into crime was imagined as a line of tumbling cards,[23] it is no surprise that added emphasis was placed on correcting the crimes of the young. Youth was the key stage in the penitential and reforming 'last dying speeches' of the condemned felon, the time of life when the first small lapse set in motion a speedy slide to the gallows.[24]

Places of confinement for the young in the early modern period included a 'prison for servants' in Norwich or the 'Little Ease' in London. Young men who dressed far above their station-in-life or who frequented alehouses or other dens of disorder were sent to a 'special gaol or prison' for apprentices in Newcastle. [25] Let us not forget, too, that bridewells or houses of correction were constructed, as Joanna Innes writes, as 'penal instruments specifically designed to correct the faults of a servant class', and that it was hoped that they would 'arrest the descent into incorrigible delinquency of those who had taken the first few steps towards a life of crime'. The young were certainly treated as a case apart in the 1576 Act that planned 'to set the poor on work' in houses of correction. In such places, it was said, 'youth may be accustomed and brought up in labour and work, and then not like to grow to be idle rogues'.[26] Also significant in this respect are the practices and principles of the charity schools at the turn of the eighteenth century and the proliferation of workhouses at the same time, which were frequently cut from the same cloth. In Bristol, the children of the poor who were spotted 'lousing like locusts in every corner of the streets' were sent to the workhouse to be turned into 'neat and wholesome' bright hopes for the future.[27] A poor children's bill to place young paupers in 'houses of industry' was put before Parliament in 1752, though it sank after some consideration.[28]

Young people also featured prominently in the early history of transportation. This ocean crossing was to some extent pioneered as an opportunity to give a second chance to street children and the children of the settled poor. 'Many cittyzens' petitioned London Common Council in 1618 to sing the praises of a scheme 'for taking upp of vagrant boyes and girles that lyve and begg in the streetes', who had 'no place of abode nor friends to relieve them, and for the transporting of them to Virginia to be imployed in some industrious courses'. A Virginia Company ship set sail two years later with a hundred children from hard-up families on board. Other ships with similar human cargoes followed later. Overseas transportation was not first planned with the offspring of the poor exclusively in mind. It was instead one aspect of policies to combat crime and poverty, but, quite quickly, apprenticeship across the Atlantic Ocean emerged as one of a number of strategies to tackle problems raised by the young.[29]

Much the same can also be said about the public punishment of crime. Though never kept as an exclusive penalty for the delinquent young, these rituals with their scope for audience participation provided good opportunities through sermons and symbols to articulate the politics of age-relations in situations where its principles had been turned upside down. So it was that a Norwich apprentice was 'whipped with rodds' in 'the face of other servants'. Other symbolic touches were sometimes added to these juvenile-centred punishments to make messages even more powerful. James Ure, 'a ladde of xvi yeares', who planned to poison his master and mistress, was 'appointed to be strippd nakyd and tyed to a poste with a rope and whipped with rodds by two ladds'.[30]

In such ways, then, administrators of punishment in the early modern period could be creative and even innovative when producing youth-centred penalties. Highly significant, too, were policing techniques that were planned to curb the disorders of the young. In towns, as well as in rural districts, the sharpest anxiety expressed in orders setting up night-time curfews usually concerned the rowdy exploits of young people. In addition, special officers or watches were instructed to keep a close eye on the young in tense times or situations, and they included parish officers equipped with 'a wand to correct stubbornnes' and powers to 'admonish' napping or chatting servants in church, patrols set-up on busy streets and strategic corners in London to stop young people walking the streets dressed in 'monstrous' clothing, or special measures to police the capital's apprentices and servants on festive days like Shrove Tuesday or ritual events like the mayor's parade.[31]

As well as punishing and policing delinquent juveniles, contemporary moralists and magistrates also produced procedures to reform, reclaim, protect, and even, in the words of a later century, to 'save' them. It must be remembered that it was hoped that service would both regulate and educate young people. The emphasis on reforming the offender was a keynote theme in the practices and principles of punishment in the sixteenth and seventeenth centuries, most notably in the correction of misdemeanours, the usual first breach of the law for most young delinquents.[32] The malleability of youth in contemporary moral and intellectual images seemed to provide a golden opportunity to reform souls, an intervention that was imagined as massaging wax into more manageable shapes or bending twigs while they were still brittle. Unlike older adults who were too deeply sunk in the wicked ways of the world, it was thought that there was still a possibility of reforming people in their youth.[33] After a string of allegations about his 'disorderly carriage' and abuses to his master and mother in 1639, Francis Taylor promised magistrates that he would 'become a new man'. It was said in 1632, that 'nothing will reclaime' the apprentice John Baldwin who had 'been oftentimes before the [London] chamberlaine'.[34]

The better chances of reform in youth offered a glimmer of hope, but it was also felt that the young needed protecting from poisonous environments that would possibly put them on the road to a life-time of crime and deprivation. This was one reason why child paupers were plucked from their squalid home-life and put in service. To this extent, the twin calamities of crime and poverty were felt to be hereditary. So it was that the authorities intervened in pauper households and in others where young people were the victims of cruel abuse or neglect that threatened their life-chances. The London fishmonger, Arthur Mouse, was sharply rebuked by his company court because he 'taketh many apprentizes and bringeth them upp very few or none to any purpose'. The clothworker ,William Standish, was cautioned to treat his apprentice 'in better sort hereafter ... to use reasonable correction towardes him, and not to be over furious for every little faulte'. In situations such as these the courts acted as umpires of domestic disorders, and they were perfectly prepared to rule against rogue masters or parents.[35] In similar ways, 'enticers', 'corrupters', or 'seducers' of young men or women like bawds, nightwalkers, lecherous masters, 'brokers' who placed servants with the sole intention that they would steal from their master, beggars who used children to squeeze sympathy from passers-by, or adult thieves who passed on the tricks of the trade, were prosecuted in the courts and lampooned in texts or visual images. As well as these polluting individuals, magistrates and moralists also targeted corrupting institutions like bowling alleys or dancing-, dicing-, and fencing-schools. Again, the environmental and hereditary nature of the causes of crime are apparent, and this list of family, workplace, and moral blemishes is a near reproduction of the causes of juvenile delinquency outlined in nineteenth-century investigations of this 'new' social disease.[36]

Finally, I want to reiterate the significance of service in households, hospitals, or workhouses, not just as a preparation for full participation in the adult world, but, as in the most optimistic contemporary formulations, as a process of cultural and social engineering that would reclaim and reform lost youth. This was why the courts took steps to patch up shattered master/servant relations; why the rootless and independent young were pressured to settle down with a master; and why service was considered to be a linchpin of political and social order. Thus vagrant young people were shifted from the streets and put to work in bridewells; and abandoned, needy and sick children were moved to the Children's Hospital in Norwich and Christ's Hospital in London. A part of the day was usually spent in moral and religious teaching in such places. At London Bridewell work discipline was supplemented by a diet of preaching and catechising that spread 'the principles of religion'. One hundred bibles were handed to the apprentices 'as can reade' in 1652, 'for their better instruction in the knowledge of God and the edifyinge of their fellows which cannot reade'; it was expected that apprentices would spend Sunday indoors 'readinge and repeatinge what they learned att the chappell'.[37] Much the same commitment to moulding character and imparting work skills motivated those who set up apprenticeship schemes across the ocean in the American colonies.

Clear identifications of 'problem' groups of youth together with less specific conceptualisations of youth as a distinctive, threatening presence in the early modern period gave rise to a bundle of policies and penalties that were devised to tame and reform delinquent juveniles. That much is certain and essential to situating juvenile delinquency in time. In many respects, however, the types of behaviour described in later panics about juvenile delinquency were not in any radical sense qualitatively different to the ones that filled early modern commentators with dread. It is now time to wonder exactly what was different about the treatment of the disorderly young after the turn of the nineteenth century.

Juvenile Delinquency

'Problems' of youth were recast yet again in the nineteenth century, and it seems to me that we must follow a two-tier point of entry when investigating these reconfigurations of age-relations. In the first place, and especially with regard to policies and penalties, extensions of practices already followed in the early modern period are very apparent. Second, significant shifts occurred most notably in, language and conceptualisation, the precise age-group under consideration in these ritual rants about delinquent youth, and in the material circumstances in which most young people were groomed for adulthood. There was therefore no continuous stream of change over time or any inevitable progression. A more muddled yet accurate impression would lay emphasis on simultaneous patterns of cumulative change and seemingly sudden turns when the nature of perceptions took a quite different course.

As befits a complicated question, the rise of juvenile delinquency has spawned many explanations. As mentioned, several of them pinpoint extensions of practices that, if only spasmodically, were followed in the early modern past, including the accelerated establishment of age-specific penalties and corrective institutions like Parkhurst (1838) and reformatory schools.[38] Equally important was the space created inside the criminal justice system for juvenile courts and the processing of young offenders by summary justice - though this last manoeuvre was by no means new.[39] One offshoot of these developments at a time when statistics were put on a more scientific footing was a regular record of the ages of offenders. Ages were noted in the records of some early modern courts but not as a general rule of thumb. Records also described suspects through age-titles like 'boy', 'servant', or 'wench', which directly derived from the life-course and assisted in constructions of the most likely sources of crime.[40] But new possibilities for the classification and categorisation of juveniles were opened up by record-keepers, social investigators, and statisticians after 1800, even though it is still difficult to agree with Peter Rush that a quickening anxiety about life-course crime signalled 'a novel problem' - a rising tide of juvenile crime.[41]

Nor are any of the following ideas that have been pushed forwards to explain the sudden coining of juvenile delinquency the exclusive property of the decades after 1800 - the brand new push to reform offenders with its implications for the young;[42] a crystal-clear sense of the young as the bright hope of the uncertain future and as mirrors of society;[43] the 'domino-theory' of criminality in which dangerous felonies followed quickly on the heels of minor lapses in youth;[44] and an environmental understanding of crime, that discourses of criminality became 'the repository for broader fears about social change'.[45] What might be more convincing is the cumulative impact of these perceptions or strategies over a period of some innovation within the criminal justice system that had substantial repercussions for the treatment of young offenders.

There were changes, too, in the material circumstances affecting the lives of the young in the eighteenth and nineteenth centuries. Again, few of these situations had not existed in previous centuries, including the waves of quick population growth that tipped the balance of the age-structure towards the young,[46] or the speedy growth of trouble-torn towns where it was felt that tribes of street children roamed free.[47] But it is the near synchronicity of such far-reaching changes with the other ones under review here that collectively raised unease about juveniles and resulted in new departures in the conceptualisation and management of the problems which these situations raised. There were also further changes in social relations and authority structures that might well have resulted in a narrowing of perceptions of the age-range of 'problem' youth. These were the long drawn-out but steady decline in apprenticeship and service, and the leap in the number of young wage-workers.[48] The visibility of the young and senses of them as escalating financial and social costs sharpened as population growth zoomed upwards after 1750, as already bulging towns kept growing, and as the nature of work and subordination through socialisation altered forever.

A long familiar and cherished control over young people was disappearing in the eighteenth and nineteenth centuries. Service was called 'both a moral and political institution' and a 'custom' in the early nineteenth century.[49] Edward Thompson writes that the fall in the number of servants and apprentices 'was not an easy or quick transition'. It spread deep-rooted concerns about socialising youth, however, at a time when waged work (or schooling) had yet to fully satisfy contemporaries that it had the full potential to discipline workers of any age-group.[50] This scare about authority structures and the regulation of employment was broadcast by Defoe, Fielding, 'the manufacturing interest' and, memorably, in the fuss that flared-up over the repeal of the Statute of Artificers (1814), which fits neatly with the most recent chronology of the rise of juvenile delinquency. This Statute had been a planned brake on the 'unadvised rashness and licentiousness of youth' for almost exactly 350 years. One MP claimed that its loss would be 'ruinous to the morals of youth'; another dryly commented that 'it was much better that young people should not be left without some controule'.[51]

It is unlikely that this sharp concern about 'masterless' young people, which was energised by more general anxieties about the moral and physical condition of the working class, did not have a connection with the first entry of juvenile delinquency into regulatory vocabularies after 1800. One apparent difference between this latest cycle in conceptualising delinquent youth and its Tudor and Stuart counterparts was a shortening of the age-span under consideration.[52] This was in part the consequence of life-course shifts that were to eventually prune the duration of youth and prompt much rethinking about pre-adult stages of life. These included the drop in the average age at first marriage which was already bringing forward the leap from youth into adulthood before 1800. The long decline of service also altered the nature of experiences and perceptions. Arguably, it directed fresh attention towards pre-teenage and teenage years, especially in the pressing circumstances that followed its regionally patterned decline. For example: the growing number of teenagers who stayed at home, the tough afflictions of children working long hours in factories, the rising vulnerability of the young to economic slumps, their insufficient poor relief provision, and their marginal status in occupational structures that resulted in their unemployment and under-employment.[53] Specific senses of children and teenagers as victims and villains were by now among the burning issues of the day, and in different ways to those in which similar preoccupations were expressed three centuries earlier.

So, service, once the cornerstone of age-discipline, was falling away and this was one of the reasons why 'problems of youth' were redefined both in terms of age and substance. Nevertheless, this was no tidy displacement, as service continued to be a cause of concern in the nineteenth century. It has also recently been suggested that not only was the range of years cut by perceptions of juvenile delinquency, but that the scope of offending was limited too. The soaring rates of indicted theft by young people at the turn of the nineteenth century have received special emphasis. So much so, that Peter King argues that it was 'juvenile depradators' who sent contemporary concerns rocketing skywards after 1800.[54] It certainly seems that, from Patrick Colquhoun on, social investigations, including later Parliamentary reports, dwelt at some length on light-fingered juveniles and that, in so doing, they interpreted juvenile delinquency in a less comprehensive way than we might expect today.

Yet this narrowing of the compass of offending is to some extent the outcome of the selection of sources as well. Most recently, Peter King's important interpretation of the rise of juvenile delinquency draws upon the records of serious crime (felony) alone. The contemporary sense of crime levels, he notes, 'was based on the number of felons tried before the major [felony] courts'.[55] One possible flaw here is that, given its case profile, this felony focus is not without its pitfalls and it will inevitably reproduce a massive concern with theft in any century for which records survive (theft is always the largest category of crime prosecuted in the felony courts). The chance recording of a run of ages in the London Criminal Registers (1791) where juveniles were a smaller pool of offenders than in later Assize and Quarter Sessions records drawn from other districts before the nationwide compilation of age information (1834), not unfairly creates an impression of a leap in indicted property crime by juveniles.[56] But the suddenness or novelty of this burst of juvenile theft is partly formed by silences in the sources. Comparative age information is missing for the early modern period, a position that is complicated still further by the sparse age data in the records of petty crime between the sixteenth and nineteenth centuries.[57]

If the common denominator in early ideas of juvenile delinquency was theft, then this represents a sharp break from descriptions of 'problems of youth' in the early modern past and a thinner understanding than the ones that emerged over the next 150 years. Present-day senses of juvenile delinquency are loose and flexible, with the result that they can be stretched to cover a multitude of situations. Demmie Vonghel in Saul Bellow's *Humboldt's Gift* (1975) calls juvenile delinquency 'the whole works'.[58] The last few generations of social scientists seem satisfied with matching catch-all meanings - juvenile delinquency is 'the failure of children and youth to meet certain obligations expected of them by the society in which they live', 'the characterisation of an act by a juvenile as a violation of delinquency laws', 'illegal behaviour by youths', 'crimes committed by young people'; or the 'anti-social acts of children and young people'.[59]

In a nutshell, then, juvenile delinquency is today imagined in an open-ended manner as 'the whole works'. This ample scope is precisely what early modern moralists had in mind when they moaned about 'ill-advised and ill-nurtured youth'.[60] The conceptual migration that seems to have occurred after 1800 raises a couple of possibilities. That the sorts of misdemeanour and street disorder that we now think of as juvenile delinquency became more prosecuted and visible as time passed, perhaps as a result of the activities of the Police Courts in the second half of the nineteenth century where high numbers of victimless misdemeanours were prosecuted;[61] or, more likely, that they existed side-by-side with the property crime that was so noticed in the early nineteenth century, but had yet to be fully incorporated into understandings of juvenile delinquency.[62] One suspects that a more complete study of the records of petty crime and summary justice might well reveal an absorption with the anti-social juvenile offender in the early nineteenth century. In this respect, the growing pains of manufacturing and the towns raised challenging questions about the control of youth for governors, and it is difficult to imagine that, like elites in seventeenth-century London for example, they did not imagine crime and its extent in terms far broader than the rate of prosecuted felony.

Conclusions

Delinquent youth can be found in all centuries. Young people in the early modern past were not silent lambs, drained of creativity by a powerful patriarchy in all situations. Socialisation was never inevitable or natural then. Delinquency as well as conformity was widespread, and a clutch of youth-related perceptions and policies emerged as a result of this situation.

My purpose in saying this is not to suggest that sluggish continuities are the principal features of juvenile delinquency in time. 'Problems of youth' and their conceptualisation move through cycles where meanings are never stationary but shift as circumstances, cultures, and ideologies alter. These reconfigurations continue today.[63] And, finally, to return to my original question - can something exist without the power of prior definition? Juvenile delinquency was not legislated into existence in the early nineteenth century, though this new form of words signalled a conceptual twist.[64] This idea resulted from the convergence of changes in society and the criminal justice system that pushed juvenile delinquents into the spotlight. Few of these changes were unique, and most of the patterns of behaviour that concerned the people who first coined the term juvenile delinquency raised storms of protest as far back in time as the stories in our surviving sources begin.

* I must thank Peter King for many highly profitable chats about juvenile delinquency in time.

Endnotes

1   For the sixteenth and seventeenth centuries see P. Griffiths, *Youth and Authority: Formative Experiences in England, 1560-1640* (Oxford, 1996), chaps 3-7.

2   J. Habermas, 'Modernity - an incomplete project', in H. Foster ed., *Postmodern Culture* (1983), pp. 3-15, quoting p. 4. Let us not forget that an ESRC funded research-project is called 'Youth, Crime, and the Coming of Modernity'. The many problems in following modernity as a conceptual point of entry for studies of the family and its parts are noted by Keith Wrightson, 'The family in early modern England: continuity and change', in S. Taylor, R. Connors, & C. Jones eds., *Hanoverian Britain and Empire: Essays in Memory of Philip Lawson* (Woodbridge, 1998), esp. pp. 5-10 & 12-13.

3   P. King & J. Noel, 'The origins of the "problem of juvenile delinquency": the growth of juvenile prosecutions in London in the late eighteenth and early nineteenth centuries', *Criminal Justice History*, 14 (1993), pp. 17-41, quoting p. 17. See also P. King, 'The rise of juvenile delinquency in England 1780-1840: changing patterns of perception and prosecution', *Past and Present*, 160 (1998), pp. 116-66, esp. pp. 116, 154-5; M. May, 'Innocence and experience: the evolution of the concept of juvenile delinquency in the mid-nineteenth century', *Victorian Studies*, 17 (1973), pp. 7-29, esp. p. 14; S. Margery, 'The invention of juvenile delinquency in early nineteenth-century England', *Labour History*, 34 (1978), pp. 11-27; P. Rush, 'The government of a generation: the subject of juvenile delinquency', *Liverpool Law Review*, 14 (1992), pp. 3-43, esp. p. 10.

4   J.H. Plumb, 'The new world of children in eighteenth-century England', *Past and Present*, 67 (1975), pp. 64-93.

5   King, 'Rise of juvenile delinquency', pp. 158-9. See also H. Shore, *Artful Dodgers: Youth and Crime in Early Nineteenth-Century London* (Woodbridge, 1999), p. 150. Earlier child-centred approaches are discussed in N. Orme, 'The culture of children in medieval England', *Past and Present*, 148 (1995), pp. 48-88; A. Bryson, *From Courtesy to Civility: Changing Codes of Conduct in Early Modern England* (Oxford, 1998), p. 67.

6   See, for example, E. Shorter, *The Making of the Modern Family* (New York, 1975); L. Stone, *The Family, Sex and Marriage in England* (London, 1977); T. Laqueur, *Making Sex: Body and Gender from the Greeks to Freud* (Cambridge, Mass., 1990); id., 'Sex and desire in the Industrial Revolution', in P. O'Brien & R. Quinault eds., *The Industrial Revolution and*

British Society (Cambridge, 1993), pp. 100-23; A. Fletcher, *Gender, Sex, and Subordination in England, 1500-1800* (New Haven & London, 1995); and, most recently, T. Hitchcock, 'Redefining sex in eighteenth-century England', *History Workshop Journal*, 41 (1996), pp. 72-90; id., *English Sexualities, 1700-1800* (Basingstoke, 1997).

[7] M. Mitterauer, *A History of Youth*, trans. G. Dunphy (Oxford, 1992), pp. 132, 236.

[8] See esp. Griffiths, *Youth and Authority*, chaps 3-7; M. Thornton Burnett, *Masters and Servants in English Renaissance Drama and Culture: Authority and Obedience* (Basingstoke, 1997); K. Thomas, 'Children in early modern England', in G. Avery & J. Briggs eds., *Children and Their Books: A Celebration of the Work of Iona and Peter Opie* (Oxford, 1989), pp. 45-77.

[9] Rush, pp. 3, 8; King & Noel, 'Origins of the "problem of juvenile delinquency"', pp. 35-6; King, 'Rise of juvenile delinquency', p. 166.

[10] B.M. Berger, 'On the youthfulness of youth culture', *Social Research* 30 (1963), pp. 319-42, quoting p. 319.

[11] Heather Shore detects 'a strong continuity in the debates about adolescent and disorderly youth which can be traced through the early modern period' (*Artful Dodgers*, p. 148). See also Ibid., pp. 2, 17; King, 'Rise of juvenile delinquency', p. 116. The best account of the nature of early modern youth in work on later centuries is still J. Springhall, *Coming of Age: Adolescence in Britain, 1860-1960* (Dublin, 1986).

[12] J.R. Gillis, 'The evolution of juvenile delinquency in England, 1890-1914', *Past and Present*, 67 (1975), pp. 96-126, quoting p. 96; H. Cunningham, *Children and Childhood in Western Society Since 1500* (London, 1995), p. 145; M.H. Neumeyer, *Juvenile Delinquency in Modern Society* (Toronto, 1949), p. 3.

[13] T. Barnes, *The Wise-Mans Forecast Against the Evill Time* (1624), p. 59. Stubbes is quoted in D. Underdown, *Revel, Riot and Rebellion: Popular Politics and Culture in England, 1603-1660* (Oxford, 1985), p. 48.

[14] P. Slack, *Poverty and Policy in Tudor and Stuart England* (1988), p. 98; A.L. Beier, *Masterless Men: The Vagrancy Problem in England, 1560-1640* (London and New York, 1985), pp. 54-5.

[15] P. Griffiths, 'Masterless young people in Norwich, 1560-1645', in P. Griffiths, A. Fox & S. Hindle eds., *The Experience of Authority in Early Modern England* (Basingstoke, 1996), pp. 146-86; Beier, *Masterless Men*, esp. pp. 55-6; id., 'Social problems in Elizabethan London', *Journal of Interdisciplinary History*, 9 (1978), pp. 203-21, esp. pp. 203-5; I. W. Archer, *The Pursuit of Stability: Social Relations in Elizabethan London* (Cambridge, 1991), pp. 206-8; D. Andrew, *Philanthropy and Police: London Charity in the Eighteenth Century* (Princeton, 1989), pp. 182-3.

[16] R. von Friedeburg, 'Reformation of manners and the social composition of offenders in an East Anglian village: Earls Colne, Essex, 1531-1642', *Journal of British Studies*, 29 (1990), pp. 347-79; P. Collinson, *The Religion of Protestants: The Church in English Society, 1559-1625* (Oxford, 1982), pp. 224-5; M. Ingram, *Church Courts, Sex, and Marriage in England, 1570-1640* (Cambridge, 1987), esp. pp. 123, 354-5; D. Underdown, *Fire From Heaven: Life in an English Town in the Seventeenth Century* (1992), pp. 79-84; Griffiths, *Youth and Authority*, esp. chap. 4.

17 J.M. Beattie, *Crime and the Courts in England, 1660-1800* (Oxford, 1986), pp. 243-7. Cf. M.B. Boes, 'The treatment of juvenile delinquents in early modern Germany: a case study', *Continuity and Change*, 11 (1996), pp. 43-60, esp. p. 50.

18 M. Ingram, 'Reformation of manners in early modern England', in Griffiths, Fox, & Hindle eds., *Experience of Authority*, pp. 47-88, esp. p. 75; R.B. Shoemaker, 'Reforming the city: the reformation of manners campaign in London, 1690-1738', in L. Davison et al eds., *Stilling the Grumbling Hive: The Responses to Social and Economic Problems in England, 1689-1750* (Stroud, 1992), pp. 99-120, esp. p. 110.

19 M.E. Wiesner, *Women and Gender in Early Modern Europe* (Cambridge, 1993), esp. pp. 23, 62, 89, 99; Beier, *Masterless Men*, pp. 54-5; Griffiths, 'Masterless young people'.

20 J. Beattie, 'London crime and the making of the "bloody code", 1689-1718', in Davison et al eds., *Stilling the Grumbling Hive*, pp. 49-76, esp. p. 69; B[ridewell] H[ospital] C[ourtbook] 8, fo. 44.

21 The literature on this aspect of early modern society is neatly summarised in G. Mayhew, 'Life-cycle, service and the family unit in early modern Rye', *Continuity and Change*, 6 (1991), pp. 201-26.

22 See Griffiths, *Youth and Authority*, esp. chaps 5-6; P. Seaver, 'A social contract? Master against servant in the Court of Requests', *History Today*, 39 (Sept. 1989), pp. 50-6.

23 J.A. Sharpe, *Crime in Early Modern England, 1550-1750* (1984), esp. pp. 162-4; Beattie, *Crime and the Courts*, p. 60; R.B. Shoemaker, *Prosecution and Punishment: Petty Crime and the Law in London and Rural Middlesex, c.1660-1725* (Cambridge, 1991), p. 250; Archer, pp. 206-7.

24 Griffiths, *Youth and Authority*, pp. 35-6; J.A. Sharpe, '"Last dying speeches": religion, ideology, and public executions in seventeenth-century England', *Past and Present*, 107 (1985), pp. 144-67; N. Wurzbach, *The Rise of the English Street Ballad, 1550-1650*, trans. G. Walls (Cambridge, 1990), pp. 112-13, 126, 129.

25 N[orfolk] R[ecord] O[ffice] Norwich Chamberlain's Accounts, 1551-67, fo. 225; BHC 8, fos 203, 282v; J.R. Boyle & F.W. Dendy eds., *Extracts from the Records of the Merchant Adventurers of Newcastle-upon-Tyne* (2 vols., Surtees Society, 93, 101, Durham, 1895, 1899), i, pp. 20-3.

26 J. Innes, 'Prisons for the poor: English bridewells, 1555-1800', in F. Snyder & D. Hay eds., *Labour, Law and Crime: A Historical Perspective* (Oxford, 1987), pp. 42-122, quoting pp. 47, 101. See also Shoemaker, *Prosecution and Punishment*, esp. pp. 174-5, 184 n.70, 184-5; Griffiths, 'Masterless young people'.

27 T. Hitchcock, 'Paupers and preachers: the SPCK and the parochial workhouse movement', and M. Fissell, 'Charity universal? Institutions and moral reform in eighteenth-century Bristol', in L. Davison et al eds., *Stilling the Grumbling Hive*, pp. 145-66, esp. pp. 152, 156, & pp. 121-44, esp. pp. 124, 126, 129; id., *Patients, Power, and the Poor in Eighteenth-Century Bristol* (Cambridge, 1991), chap. 4; Slack, *Poverty and Policy*, p. 198; Beattie, 'London crime and the making of the "Bloody Code"', p. 61.

28 N. Rogers, 'Confronting the crime wave: the debate over social reform and regulation, 1749-1753', in L. Davison et al eds., *Stilling the Grumbling Hive*, pp. 77-98, esp. pp. 90-1.

29 C[orporation of] L[ondon] R[ecord] O[ffice] Jour[nals of Common Council] 30, fos 374, 382, 396, 397v; 31, fos 125-5v, 129; Rep[ertories of the Court of Aldermen] 36, fos 170,

275; BHC 6, fo. 101v. See also R.C. Johnson, 'The transportation of vagrant children from London to Virginia, 1618-1622', in H.S. Reinmuth ed., *Early Stuart Studies* (Minneapolis, 1970), pp. 137-51. The most helpful summary of the early history of transportation is J. Innes, 'The role of transportation in seventeenth- and eighteenth-century English penal practice', in C. Bridge ed., *New Perspectives in Australian History* (1990), pp. 1-24.

30 NRO N[orwich] M[ayor's] C[ourtbooks] 9, fo. 148; 8, fo. 430.

31 For church-officers see G[uildhall] L[ibrary, London] MSS 1175/1, fos 40v, 51; 1431/2, fo. 187; 1175/1, fo 51; CLRO Jour. 22, fos. 76v-7; W.H. Frere ed., *Visitation Articles and Injunctions of the Period of the Reformation, 1536-1575* (3 vols.; Alcuin Club Collections, 14-16, 1910), iii, p. 168. For examples of clothing officers see CLRO Jours 21, fo. 428; 24, fos 227, 237v; Rep. 14, fo. 332v; 15, fos 77, 86; 16, fo. 48v; GL MS 11,588/1, fos 46, 48, 128.

32 P. Griffiths, 'Bodies and souls in early modern Norwich: punishing petty crime, 1560-1700', in P. Griffiths & S. Devereaux eds., *Punishment, Pardon, and Pain: The Production and Selection of Penalty in England, 1500-1850*, forthcoming; Boes, 'Treatment of juvenile delinquents', esp. p. 55.

33 Griffiths, *Youth and Authority*, esp. chap. 1; I. Krausman Ben-Amos, *Adolescence and Youth in Early Modern England* (New Haven, London, 1994), esp. chap. 1; S.R. Smith, 'Religion and the conception of youth in seventeenth-century England', *History of Childhood Quarterly*, 2 (1975), pp. 493-515.

34 BHC 8, fo. 234; 7, fo. 304. The importance of reformation in the considerations of sixteenth- and seventeenth-century courts will be explored in much greater depth in my forthcoming *The First Bridewell: Petty Crime, Policing, and Prisons in London, 1545-1660*.

35 GL MS 5770/1, fo. 255; Clothworkers' Hall, London, company minute book 1581-1605, fo. 81v. See also Griffiths, *Youth and Authority*, chap. 6.

36 H. Shore, 'Home, play and street life: causes of, and explanations for, juvenile crime in the early nineteenth century', in A. Fletcher & S. Hussey eds., *Childhood in Question: Children, Parents, and the State* (Manchester, 1999), pp. 96-114; id., *Artful Dodgers*, pp. 20, 22; D. Taylor, *Crime, Policing, and Punishment in England, 1750-1914* (Basingstoke, 1998), p. 63.

37 BHC 9, fos 147, 187, 528, 532, 583.

38 This age-angle to the development of penalty is emphasised by King, 'Rise of juvenile delinquency', esp. pp. 133-7; Margery, pp. 24-5; May, pp. 7, 13. The development of institutions is described in L. Radzinowicz & R. Hood, *A History of English Criminal Law and its Administration from 1750: Volume 5, The Emergence of Penal Policy* (1986), esp. chaps 6-7 & 19; and more briefly in P. Rawlings, *Crime and Power: A History of Criminal Justice, 1688-1998* ((Harlow, 1999), pp. 96-8.

39 These developments within the criminal justice system are stressed by King, 'Rise of juvenile delinquency'; and Shore, *Artful Dodgers*, pp. 29-34.

40 See Griffiths, *Youth and Authority*, esp. pp. 24-6. A quite similar process of patchy age-recording but far more frequent age-title registration is also evident in the criminal records of early modern Frankfurt. Maria Boes writes that 'References to the young age of an offender were diligently recorded [in the criminal records of Frankfurt] either by stating the precise or approximate age of a young suspect or by referring to the delinquent as either a young boy or a young girl. This recording method [she notes], is itself indicative of the fact that

contemporaries were at least aware, if not convinced, of the importance of the age-factor [in law-breaking]' ('Treatment of juvenile delinquents', p. 47).

41 Shore, *Artful Dodgers*, pp. 18-19; Rush, p. 10. See also May, esp. pp. 15-17. The splitting of criminals into 'classes' and its implications for juvenile delinquency are discussed in King, 'Rise of juvenile delinquency', pp. 154-5.

42 King, 'Rise of juvenile delinquency', pp. 153, 156, 159; M.J. Wiener, *Reconstructing the Criminal: Culture, Law, and Policy in England, 1830-1914* (Cambridge, 1990), pp. 131, 358-9; May, pp. 8, 11, 28; H. Shore, '"An old offender tho' so young in years": the criminal careers of juvenile offenders in Middlesex in the 1830s', in T. Hitchcock, P.King, & P. Sharpe eds., *Chronicling Poverty: The Voices and Strategies of the English Poor, 1640-1840* (Basingstoke, 1997), pp. 192-210, esp. 204; Gillis, 'Evolution of juvenile delinquency', p.97; G. Fisher, 'The birth of the prison retold', *The Yale Law Journal*, 104 (1995), pp. 1236-324, esp. pp. 1238, 1243, 1277, 1279, 1290, 1306.

43 Rush, pp. 11-12; King, 'Rise of juvenile delinquency', p. 157.

44 Fisher, 'Birth of the prison', esp. pp. 1242, 1281, 1282-3.

45 Quoting King, 'Rise of juvenile delinquency', p. 157, who is following V.A.C. Gatrell, 'Crime, authority, and the policeman-state', in F.M.L. Thompson ed., *The Cambridge Social History of Britain 1750-1950: Volume 3, Social Agencies and Institutions* (Cambridge, 1990), pp. 243-310, esp. pp. 250, 251-2, 254.

46 Wiener, esp. pp 14, 17; Taylor, *Crime, Policing, and Punishment*, p. 62. Earlier demographic situations featuring large proportions of young people are examined in E.A. Wrigley & R.S. Schofield, *The Population History of England, 1541-1871: A Reconstruction* (Cambridge, 1989), esp. pp. 215-19 & 443-50.

47 King, 'Rise of juvenile delinquency', pp. 138-40; J. Walvin, *A Child's World: A Social History of English Childhood, 1800-1914* (Harmondsworth, 1982), p. 57 & chap. 10.

48 A. Kussmaul, *Servants in Husbandry in Early Modern England* (Cambridge, 1981), pp. 114-29; K. Snell, *Annals of the Labouring Poor: Social Change and Agrarian England, 1660-1900* (Cambridge, 1985), esp. pp. 67-103 & 228-69; id., 'The apprenticeship system in British history: the fragmentation of a cultural institution', *History of Education*, 25 (1996), pp. 303-21; P. Horn, *Children's Work and Welfare, 1780-1890* (Cambridge, 1994), chaps 1-2; H. Cunningham, 'The employment and unemployment of children in England, c.1680-1851', *Past and Present*, 126 (1990), pp. 115-50; King, 'Rise of juvenile delinquency', pp. 140-5; Fisher, p. 1242.

49 Randle Jackson, speaking before a committee of the House of Commons in 1806, is quoted by A. Randall, *Before the Luddites: Custom, Community and Machinery in the English Woollen Industry, 1776-1809* (Cambridge, 1991), p. 243.

50 E.P. Thompson, 'The patricians and the plebs', in his *Customs in Common* (1991), pp. 16-96, quoting p. 36. More general concerns about the subordination of labour and youth are discussed in J. Rule, 'Employment and authority: masters and men in eighteenth-century manufacturing', in Griffiths, Fox, & Hindle eds., *Experience of Authority*, pp. 286-317; Thompson, esp. pp. 36-42; Wiener, pp. 17-19, 51.

51 Defoe and Fielding are discussed in Rule, pp. 288-9. The description of the Statute is quoted from a memorandum on it which is reprinted in R. Tawney & E. Power eds., *Tudor Economic Documents* (3 vols.; 1924), iii, p. 363. Parliamentary proceedings concerning the

repeal are reprinted in *Hansard, 1813-1814*, pp. 879, 892-3. See also D. Hay & N. Rogers, *Eighteenth-Century English Society: Shuttles and Swords* (Oxford, 1997), pp. 102-9; Randall, *Before the Luddites*, chap. 7; H. Hendrick, *Images of Youth: Age, Class, and the Male Youth Problem, 1820-1920* (Oxford, 1990), pp. 15-16.

[52] Peter King remarks that 'the growing debates about 'the alarming increase of juvenile delinquency' in the early nineteenth century focused on an earlier part of the lifespan', in the main the years up to age 17 ('Rise of juvenile delinquency', p. 121). See also H. Shore, 'The trouble with boys: gender and the 'invention' of the juvenile offender in early nineteenth-century Britain', in M.L. Arnot & C. Usborne eds., *Gender and Crime in Modern Europe* (1999), pp. 75-92, esp. p. 76.

[53] Cunningham, 'Employment and unemployment of children'; M. Anderson, 'The emergence of the modern life-cycle in Britain', *Social History*, 10 (1985), pp. 69-87; M. Winstanley ed., *Working Children in Nineteenth-Century Lancashire* (Preston, 1995); Horn, *Children's Work and Welfare*, chaps 1-2; King, 'Rise of juvenile delinquency', pp. 137-51, who warns against simple generalisations connecting socio-economic change and the rise of juvenile delinquency.

[54] Ibid., quoting p. 122. See also Ibid., esp. pp 125-6, 128, 130, 132, 151, 161; King & Noel, 'Origins of the 'problem of juvenile delinquency', esp. pp. 19, 21-2, 29, 30-1, 34, 35; Shore, *Artful Dodgers*, p. 18.

[55] King, 'Rise of juvenile delinquency', p. 120. King remarks that there are 'good theoretical as well as practical reasons' fort his felony focus. See also Fisher, esp. p. 1321.

[56] King, 'Rise of juvenile delinquency', esp. pp. 119-42.

[57] Cf. Shore, *Artful Dodgers*, p. 17.

[58] S. Bellow, *Humboldt's Gift* (Harmandsworth, 1996), p. 19.

[59] W.B. Sanders, *Juvenile Delinquency: Causes, Patterns and Reactions* (New York, 1981), p. 8; R. Shonie Cavan, *Juvenile Delinquency: Development, Treatment, Control* (Philadelphia, 1962), p. 15; H.B. Kaplan, *Patterns of Juvenile Delinquency* (Beverly Hills, London, 1984), p. 16; C. Bartollas, *Juvenile Delinquency* (New York, 1985), p. ix; Neumeyer, p. 16. See also M. Rutter & H. Giller, *Juvenile Delinquency: Trends and Perspectives* (Harmandsworth, 1983); *The Oxford English Dictionary* (second edition., Oxford, 1989), s.v. juvenile.

[60] T. Beard, *The Theatres of God's Judgement* (1631), p. 216.

[61] J. Davis, 'A poor man's system of justice: the London Police Courts in the second half of the nineteenth century', *Historical Journal*, 27 (1984), pp. 309-35; id., 'Prosecutions and their context: the use of the criminal law in later nineteenth-century London', in D. Hay & F. Snyder eds., *Policing and Prosecution in Britain, 1750-1850* (Oxford, 1989), pp. 397-426, esp. pp. 419-24. Later nineteenth-century panics about juvenile delinquents and the street life of the young are discussed in G. Pearson, *Hooligan: A History of Respectable Fears* (Basingstoke, 1983); J. Springhall, *Youth, Popular Culture and Moral Panics: Penny Gaffs to Gangsta-Rap, 1830-1996* (Basingstoke, 1998), esp. chaps 1-3; A. Davin, *Growing Up Poor: Home, School, and Street in London, 1870-1914* (1996).

[62] King, 'Rise of juvenile delinquency', p. 122; Shore, *Artful Dodgers*, p. 18; id., 'The trouble with boys', esp. pp. 78-86; Taylor, *Crime, Policing and Punishment*, p. 66.

[63] See V. Bailey, *Delinquency and Citizenship: Reclaiming the Young Offender, 1914-1948* (Oxford, 1987), p. 12; Kaplan, pp. 16-17; Gillis, 'Evolution of juvenile delinquency', p. 96.

[64]   Margery, 'Invention of juvenile delinquency', pp. 24-5.

Chapter 2

On *Not* Becoming Delinquent: Raising Adolescent Boys in the Dutch Republic, 1600-1750

Benjamin Roberts

Youth delinquency in urban areas is not a modern phenomenon. Its roots are deeply embedded in the collective socialisation of youth in the middle ages and early modern period. Dutch municipal officials, moralists, and parents in the seventeenth and eighteenth century were frequently concerned about the behaviour of their adolescent children, fearing the delinquent activities in which they might indulge. Many early modern boys often left the parental home in their early teens to attend a Latin School in another city or became apprentices in other households. Because of this they gained much more freedom at an earlier age than many youths today. This group of young, adolescent males caused great distress to the municipal authorities, ministers, and parents in Dutch cities in the seventeenth and eighteenth centuries. This chapter will focus on three families - Huijdecoper, Van der Muelen, and Huygens - to examine the methods they used to guide and govern their adolescent sons after they left the parental home. These families were members of the urban elite of the Dutch and had a representative function in society: it was therefore extremely important that their children be raised to uphold that image.[1] Delinquent and inappropriate behaviour displayed by such urban elite adolescents not only jeopardised their own good name and reputation, but also that of their families, the consequences of which could mean exclusion from the political arena and damage to their economic position. This chapter will address three matters. First, how were adolescents and youths in the early modern period socialised? Second, how, in urban areas, did they become delinquent? And third, how did urban elite parents try to control their offspring?

Collective Socialisation

Delinquency among young people has often been regarded as part of a collective process. In the middle ages when most of Europe resided in rural communities, male youths socialised in large groups with other juveniles, outside the parental home. Thus adolescent boys and young men of all social backgrounds formed youth groups that generally congregated at town squares or inns. The follies of these homogenous youth groups, which often included excessive drinking, fighting, and tomfoolery, were seen by the community as an accepted outlet for sexual frustration.[2] In rural French villages during the middle ages, such male youth groups had jurisdiction over their peers, including girls of marrying age as well as their elders. According to Natalie Zemon Davies, they fulfilled an important function as guardians of village norms and values. For example, when there was a large gap between the age of a bride and groom, 'the masked youth with their pots, tambourines, bells, rattles and horns might make their clamour for a week outside the house of their victims, unless they settled and paid a fine'. Further, local adults 'gave youths rituals to help control their sexual instincts and also allowed them some limited sphere of jurisdiction or 'autonomy' in the interval before they were married'.[3] In Dutch rural areas this tradition continued until the nineteenth century. Rural male youths were initiated into the world of adulthood by a series of rituals, such as 'spinning bees', 'abbeys', and 'charivaris' that were often organised by secular and church authorities.[4]

During the sixteenth century, the socialisation of adolescents and youths in Europe underwent a radical shift. The increasing migration of rural inhabitants to the cities and urban centres, meant that the 'autonomy' that youth groups had been allowed in rural society was no longer permissible. Urban authorities felt that their power was being challenged, and the city became a battlefield where the old youth culture of rural society with its collective socialisation and wild behaviour clashed with the more constrained and 'civilised' culture of urban society.[5] In the cities and urban areas young men were much less commonly socialised within old-style youth groups but increasingly within the family group and through their fathers in particular. New collective cultures and rituals nevertheless developed, in part because of the new opportunities afforded by the city and in part, perhaps, as a way of challenging this 'new' parental authority.[6]

Urban Constraints

This development was strongest in the highly urbanised areas of Europe such as the Dutch Republic of the seventeenth century. Arguably, the Dutch Republic of this so-called Golden Age represented much of Europe's future. This was a primarily urban society, with affluent burghers in nuclear families dominated by emerging bourgeois norms and values.[7] During the course of the seventeenth century the population of Dutch cities grew dramatically. At the beginning of the century Amsterdam was a small trading port of 30,000 inhabitants; by the end of the century it had exploded into the third largest city in Europe with 200,000 residents.[8] Amsterdam was not alone in this growth. In the early seventeenth century other cities such as Leiden and Middelburg also attracted large numbers of religious, political, and economic refugees, particularly from the southern Netherlands and German states during the Dutch Revolt and the Thirty Years War. The economic boom in the northern Netherlands at this time not only lured rural people from across Europe seeking employment in expanding sectors such as the Dutch East India Company, but also attracted social 'misfits'. such as prostitutes, vagabonds, and petty criminals.[9]

In response to concerns about disorder, Dutch urban authorities attempted to restrict the freedom of youths in a number of ways: judicially (by passing municipal ordinances); institutionally (by setting up correctional homes and orphanages); morally (by church sermons and catechisation books addressing adolescents); pedagogically (through parental upbringing at home); and, in drastic cases, by expulsion (through banishment from cities or deportation to the Dutch Indies). Urban officials were quite aware of the potential threat that youths posed to public order. During periods of religious and political struggle, city youths engaged in riots and other disturbances, and were apparently involved in plundering, stone throwing and window breaking. Moreover, these activities did not only involve youths from the lower echelons of Dutch society. During a riot in Amsterdam in 1696, witnesses reported seeing many boys from 'decent burgher families'.[10] Increased policing of youth specifically, and of burghers more generally, in Dutch cities in the seventeenth century is evidenced by the sheer number of laws passed by municipal councils aiming to curb public conduct. Successive town councils in the city of Utrecht, for example, introduced several new measures in the course of the century. It first prohibited holidays that were not recognised by the Dutch Reformed Church (such as the papal feasts of St. Martin, St. Nicolas, and Epiphany). Thereafter it tried to police public conduct by attacking neighbourhood games, meals, funerals, fairs, and activities that took place in and around the churches, or on public roads or waterways (such as walking, playing, fighting, rowdiness, and swimming). It strove for a more serene and meditative use of church buildings which were traditionally used as public meeting places. It subsequently aimed to control secular areas through the control of noisy neighbourhood parties, the playing of popular music, and boisterous funerals. Finally it aimed to curb vandalism and vagrancy and to regulate those who, for various reasons, were outside the prevailing economic order.[11]

One key way in which Dutch urban authorities tried to keep the streets free of rowdy youths was to set up correctional homes and orphanages. The first of its kind on the European continent, Amsterdam's correctional home - *Rasphuis* (Rasp house) - was given the task of reforming the city's criminal element, as well as those on its periphery.[12] The institution had a special ward for what were known as 'white bread children'. For a price the wealthy could confine young wayward family members in the hope of securing their reform. Urban elite families sought to protect their good name by having their sons (and other aberrant family members) incarcerated in cases of excessive drinking, womanising, and other deviant conduct. This was often a final sanction for parents who thought they had no other way of keeping their children on the right moral path.[13] Incarcerating and reforming delinquent family members was not unique to the Dutch Republic. In eighteenth century Seville an institution called the *Toribios* was used to prevent and correct juvenile delinquency and was used similarly by elite families.[14] In the Dutch Republic, orphanages in general fulfilled an important role in educating and steering adolescents in the right direction. These often operated as miniature societies with rules and regulations by which the 'orphans' had to abide. Whether a municipal, Protestant or alms orphanage, all intended to give children and young people a proper religious education and to provide them with a useful profession so that they could support themselves when they became adults. Besides being trained to become devout Christians, they were also trained to become disciplined city residents.[15] Their uniforms, compulsory and in the colours of the city, demarcated their public parameters. An 'orphan' inside a tavern or brothel was easily spotted, and could be expelled from the institution.[16]

Another means of maintaining public order was by filtering out social undesirables. According to criminal records, both juvenile and adult delinquents could be banished from the municipal and/or provincial boundaries as a punishment.[17] A more extreme measure allowed for them to be shipped off to the Dutch East Indies. That was the fate of five 'orphans' from Amsterdam's *Diachonie* orphanage in 1762. They had been caught red-handed by other orphans stealing valuables ranging from gold rings to pistols to shoes. Most of the goods were taken from fellow orphans and shopkeepers, and the culprits were not first-time offenders. In considering their case, the orphanage's 'house father' instructed that the boys be sent to either the West or East Indies since he feared that to allow them to stay would allow them to exercise a bad influence over other orphans, and that to release them into society would only give the orphanage a bad name.[18] For the Protestant orphanage in Delft, deportation to the East Indies was a common method of disposing of incorrigible orphans.[19] However, the Dutch East and West Indies were not only used for removing the 'criminal' element. They were also an outlet for 'surplus' youths without families or other 'acceptable' social networks. The Dutch East India Company regularly recruited orphans from Amsterdam's municipal orphanage because it needed boys for trade and service; this reached a peak in 1637 when 41 orphans entered the company's services.[20] The Dutch West India Company was also in desperate need of young apprentices to man its New Netherlands colony in North America. In 1651 the company approached the burgomasters of Amsterdam for their help in enlisting some three to four hundred orphans from the alms orphanage. The burgomasters were all too willing to comply to reduce the cost of running the orphanage, but qualified candidates were hard to find, and many did not want to go.[21]

Besides these extreme efforts (confinement, deportation and bonded labour) to prevent youths from becoming delinquent, other efforts were made to encourage them to internalise proper social values. Sermons and catechism, for example, represented more subtle moralising tactics. The 1602 *Schatboeck* [Treasure book], a handbook for the Heidelberg catechisation, openly appealed to the church to target youths as a way of maintaining social order. And the church continued this targeting, especially in periods of crisis and disaster, when it seemed that to discipline young people was to solve more generally defined social ills.

Leisure Activities

But now let us turn our attention to those who were most responsible for the everyday policing of youths - parents. Parental concern was very apparent in the Van der Muelen family, a wealthy and prestigious merchant family in Utrecht. Their 15 year old son Willem van der Muelen left the parental home in 1646 to attend the Latin School in Elbing, Prussia. In this period it was not unusual for elite Dutch parents to send an adolescent son to a Latin School in another city although it was very rare for them to choose a school outside the Republic. However, Willem's parents believed Prussian schools to be superior and entrusted him to the care of his brother-in-law, who lived in Prussia and who accompanied him on the journey. Soon after his arrival in June 1646, Willem received his first letter from his mother, Catharina van Santen. She reminded Willem of his duty to obey his brother-in-law, emphasised his religious duties, instructed him to be polite, and to observe the norms of Prussia. She urged Willem to behold God before him and to be alert to good and evil. She reminded him to pray to God on his knees in the morning and evening, and to be aware of all his actions, because they would be recorded by God, for eternity. He was advised to read a chapter of the Bible and to live by God's salvation as much as he could. She most likely brought these religious duties to Willem's attention in an attempt to protect him from the corrupt temptations which she feared loomed on his horizon - namely playing cards, drinking, idleness, and bad company.[22] Letters from Willem's father warned him to uphold the family reputation and stressed the necessity of unity and friendship.[23] When he reached the age of 17, his mother warned him in further letters about 'drinking, playing cards, and *débauche*'. If Willem was careless about such matters then his life would be, as she reminded him, 'a great sadness to him and to his parents'.[24] There was no indication in the correspondence that Willem's behaviour was anything but exemplary.

In Paris, while on the *grand tour*, 22 year old Johan Huijdecoper Jr, son of the burgomaster of Amsterdam, was apparently having a good time. Yet despite the distance between Paris and Amsterdam young Johan was still under the watchful eye of his father, who was kept informed of his gallivanting. The Dutch ambassador with whom he was staying kept a check on his behaviour, and reported back to his father. In the letters from his father, such as this one written in 1678, he was admonished:

...it would contribute much to my health if you are modest and respectful concerning the ambassador by refraining from all bad company...stay away from game of dice, and be frugal with drinking by sometimes mixing water in the wine...[25]

This was not the only time Johan Huijdecoper was reprimanded about his gaming. Five months later his father warned him again about 'fraternising with those playing dice and games'.[26] The parental advice to the young Huijdecoper was well intended. By contemporary standards he was still a minor (in the seventeenth century the age of majority for men was 25, and for women 23).[27]

The parents of 15 year old Constantijn Huygens were even more concerned that their adolescent son might turn into a delinquent. Constantijn Huygens, or Tien, was the son of the Constantijn Huygens Jr, the secretary of stadholder Willem III (who later became King William III of Great Britain and ruled with his wife, Queen Mary). After William ascended to the throne in 1689, Constantijn Huygens was called to England, leaving his 15 year old son Tien and wife Susanna behind in Holland. When Tien left home to attend the University of Leiden, Susanna kept her husband well informed of his activities. Neither parent found him easy.[28] Shortly after starting in Leiden, Huygens reported that his son 'has acquired a taste for wine' because he had been seen drunk a number of times. When he received news that his son was not interested in studying Huygens hired a new 'governor' for him. Two weeks later the governor resigned from his position because he did not think he 'could steer Tien on the right path', though he had himself had apparently introduced the young man to smoking. In his despair Huygens recorded in his diary that 'Tien was the most immoral student in Leiden'. Huygens tried to steer his son into what he regarded as more respectable behaviour by forbidding him from frequenting coffee-houses and fencing schools. He prohibited Tien from smoking and from drinking, which he apparently did in excess. Occasionally when drunk he would fight and challenge other men to duels. Whilst this youthful misbehaviour was not always taken seriously, Tien's conduct was a great sadness to his father, who, in his anger, threatened to have him locked up in a correctional home. His father thought that Tien associated with the wrong kind of people. Time and time again, according to his father's diary, Tien would promise to be better but within a short time returned to his old ways.[29]

Were parents making much ado about nothing? Early modern parents believed they had valid reasons to be worried about their adolescent children.[30] They and their seventeenth century contemporaries believed that youths on the threshold of adulthood underwent a troubled time, characterised by unbalanced, unstable, and often ambivalent behaviour. Adolescents were generally felt to be reckless, to have unrealistic expectations, to be gullible. Their feelings of love and hate were unbalanced, yet keenly experienced.[31] Parents were not alone in their concern for adolescent boys in particular. Throughout the seventeenth century Protestant ministers and moralists aimed to police the behaviour of urban youths, although their campaigns escalated during periods of perceived national calamity. Public unrest mounted, for example, during the 1650s and 1660s, as a result of a series of crises including the first Anglo-Dutch War (1652-1654), the outbreak of smallpox in 1665, the loss of influence in Brazil, a dwindling economy and a growing tolerance of Catholics. For Protestants such adversity was reason enough to kindle moral panic, and to conclude that God's commandments had been violated. Drinking, whoring, adultery, dancing, and playing dice were taken as evidence of more general moral decay. In the face of such decay, the States-General supported the church council in issuing official days of prayer.[32] Moreover, as early as 1654, Amsterdam's city council revoked its policy of tolerance, and, yielding to religious protest, banned Vondel's 'blasphemous' play, *Lucifer*.[33]

Cards and Gaming

In seventeenth and eighteenth century Amsterdam, youths frequented dance, music, and amusement halls. It was no secret to many parents, such as Willem van der Muelen's, that card games were played in amusement halls and that these places were occasionally raided by the authorities, who believed that they operated as covers for brothels.[34] In *Oeconomic Christiana* (1655), the Pietist reverend Petrus Wittewrongel, condemned dancing, theatre, and card games. Wittewrongel outlined specific guidelines for adolescent leisure activities. He argued that youths should not become too preoccupied with leisure, and that leisure should be viewed as a reward for achieving something else rather than as a goal in its own right. Furthermore it was not supposed to be enjoyed on Sundays or religious holidays, and should certainly not interfere with religious lessons.[35] In the popular *Catechizatie over den Heidelbergschen catechismus* (Catechisation of the Heidelberg catechisms) by Petrus de Witte, which was reprinted many times in the seventeenth and early eighteenth centuries, the playing of cards and dice was said to lead to insulting, lying, drinking, cursing, swearing, quarrelling, fighting and even killing.[36] Chance games raised ethical issues for many theologians in the Dutch Republic. Their main concern was that they were played for money, and won by dishonourable means. Moralists did not only use theological and ethical justifications in their crusades against such games. Some believed that these games invited direct and dark divine vengeance. In his 1632 treatise, G.C. Udemans told of the fate of a group of card-players gathered at an inn, 'On the 7th of August 1546 lightening struck the Santpoort [Inn] in Mechelen where 800 tons of gunpowder was stored. Among the victims was the innkeeper himself, found with a deck of cards in his hands...'.[37]

Most moral messages were more subtle, and parents did not have to look far for suitable didactic material for use in everyday child-rearing. In *Sinnepoppen* (1614), an album of emblems by Roemer Visscher, the message was made quite clear in an illustration entitled *Leert het u kinderen niet* ('Don't teach your children this').[38] It portrays a crab crawling towards dice and a stack of cards. According to Visscher, parents who strayed from the moral path by playing dice, drinking, and being promiscuous set bad examples for their children, who, like a crab, would fixedly follow their line.[39] In *Two children playing cards* by the seventeenth century painter Dirck Hals, a boy is enticed into a game of cards while the young girl with whom he is playing mischievously smiles out at the observer.[40] According to Simon Schama, such illustrations of card and dice games made clear connections with greed and violence, and 'were thought peculiarly dangerous for the addictive way in which [they] dispossessed men of their will and reason, and so gave the devil, in the guise of Fortuna, sovereignty over the Christian way'.[41] Perhaps the low-life associations of such games was the reason why Willem van der Muelen's mother warned him about staying away from bad company, which could only, apparently, lead to drinking, debauchery, and idleness.

Dice, Drink and Debauchery

In *Parallelon Republicarum* (Comparing Republics; 1602) the Dutch statesman, Hugo de Groot, portrayed his people as a folk fond of honest games and amusement. However, one of those less virtuous games was dice, condemned by De Groot because the last throw determined the fate of the loser who was doomed to a kind of voluntary slavery.[42] Throughout the seventeenth century reverends had complained to the Amsterdam town council about the evils of playing with dice. In the eyes of the Amsterdam church council the game was a sin. In 1681 they presented the city burgomasters with a petition seeking legal action against violators of dice, buoyed by the fact that, four months earlier

> ...the city magistrates had ruled that dice playing and other high risk games not only lead to swearing and alcoholism as well as a waste of time and money but also to the downfall of whole families.[43]

Church leaders, parents, and society in general regarded dice and other games as having a domino effect. Gambling would inevitably lead, it was felt, to other vices such as drinking and swearing. Swearing in the seventeenth century was a sin, and, depending on the nature of the profanity, punishable as an offence.[44] The connection between dice and drinking was commented upon in the case of Johan Huijdecoper, the son of the burgomaster of Amsterdam. Drinking was regarded as a *moederzonde* - the mother of other sins - because intoxication could lead to other vices such as violence and promiscuous sexual behaviour.[45] The authorities therefore tried to restrict adolescents' access to alcohol.[46] In the village of Graft in North Holland moderate drinking, especially that of young adults, was enforced by prohibiting innkeepers from allowing anyone under the age of 25 (those below the age of majority) of running a tab or buying on credit.[47] In the eighteenth century excessive use of alcohol was reason enough for many of the middling sort to have family members committed to a reform institution.[48] It should be noted, however, that the consumption of alcohol in the middle ages and early modern period did not carry the same moral weight that it was later given by the temperance movements of the nineteenth and twentieth centuries.[49] In the seventeenth century moderate consumption of alcohol was accepted. Drinking beer and other distilled beverages was regarded as safer than drinking water from the canals, which could be contaminated. Calvinists were not necessarily against the consumption of alcohol, but, rather, were against *excess* of any kind.[50] It was the connection between excessive alcohol and other vices which was a key cause of concern. This connection was not only made by Dutch Calvinists. In eighteenth century Paris, wives complained about husbands who closed their shops early to play boules and frequent the taverns.[51] Parisian magistrates condemned the link between drunkenness and debauchery, a link also made by the parents of adolescent Dutch boys.[52]

Debauchery was a euphemism for fornication, a source of genuine anxiety for early modern parents.[53] Premarital sex was regarded as both immoral and materially detrimental to urban elite young men and their families. Thus according to seventeenth and eighteenth century litigation, if 'bodily conversation' occurred in a relationship between female servants and their employers or their sons, and resulted in pregnancy, a paternity suit could be filed against them. If found guilty the men concerned were often obliged to marry, which dealt a considerable blow to the marital manoeuvrings and delicate alignments of financially and politically powerful families.[54]

That early modern society was ruled by strict moral conventions in regard to sexuality appears to be obvious. The practical side of this moral code, however, is rather more open to question. For example, blind eyes were often turned towards young men's use of prostitutes. In Amsterdam, any legal action was more often filed against the prostitutes, while their young male visitors were exonerated. Police officials received bribes and back-handers for omitting the names of elite young men from police records of immoral crimes.[55] As in other university towns in the Dutch Republic, students in Leiden found guilty of criminal acts were tried *not* by municipal judges but by university officials. This protected the names and reputations of the sons of the affluent families. Moreover, university officials used kid-gloves when passing sentence on such students. Research into criminal cases tried at the University of Leiden in the seventeenth century shows that numerous serious incidents occurred, including sexual violence (mainly actual or attempted gang-rapes), excessive drunkenness, force of arms, destruction of property (such as window breaking) or petty larceny (such as stealing chickens). University judges were often lenient when punishing such incidents because they considered the student 'phase' as a transitional period between dependence and independence in which passions were more or less given free reign - a view more generally accepted by society.[56]

Judges in municipal courts were certainly less sympathetic towards less elite juveniles, but were still far more tolerant towards them than towards adults. Youths found guilty of stealing were, for example, exempt from the death penalty, a common punishment for such an offence. One punishment reserved for adolescents was a whipping on a 'wooden horse' which was conducted indoors in private rather than outside in public with all its attendant public humiliation.[57] In the city of Leiden, for example, most of the juveniles featured in municipal court records in the period 1533-1811 were detained for the same crimes as students - petty theft and destruction of property (again, mainly breaking windows). Yet their sentences were much harsher than those of the students, if milder than those of adults committing the same crimes.[58] This tolerance of young offenders was also evident in Renaissance Florence where officials passed milder sentences on adolescents found guilty of sodomy. Their 'adult' companions were either publicly humiliated and banned from the city or had to pay a substantial fine and sentenced to the city mental hospital on a diet of bread and water for the rest of their lives.[59] According to Maria Boes, the same tolerance was shown towards juveniles in early modern Germany, where gentler and milder sentences were given to adolescents and youths. Punishment often took place in private, thus protecting them from public exposure.[60]

Billiards and Coffee-houses

Whilst the wayward leisure pursuits of adolescent boys of the Dutch urban elite were not necessarily of the same order as those discussed above, they nevertheless caused their parents much genuine concern. Parents feared that even their sons' association with the 'wrong people' could lead to delinquent behaviour. For example, 15 year old Jan Carel van der Muelen started at the University of Utrecht in 1753. Jan stayed with his uncle who lived in Utrecht and kept his father informed of his progress. Jan Carel's parents were informed that he had a good professor who kept his students from drinking and from playing billiards. At that time billiards was a favoured past time for students. Whilst billiards was not associated with gambling, like many of the card games, it did tend to be played in coffee-houses, which, at the time, had dubious reputations. By the mid-eighteenth century these establishments had evolved into intellectual bastions where educated men could read newspapers and journals and discuss political and philosophical matters, as well as drink coffee. Some even had special chambers where literary societies gathered. Coffee-houses, in this sense, played a pivotal role in dispersing Enlightenment thought. However, they were also noted for the less savoury activities of their male customers who tended to have both time and money and who tended to indulge in other past-times such as smoking, cards, checkers, dice and gambling for large sums of money. Respectable women shunned the coffee-houses, fearful of being linked to those women who did frequent them and who were regarded as prostitutes.[61] When the first establishments opened in the late seventeenth century, coffee-houses became particularly popular amongst students. The university cities of Leiden and Utrecht had the largest number, which generated great anxiety about the amount of time students and other young men spent in them. Moralists complained that students neglected their studies in favour of the pleasures of gaming in such places.[62] In 1712 gambling in coffee-houses had become such a problem in Utrecht that it was blamed for 'corrupting the youth and schools', resulting in an inspection by the city council.[63] However, municipal authorities recognised their popularity (and no doubt their commercial importance), and instead of calling for outright closure, tried to restrict the opening of new establishments.[64]

In the mid-eighteenth century, moralists of the *Spectatoriale geschriften* (Spectators) blamed the urban elite for perpetuating moral decay. In particular, they blamed the sons of that elite and their passion for coffee-houses. However, it was not necessarily the indolence of these young men that most concerned these moralists. Rather moral decay was identified with two 'new' kinds of male, both products of establishments such as the coffee-houses. Young men known as *petits-maîtres* and others as *lichtmissen* were perceived to present a real danger to bourgeois society. The *petits-maîtres* were young men known for their cultivated manners, modish outfits, frivolous talk, and preference for the company of women. They were condemned for their effeminate behaviour, cowardliness, lack of character, and their obsession with narcissistic and superficial matters. The *lichtmissen*, or womanisers, also enjoyed the company of women but were regarded as seducers always on the lookout for new prey. They tempted married women into adultery, sought out prostitutes, and tried to seduce young maidens. Unlike the *petits-maîtres* the *lichtmissen* also enjoyed the company of men and to boast, brag, fight, drink, and gamble. The Spectators were especially anxious about their influence because they frequented coffee-houses in university towns where, it was feared, they would coax vulnerable students into adventurous escapades.[65]

Conclusions

Over the course of the seventeenth and early eighteenth centuries the sites where adolescent leisure activities took place shifted. Whereas in the seventeenth century moralists had condemned theatres, inns, dance, music, and amusement halls where cards and dice were played, in the early eighteenth century they focused on coffee houses where billiards were played. And it was the 'bad company' that these establishments attracted that so concerned urban elite parents. Indeed, they were particularly explicit about the consequences of associating with such company. Willem van der Muelen's father was quite frank: he cautioned his son to uphold the family name and reputation which could be easily tarnished by any engagement in degenerate activity.[66] Keeping the family name free of disgrace and dishonour was especially important within the Dutch urban elite. Honour was, here and across urbanising

Europe, 'essentially someone's reputation, someone's good name with others'. Personal value in early modern society relied upon name and reputation.[67] For the Dutch urban elite, family connections were the primary means of obtaining political positions as well as retaining and enhancing economic resources. Individual disgrace through gambling, excessive drinking, or unrestrained sexual promiscuity would, in turn, disgrace the entire family. Indeed parents in some families went so far as to have their sons committed to correctional homes. The defiant behaviour of these black sheep jeopardised the long-term security of elite families in early modern Dutch society.[68]

If we compare the concerns of these Dutch parents with other European parents in the middle ages and early modern period, we find many similarities. According to Barbara Hanawalt moralists in medieval London were similarly alarmed about dice-playing, 'lust-longing', and alcohol-thirsty youths.[69] For Ilana Krausman Ben-Amos parents in early modern England expressed similar anxieties about the spirituality, sexuality, and leisure activities of their adolescent children.[70] This anxiety is captured in Paul Griffiths' research on 'masterless' youth in sixteenth century Norwich, a city which attracted a steady flow of young migrants. Without economic means, they often resorted to criminal acts to survive. Vagrants, many of whom were youths, 'begged and stole their way along the streets, always trying to keep one step ahead of officers. They were found drunk and playing unlawful games, having sex, extending 'ill-rule', and committing other offences gathered under a catch-all like misdemeanour, misbehaviour, or idles'.[71] As Joel Harrington has shown, the authorities in early modern Nuremberg were confronted with many of the same youthful transgressions, namely vandalism and petty theft.[72] It would appear that old forms of collective socialisation in rural society had taken on new forms in emergent urban society. New rituals - some linked to poverty, some to affluence, some condemned, some tolerated - were shaping ways of becoming an adult man in the city.

Endnotes

[1]   These three families were examined in: B.B. Roberts, *Through the keyhole. Dutch-child-rearing practices in the 17th and 18th century. Three urban elite families* (Hilversum, 1998). See also: L. Kooijmans, *Vriendschap en de kunst van het overleven in de 17de en de 18de eeuw* (Amsterdam, 1997).
[2]   R. Muchembled, *De uitvinding van de moderne mens. Collectief gedrag, zeden, gewoonten en gevoelsleven van de middeleeuwen tot de Franse revolutie* (Amsterdam, 1991), Dutch translation, pp. 236-41.
[3]   N. Zemon Davis, 'Youth groups and charivaris', *Past and Present* 50 (1971), 53-4. See also: E. Muir, *Ritual in early modern Europe. New approaches to European history* (Cambridge, 1997), pp. 98-104.
[4]   G. Rooijakkers, *Rituele repertoires. Volkscultuur in oostelijk Noord-Brabant 1559-1853*

5   (Nijmegen, 1994).
    H. Pleij, *De sneeuwpoppen van 1511. Literatuur en stadscultuur tussen middeleeuwen en modernetijd* (Amsterdam, 1988).
6   R. Muchembled, *De uitvinding van de moderne mens.* pp. 236-41.
7   J. Israel, *The Dutch Republic. Its rise, greatness, and fall 1477-1806* (Oxford, 1995). S. Schama, *The Embarrassment of Riches. An interpretation of Dutch culture in the Golden Age* (London, 1988). J.L. Price, *Dutch Society, 1588-1713* (London/New York, 2000).
8   J.I. Israel, *The Dutch Republic. Its rise, greatness, and fall 1477-1806* (Oxford, 1995), pp.619-627. J.G.C.A..Briels, *De Zuidnederlandse immigratie in Amsterdam en Haarlem omstreeks 1572-1630* (Utrecht, 1976).
9   L. van de Pol, *Het Amsterdams Hoerdom. Prostitutie in de zeventiende en achttiende eeuw* (Amsterdam, 1996), pp. 293-97. P. Spierenburg, 'Knife fighting and popular codes of honor in early modern Amsterdam' *Men and violence. Gender honor, and rituals in early modern Europe and America* ed. P. Spierenburg (Columbus, Ohio, 1998), pp.103-27.
10 R. Dekker, *Holland in beroering. Oproeren in de 17de en 18de eeuw* (Baarn, 1982), p.61. A.Th. van Deursen, *Bavianen en slijkgeuzen. Kerk en kerkvolk ten tijde van Maurits en Oldenbarnevelt* (Franeker, 1998 3rd Print), pp.336-40. For the disturbance of the peace in the city of Haarlem see: G. Dorren, *Eenheid en verscheidenheid. De burgers van Haarlem in de Gouden Eeuw* (Amsterdam, 2001), pp. 73-78.
11 F.A. van Lieburg, *De Nadere Reformatie in Utrecht ten tijde van Voetius. Sporen in de gereformeerde kerkeraadsacta* (Rotterdam, 1989), pp. 63-64. L. Bogaers, 'Een kwestie van macht? De relatie tussen de wetgeving op het openbaar gedrag en de ontwikkeling van de Utrechtse stadssamenleving in de zestiende en zeventiende eeuw' *Volkskundig Bulletin* 11 (1985), pp. 102-126. For this problem in urban areas in general see: A. Cowan, *Urban Europe, 1500-1700* (London, 1998), p.76. G. Dorren, 'Communities within the community: Aspects of neighbourhood in seventeenth-century Haarlem', *Urban History* 28 (1998), pp. 173-88.
12 P. Spierenburg, *The Prison Experience. Disciplinary institutions and their inmates in early modern Europe* (New Brunswick, 1991), pp. 25-6. S. Faber, 'Het Rasphuis: wat was dat eigenlijk?' in: C. Fijnaut & P. Spierenburg eds., *Scherp toezicht. Van 'Boeventucht' tot 'Samenleving en criminaliteit'* (Arnhem, 1990), pp. 127-43.
13 P. Spierenburg, *Zwarte schapen. Losbollen, dronkaards en levensgenieters in achttiende eeuwse beterhuizen* (Hilversum, 1995), pp. 44-69.
14 V.K. Tikoff, 'Before the Reformatory: A Correctional Orphanage in Old Regime Seville', in this volume. M.E. Perry, *Crime and society in early modern Seville* (Hanover, New Hampshire, 1980), pp. 209-11.
15 S. Groenveld, "Tot een godsalig ende eerbaar leeven'. Immateriele zorg' *Wezen en boefjes. Zes eeuwen zorg in wees-en kinderhuizen* eds. S. Groenveld, J.J.H. Dekker & Th.R.M. Willemse (Hilversum, 1997), pp. 182-3.
16 T. G. Kootte, 'Kleding' *Wezen en boefjes. Zes eeuwen zorg in wees-en kinderhuizen* eds. S. Groenveld, J.J.H. Dekker & Th.R.M. Willemse (Hilversum, 1997), pp. 151-4.
17 H.M. van den Heuvel, *De criminele vonnisboeken van Leiden, 1533-1811* (Leiden, 1977-1978).
18 Gemeenearchief Amsterdam (Municipal archive of Amsterdam), Archive of the Diachonie

19 Orphanage of the Reformed Church of Amsterdam, nr.1436.
    A. Hallema, *Geschiedenis van het Weeshuis der Gereformeerden binnen Delft* (Delft, 1964), pp. 244-5.
20 A.E.C. McCants, *Civic charity in a Golden Age. Orphan care in early modern Amsterdam* (Urbana, Ill., 1997), pp. 64-70.
21 J. Jacobs, *Een zegenrijk gewest. Nieuw-Nederland in de zeventiende eeuw* (Amsterdam, 1999), pp. 96-100.
22 Provincial Archives of Utrecht (RAU), (F)amily (A)rchive Van der Muelen (hereafter FA Van der Muelen) nr. 81, 2 July 1646.
23 RAU, FA Van der Muelen nr.81. 2 July 1646.
24 RAU, FA Van der Muelen nr. 81, 1 February 1648.
25 RAU, FA Huijdecoper nr. 58, 21 Dec. 1678.
26 Ibid.
27 D. Haks, *Huwelijk en gezin in Holland in de 17de en 18de eeuw. Processtukken en moralisten over apsecten van het laat 17de-en 18de eeuwse gezinsleven* (Assen, 1982), p. 158.
28 R. Dekker, *Uit de schaduw in 't grote licht. Kinderen in egodocumenten van de Gouden Eeuw tot de Romantiek* (Amsterdam, 1995), p. 67.
29 R. Dekker, *Uit de schaduw in 't grote licht.* pp. 68-72.
30 R. Dekker, *Uit de schaduw in 't grote licht.* pp. 68-69. According to German Reformation moralists besides sex and alcohol, the theatre was the third 'horsemen of adolescence' with which youth were tempted. S. Ozment, 'The private life of an early modern teenager: a Nuremberg Lutheran visits Catholic Louvain (1577) *Journal of Family History* 21, 1 (1996), p. 31. S. Ozment, *Protestants. The birth of a revolution* (London, 1993), p. 109.
31 H.F.M. Peeters, *Kind en jeugdige in het begin van de moderne tijd.* pp. 254-57.
32 Leendert F. Groenendijk, 'Salomo's raad aan de jeugd'. 247-258. J. Springhall, 'Corrupting the young?' Popular entertainment and 'moral panics' in Britain and America since 1830', *Aspects of Education* 50 (1996), pp. 95-110. F. van Lieburg, *De Nadere Reformatie in Utrecht ten tijde van Voetius.* pp.53-4. L. Noordegraaf, 'Of bidden helpt? Bededagen als reactie op rampen in de Republiek' *Of bidden helpt? Tegenslag en cultuur in Europa, circa 1500-2000* eds. M. Gijswijt-Hofstra & F. Egmond (Amsterdam, 1997), pp. 29-42.
33 Leendert F. Groenendijk, 'Het Puritanisme en het gezinsagogisch offensief van de nadere reformatie in de zeventiende eeuw' *Nederlands tijdschrift voor opvoeding, vorming en onderwijs* 3, 1, (1987), pp. 168-79.
34 L. van de Pol, *Het Amsterdams hoerdom. Prostitutie in de zeventiende en achttiende eeuw* (Amsterdam, 1996), p. 278.
35 L.F. Groenendijk, *De nadere reformatie van het gezin. De visie van Petrus Wittewrongel op het christelijke huishouding* (Dordrecht, 1984), pp.145-6.
36 P. de Witte, *Catechizatie over den Heidelbergschen catechismus* (Amsterdam, 33rd Print, 1728), pp. 702-3.
37 Leendert F. Groenendijk, 'Kansspelen in het ethische discours van gereformeerde theologen in de Noordelijke Nederlanden' *De Zeventiende Eeuw* 15, (1999), pp. 74-85 (quote from p.83).
38 R. Visscher, *Sinnepoppen* (The Hague, [Modern reprint],1949), p. 101.

39 R. Visscher, *Sinnepoppen*, p. 101. Dutch artists also illustrated other forms of bad behaviour. I. Gaskell, 'Tobacco, social deviance, and Dutch art in the seventeenth century' *Looking at seventeenth-century Dutch art: Realism reconsidered* ed. W. Franits (Cambridge, 1997), pp. 68-77. D. Harley, 'The moral symbolism of tobacco in Dutch genre painting' *Ashes to ashes. The history of smoking and health* ed. S. Lock (Amsterdam/Atlanta, 1998), pp. 78-88.
40 D. Hals, *Two children playing cards* (Clark Institute of Art, Williamstown, Massachusetts).
41 S. Schama, *The Embarrassment of Riches. An interpretation of Dutch culture in the Golden Age* (London, 1988), pp. 505-6. See also: J.J.H. Dekker, 'A Republic of Educators: Educational Messages in Seventeenth-Century Dutch Genre Painting' *History of Education Quarterly* 36, 2 (1996), pp. 155-82.
42 M. Meijer Drees, *Andere landen, andere mensen. De beeldvorming van Holland versus Spanje en England omstreeks 1650* (The Hague, 1997), pp. 33-37.
43 Realising that dice playing had become so commonplace that any enforcement of prohibition would be an endless battle, the magistrates did not forbid the game but put concessions on the stakes of its players. H. Roodenburg, *Onder Censuur. De kerkelijke tucht in de gereformeerde gemeente van Amsterdam, 1578-1700* (Hilversum, 1990), p. 334.
44 P.G.J.van Sterkenburg, *Vloeken. Een cultuurbepaalde reactie op woede, irritatie en frustratie* (The Hague, 1997), pp. 37-40.
45 H.Roodenburg, *Onder censuur.* p. 339.
46 R. Dekker, *Uit de schaduw in 't grote licht.* p. 68.
47 A. Th. van Deursen, *Een Dorp in de polder. Graft in de zeventiende eeuw* (Amsterdam, 1995), pp. 246-7.
48 P. Spierenburg, *Zwarte schapen. Losbollen, dronkaards en levensgenieters in achttiende-eeuwse beterhuizen* (Hilversum, 1995), pp. 47-51.
49 G.J. Giles, 'Temperance before the temperance movements: some examples from eighteenth-century children's literature in England and Germany' *History of Education* 20, 4, (1991), pp. 295-305.
50 J.C. van der Stel, *Drinken, drank en dronkenschap: Vijf eeuwen drankbestrijding en alcoholhulpverlening in Nederland: een historisch-sociologisch studie* (Hilversum, 1995), pp. 55-60.
51 Th. Brennan, *Public drinking and popular culture in eighteenth-century Paris* (Princeton, New Jersey, 1988), p. 208.
52 Th. Brennan, p. 196.
53 In England, the courts were well aware that young people were likely to be 'more promiscuous and less rigid in their morals than married adults'. I. Krausman Ben-Amos, *Adolescence and Youth in Early Modern England* p. 201.
54 D. Haks, *Huwelijk en gezin in Holland.* pp. 88-89. P. Spierenburg, *De verbroken betovering. Mentaliteitsgeschiedenis van preïndustrieel Europa* (Hilversum, 1988), pp. 298-302. See also: M. van der Heijden, *Huwelijk in Holland. Stedelijke rechtspraak en kerkelijke tucht, 1550-1700* (Amsterdam, 1998).
55 L. van de Pol, *Het Amsterdams hoerdom. Prostitutie in de zeventiende en achttiende eeuw* (Amsterdam, 1996), pp. 128-131. The double moral between women and men was quite explicit in the seventeenth century. Women were expected to be chaste while men not. M-Th.

Leuker & H. Roodenburg,"Die dan hare wyven laten afweyen'. Overspel, eer en schande in de zeventiende' *Soete minne en helsche boosheit. Seksuele voorstellingen in Nederland 1300-1850* eeuw eds. G. Hekma & H. Roodenburg (Nijmegen, 1988), pp. 66-7.

56 M. Wingens, 'Jeugdige lichtzinnigheid en losbandigheid. Seksuele gedrag en seksuele beleving van studenten ten tijde van de Nederlandse Republiek' *Grensgeschillen in de seks. Bijdragen tot een culturele geschiedenis van de seksualiteit* ed G. Hekma (Amsterdam/Atlanta, 1990), pp. 8-28. M. Wingens, 'Deviant gedrag van studenten: verkrachters in de zeventiende en achttiende eeuw' *Batavia Academica* 6 (1988), pp. 9-26. Students were often distracted from the purpose of philosophy and other subject matter for the pleasure of 'toping, wenching, and gambling'. W.W. Brinkman, 'The socio-cultural context of education in the seventeenth-century Netherlands (1)' *Paedagogica Historica* 24, 2 (1984), p. 398.

57 P. Spierenburg, *The Spectacle of suffering. Executions and the evolution of repression: from a preindustrial metropolis to the European experience* (Cambridge, 1984), pp. 158-60.

58 H.M. van den Heuvel, *De criminele vonnisboeken van Leiden* 1533-1811 (Leiden, 1977-1978).

59 M. Rocke, *Forbidden Friendships. Homosexuality and male culture in Renaissance Florence* (Oxford, 1996), pp. 51.

60 M. Boes, 'The treatment of juvenile delinquents in early modern Germany: a case study' *Continuity and Change* 11, 1 (1996), pp. 43-60.

61 D. Sturkenboom, *Spectators van Hartstocht. Sekse en emotionele cultuur in de achttiende eeuw* (Hilversum, 1998), pp. 57-8. M. van der Tol, 'Wat ging er om in 'Het koffy-huis der Nieusgierigen'? Vergeten periodiek (1744-1746) werpt nieuw licht op het achttiende-eeuwse koffiehuis' *Mededelingen van de stichting Jacob Campo Weyerman* 16 (1993), pp. 85-96.

62 T. Wijsenbeek, 'Ernst en luim. Koffiehuizen tijdens de Republiek' *Koffie in Nederland. Vier eeuwen cultuurgeschiedenis* eds. P. Reinders & T. Wijsenbeek (Zutphen, 1994), pp. 39-47. A.C.J. de Vrankrijker, *Vier eeuwen Nederlandsch studentenleven* (Voorburg, not dated), p. 40.

63 T. Wijsenbeek, 'Ernst en luim. Koffiehuizen tijdens de Republiek', p. 47.

64 Today this is evident in the Dutch liberal policy of drug-use. M. te Kort, *Tussen patient en delinquent. Geschiedenis van het Nederlandse drugsbeleid* (Hilversum, 1995).

65 D. Sturkenboom, *Spectators van Hartstocht.* p. 147-58.

66 B. Roberts, *Through the keyhole.* p. 176.

67 Lotte C. van de Pol, 'Prostitutie en de Amsterdamse burgerij: eerbegrippen in een vroegmoderne stedelijke samenleving' *Cultuur en maatschappij in Nederland 1500-1850. Een historisch-antropologish perspectief* eds. P. te Boekhorst, P. Burke & W.Th.M. Frijhoff, (Meppel/Amsterdam/Heerlen, 1992), pp. 180-1.

68 P. Spierenburg, *Zwarte Schapen. Losbollen, dronkaards en levensgenieters in achttiende-eeuwse beterhuizen* (Hilversum, 1995), pp. 45-6.

69 B.A. Hanawalt, *Growing up in Medieval London. The experience of childhood in History* (New York/Oxford, 1993), pp. 114-24.

70 I. Krausman Ben-Amos, *Adolescence and Youth in Early Modern England* (New Haven/London, 1994), pp.183-207.

71 P. Griffiths, 'Masterless young people in Norwich, 1560-1645' *The experience of authority*

in early modern England ed. P. Griffiths (New York, 1996), p. 161-2.

72   'Apprentices in Crime: The making and punishment of juvenile criminals in early modern Germany', paper presented by Joel F. Harrington at 'Becoming Delinquent: European Youth, 1650-1950', conference held at Fitzwilliam College, Cambridge, April 1999.

Chapter 3

Before the Reformatory: A Correctional Orphanage in Old Regime Seville

Valentina K. Tikoff

The punishment of juvenile delinquents outside domestic settings and apart from adult offenders is commonly portrayed as a phenomenon of the nineteenth and early twentieth centuries. A typical view is that of LaMar T. Empey, who has written:

> Asylums for abandoned children had been used in Europe for some time, but the idea that places of confinement could be used effectively to reform criminals or to substitute for family and community as the best method to raise children was entirely new. It was no accident either that the first houses of refuge and asylums appeared around 1825 in the most populous cities and states...Houses of refuge were to become family substitutes, not only for the less serious juvenile criminal, but for runaways, disobedient children or vagrants.[1]

This quotation incorporates several key features of the 'common wisdom' about juvenile reformatories, including the notion that the confinement of juvenile delinquents was largely a new approach in the 1820s; and that such confinement represented a substitution for the family. More recent scholarship has generally echoed these ideas. In *Children and Childhood in Western Society since 1500* (1995), Hugh Cunningham has acknowledged that 'The method dating back to the fifteenth century for dealing with abandoned or delinquent children was to place them in an institution', but nevertheless skims over much of this history to highlight the internment of juvenile delinquents principally as a nineteenth-century phenomenon.[2] Similarly, in his chapter on the juvenile reform school in the *Oxford History of the Prison* (1995), Steven Schlossman notes precursors to juvenile reformatories in early modern Europe, but still argues for the 'invention of reform schools in the nineteenth century', explaining, 'Although it is possible to identify a few institutional precedents of the reform school in sixteenth-, seventeenth-, and eighteenth-century Europe, it is clear that until the early 1800s, families, not institutions, were the principal instrument through which communities disciplined children'.[3]

While these and other scholars of juvenile reformatories briefly acknowledge precedents for the institutional treatment of young delinquents in earlier eras, the precedents themselves have received scant attention. Early modern scholars have suggested that 'juvenile delinquency' was a recognised social phenomenon long before the nineteenth-century reforms christened it with this label, but their emphasis has typically been on youthful forms of sociability and criminality, rather than the institutionalisation of delinquents.[4] Moreover, as Peter King has observed for England, early modern studies have focused on the sixteenth and seventeenth centuries, leaving the eighteenth and early nineteenth centuries largely overlooked.[5] The same is true for continental Europe. The neglect of institutionalised young people can perhaps be attributed partially to the convincing self-congratulatory rhetoric of the creators of 'modern' juvenile justice institutions, who often proclaimed the novelty of their initiatives and painted the past in tones that showed their own actions in the best light, and starkest contrast. The lack of attention to earlier forms of juvenile institutionalisation is undoubtedly also attributable in part to the fact that the institutions that filled this function were rarely identified as explicitly punitive. They were, instead, commonly institutions originally established to take in orphans and other poor young people, but which increasingly fulfilled roles as correctional or penal institutions for young people.

This chapter examines one such institution that operated in Seville, Spain precisely during the period about which so little is known, from the 1720s through the 1830s. Originally established as an asylum for orphaned and abandoned boys, it soon became better known as a correctional institution to which families as well as civil and church authorities sent misbehaving children and youths. In 1886, a half-century after this institution had closed its doors, Seville writer Francisco Collantes de Terán speculated that 'there must be few people over 50 years old who were never threatened in their childhood mischief with being sent to the Toribios'.[6] Spanish publications still frequently identify this institution as a precursor of modern juvenile reformatories.[7] Exploring heretofore untapped documentation concerning the internment of young delinquents in this institution, this case study affords a glimpse of the institutional treatment of young delinquents prior to the widespread establishment of juvenile reformatories and shows the active role of parents and families, as well as civil authorities, in shaping this charitable institution's correctional identity.

The Toribios's 'Correctional' Role and Clients

The Toribios was established in 1725 with layman Toribio de Velasco's efforts to catechise the street urchins of Seville. Support from local benefactors soon led to the foundation of an asylum for orphaned, abandoned, and poor boys commonly known simply as 'the Toribios' after its founder. Although Velasco died in 1730, the Toribios continued to exist until it was absorbed into Seville's newly created poorhouse in 1831; thereafter, it operated as a separate entity within the poorhouse until the mid-1830s. This chronology roughly parallels the last century of Spain's old regime social welfare system, just before the state appropriation (*desamortización*) of ecclesiastical properties in the 1830s effectively dismantled the traditional underpinnings of Spanish charity.[8] The fate of the Toribios varied dramatically over this century-long history. Its enrolment (including both charity and correctional cases) fluctuated wildly, ranging from 26 to over 200 residents.[9] It also moved several times, even briefly occupying the old Inquisition headquarters in Seville. While Seville's archbishop, cathedral chapter, municipal council, the city's royally appointed senior municipal official (*asistente*),[10] and even the royal court in Madrid all took an interest in this institution and supported it sporadically, there was never a completely clear chain of administrative or financial command. Its funding was chronically precarious, notwithstanding the unanimity of the city's leaders on the utility of this institution in fulfilling both charitable and penal roles.

Although begun as a refuge for poor boys, the Toribios began to be known as a 'correctional' institution almost since its inception. By the 1730s parents were already sending their 'incorrigible' sons there.[11] According to a 1766 account, even parents who never placed their sons in this institution nevertheless benefited from its existence, since 'with the mere threat of being sent to the Toribios the parent of the most mischievous and dissolute son can subject and restrain even the most loose and deviant (*libre y viciada*) behaviour. And if in the most unchecked cases the threat is not sufficient, with a stay in this institution (*hospicio*), generally not very long, the son who had left his parents' home haughty, free, disobedient and a menace to the family and the republic, returns to obey them now humbled, shamed, and sensible'.[12]

The institution's reputation as correctional establishment was well known both within and beyond Seville. In 1783, several judges of the royal chancery court (*alcaldes del crimen*) of Granada requested royal permission to establish an institution in that city based on the model of the Toribios in Seville, noting that the institution they proposed, like the establishment they sought to emulate, 'must not only be one of charity but also of correction'; it would take in not only poor children but also young people sent by families willing to board them for a fee.[13] Both local and long-distance correspondence to the Toribios and other documentation also increasingly referred to this institution not as an 'asylum'/'poorhouse' (*hospicio*) or school but as a 'house of correction' or of 'reclusion'.[14] So strongly was the institution identified as a juvenile correctional facility that one Toribios administrator, frustrated by neighbours who seemed to have forgotten that the institution also housed innocent boys taken in as acts of charity, implored: 'People of Seville[,] do not deceive yourselves: these boys are not those bad, disobedient, perverse, vicious youths who are sent to this institution by parents or the authorities[;] although there is also unfortunately this correctional mission, [the disobedient youths] are in a different section and separated from these [charity] boys'.[15]

Clearly, contemporaries of the eighteenth and early nineteenth century identified this institution as a sort of juvenile reformatory, even before such institutions officially existed. The first Spanish juvenile reformatories were not seriously considered until the 1830s,[16] and juvenile courts were not established until 1918.[17] Throughout the early modern period and well into the nineteenth century, Spanish law identified 14 as the age of criminal responsibility.[18] This was by no means an absolute boundary between childhood and adulthood, however; other ages also had social and legal ramifications for young people. The ages at which young people could be accused of sexual misconduct were 12 for females and 14 for males.[19] A royal decree of 1781 ordered that boys and young men under the age of 17 who were picked up in round-ups of vagrants should not be sent into military or shipboard service as older males were, but instead placed with 'masters' who might teach them a trade, at least until institutions that could accommodate these youths were erected.[20] A strong tradition of parental authority also shaped the rights and duties of unmarried youth, at least until they were married or reached the age of 25. In short, 'childhood' and 'youth' were not defined by precise age ranges, but more loosely associated with life stages, as Paul Griffiths has also found for early modern England.[21] Yet 'youth' (*juventud*) was generally used to describe people in their teens and early twenties (again, as in England), ages at which individuals were considered to be highly vulnerable to corruption, but also responsive to reform efforts.[22]

How then did the Spanish define and deal with young delinquents prior to the development of juvenile reformatories and juvenile courts? Historical scholarship on the topic is sparse, but two Iberian precursors of modern juvenile justice institutions are frequently noted. The earliest is the municipal post known as the 'orphans' father' (*padre de huérfanos*), which originated in the Crown of Aragon during the fourteenth century and continued to exist throughout much of early modern period.[23] In Zaragoza, at least, this official's responsibilities included the disciplining of juveniles (including non-orphans), especially servants and apprentices.[24] The other commonly cited institution serving juvenile delinquents in early modern Spain was the Toribios in Seville, the focus of this chapter. Notwithstanding its notoriety, almost all published scholarship on this institution is based on a small number of documents: Gabriel Baca's detailed account of the institution's establishment and initial decades (published 1766); plus a handful of documents at Seville's municipal archive.[25] For the present study, previously unexplored archival documentation has been consulted, including correspondence and account books, most dating from the late eighteenth and early nineteenth centuries.[26] While the institutional documentation is incomplete (and particularly scant for much of the eighteenth century), it nonetheless affords insight regarding the operations of the Toribios as a juvenile reformatory, shedding light especially on the families' and authorities' recourse to this institution as a juvenile correctional facility.

Of course, there is nothing very novel about noting the close ties among 'poverty', 'delinquency', and 'internment' in the old regime. This association is ubiquitous throughout much of the literature on early modern poor relief, in part because the institutional patrons and administrators who penned the vast majority of our extant primary sources believed relief institutions ideally served charitable, educational, and punitive objectives alike.[27] The poverty/criminality/internment nexus especially concerns those of us who are interested in juvenile delinquency, since young people consistently represented disproportionately large percentages of the assisted poor, including institutional populations.[28] Charity patrons and administrators typically sought to steer poor children away from the criminal activities to which they were believed to be inclined, and into socially acceptable adult paths instead. In addition to this 'preventive approach' to juvenile delinquency, institutions for poor young people could also perform more strictly punitive or correctional roles. As Hugh Cunningham has noted, 'It is difficult to keep a clear distinction between institutions designed for those who had been convicted of an offence and those aiming to prevent children from offending'.[29] The lines were particularly blurred when idleness and vagrancy were criminalised, as occurred throughout much of early modern Europe.

The Toribios itself performed both preventive and correctional functions in Seville. Indeed, these two roles were not always clearly distinct.[30] Some of the 'charity' residents appear to have been forcibly interned, drawn from the ubiquitous street urchins so commonly observed and complained about by residents and visitors to early modern Seville.[31] Toribios founder and namesake Toribio de Velasco was apparently already rounding up boys from the city streets and sending them to his fledgling institution in the 1720s. One eighteenth-century source reports:

Assured of the approval of ecclesiastical authorities, he began his pious captures, taking all prudent measures so that without any scandal or ruckus he could round up many boys observed and known to be vagrants, or [those] destitute of any Christian control and education, and in this way in little time the house with his school was filled with these poor little helpless ones[.] [A]nd as most of them . . . had been brought there against their own will, it was necessary to guard the door carefully to assure that they remained and to avoid any risk of escape.[32]

It is hardly surprising that some parents of the boys who had been rounded up and sent to the Toribios sometimes protested these aggressive internment measures.[33] What may be more surprising is that other parents actively sought to place sons in this institution for both educational and, especially, disciplinary purposes, even paying to do so. They were joined in their recourse to this institution by civil authorities that likewise committed a variety of young offenders to this institution. These internments are the focus of the rest of the chapter.

'Correctional' residents of the Toribios were distinguished from 'charity' residents in both name and treatment. Those interned as 'charity' cases were known as 'sons of the house'; their expenses were covered out of the institution's operating budget plus the labour they provided in the employ of artisans within and outside institutional confines. In contrast, those sent to the Toribios for punishment or reform were known as 'inmates' (*corrigendos* or *exercitantes*). They were separated from the charity cases and generally performed non-remunerative work and chores.[34] Whether committed by families or other authorities, the costs of their maintenance was usually borne by parents or other relatives.[35] Parents or other sponsors of correctional inmates at the Toribios could and did also pay for such 'extras' as schooling, clothing, shaving, and even shackles (*grillos*).[36]

Although much literature on the history of institutions serving delinquent youths draws sharp distinctions between 'punitive' and 'reformatory' functions, parents seeking to place a son at the Toribios frequently articulated both motives, and indeed often seemed to consider them almost synonymous. Insubordination was the main behaviour that parents sought to punish and correct. In 1830, for example, Felipe Parrado sought his son's admission to the Toribios, explaining that the boy ran away repeatedly, sometimes disappearing for more than a week at a time, returning without his jacket, hat or other belongings, and that the father's repeated efforts to encourage him to reform his ways only prompted the son to run away again. Parrado wanted to intern this son at the Toribios to 'contain' the youth's misbehaviour and prevent him from wasting the family's resources.[37] In another case, Don Pedro Nantet, guardian of two orphaned boys, had one of them committed to the Toribios because he was 'needing some correction of his habits' and Nantet considered that the Toribios 'may be the place where this objective could be achieved'.[38] Alcohol abuse (*embriaguez*) was another, less commonly stated offence for which sons were interned.[39] Master artisans, too, occasionally sent young charges to the Toribios, though much less frequently than parents did.[40]

Not all families embraced the correctional services that this institution increasingly provided, however. At least one mother disagreed vehemently with her husband's decision to incarcerate their 16 year old son at the Toribios, arguing that the son's transgressions were minor and incarceration was inappropriate for one expected to become a notary like his father. (While her protests did not prevent her son's incarceration, she did successfully gain permission to visit her son at the Toribios.[41]) Likewise, in 1785, the Marquis of Gelo rejected advice from the *asistente*, who had advised him to send his chronically intoxicated and otherwise 'depraved' son-in-law to the Toribios; the Marquis dissented, arguing that internment at this institution would not permanently reform his troublesome son-in-law and that it was, moreover, beneath the family's dignity.[42] The Marquis replied that he would rather seek his son-in-law's placement in a religious community.

While these cases reflect disdain for the Toribios, it was not uncommon for individuals of prominent status to be incarcerated there. In 1790, for example, a relative of Seville's *asistente* was interned there.[43] In 1792, separate quarters, policies, and boarding rates for 'distinguished' correctional inmates were established to accommodate 'sons of distinguished and noble parents who have found themselves in need of this temporary measure to preserve [their sons] from greater harm, and to oblige them to reform (*reducir a razón*) their conduct, preferring this reclusion, as more appropriate for these ends than the severe destiny they might encounter in jails or [at hard labour] in *presidios*.[44] Although many 'distinguished' inmates bore the noble title *Don*, the distinctions appear to have been chiefly economic rather than juridical, since several individuals originally interned as 'common' inmates were reclassified as 'distinguished' when additional funds were contributed for their maintenance.[45] The higher rates afforded qualitatively different treatment, including separate accommodations and different food, including chocolate.[46]

Internment in a charitable institution that also served abandoned street waifs and juvenile delinquents might seem an odd place for prominent families to send their sons, but it is useful to recall Stuart Woolf's contention that respectable families in pre-industrial Europe frequently could (and did) tap charitable resources, apparently with little stigma. Rather than imperilling family honour, recourse to charitable institutions may have helped some families preserve it, since 'the institutions of charity played a dual role, not only to substitute for the absence of family (for orphans, the sick and aged, etc.), but to bolster the public reputation of individual families...'.[47] While Toribios administrator Gómez y Medina's report in 1792 that *most* of the correctional inmates were from noble and distinguished families may have been an exaggeration,[48] it is clear that some were present. It is very conceivable that the misbehaviour of sons could be more damaging, and consequently of greater concern, to prominent than humble families, prompting the former to make relatively greater use of this facility.

In some cases, families negotiated with civil authorities over sons' internment at the Toribios. Such was the case of Miguel Ferrer, a cadet in an infantry battalion accused of having stolen a piece of silver, for which he and another young military man were sentenced to six years at the Toribios. Ferrer complained repeatedly about the conditions at the Toribios (the enclosure, 'bad air', fetters, etc.), even requesting a transfer to another facility or to naval service, remarking, It is unbelievable that, in dispensing us the grace of being sent to this institution, his majesty intended to make our imprisonment worse'. His entreaties fell on deaf ears, however, and he was apprehended after escaping. Finally, when he fell ill and his mother requested that the remaining two years of his sentence be waived, the authorities relented, in consideration of the military service his father had rendered to the crown, the trouble he was causing at the Toribios, and in the hope that four years at the institution had been sufficient to turn him away from future wrong-doing.[49] In other cases, government officials acted as brokers for parents seeking to punish or reform their sons. In 1830, for example, Pedro Rey of Jerez de la Frontera, frustrated at his own failure to correct the behaviour of his son Don Agustín, sought to have this son sent to the Philippine Islands. Royal authorities denied this request, but ordered that Don Agustín instead be committed to the Toribios for three years.[50]

Civil and church authorities also used the Toribios for punitive or correctional purposes. The city's *asistente*, neighbourhood constables, judges of the city's criminal court, and even the royal government in Madrid all sent individuals to the Toribios. Incarceration on the orders of secular authorities could be either in lieu of or in compliance with formal judicial proceedings, seemingly covering individuals both below and above 14, the legal age of criminal responsibility. Like parents, governing authorities expressed a blend of punitive and correctional motives in their orders to place boys and young men at this institution. Theft was an especially common offence precipitating internment at the Toribios. Eleven year old Antonio Nandín, for example, was sent to the Toribios in 1825 for having stolen sugar from a merchant. Committing him, the *asistente* explained, '[A]s his young age of eleven places him outside the normal [judicial] processes, I have determined that he should remain at that institution for ten days, suffering all the prescribed punishments, in the knowledge that a misunderstood charity might be very harmful, even more so because there are reports that he has committed more serious crimes, and his correction is crucial in order to avoid future ills'.[51] Two boys caught stealing in 1824, members of a throng of seemingly abandoned youngsters who gathered regularly in one of the city plazas, were sent to the city jail; when they were not admitted due to their young age, there was a request to admit them to the Toribios, 'where they can be given the correction appropriate for their age', thereby serving both 'the public good and even their own good'.[52] Graffiti, using or threatening to use a knife, and other offences also landed youngsters in the Toribios.[53] Like parents, governing authorities clearly saw the Toribios as an appropriate place to send young people for punitive and/or correctional reasons, and used it as such.

While some of the boys interned at the Toribios were under 14, not all were this young, as hinted by the extra payments for 'shaving', noted earlier. Among the older Toribios residents were university students and, as we have seen, young military personnel.[54] Abusive husbands and fathers were also interned on the request of their wives and other family members; as pointed out earlier, the *asistente* recommended that the Marquis of Gelo commit a son-in-law to the Toribios.[55] The Archbishop sent clergy there for punishment,[56] and at least one deaf-mute was transferred from an adult penal facility. In 1823, we even find that 'An English general had a negro servant of his in this house for several days, paying 23 *reales* for his food'.[57] Like the boys committed to the Toribios because of their young ages, all these residents were individuals deemed deserving of punishment, but for whom the penal measures generally applied to adult males were viewed as unfeasible or inappropriate.

Notwithstanding the wide range of ages and types of inmates at the Toribios, this institution was primarily associated with boys and young men. While institutional documentation indicates that children as young as eight had been interned for correctional purposes, individual records frequently lack ages, typically referring to inmates only as 'boys' (*niños, muchachos*) or 'youths' (*jóvenes*). Documentation for 1833, however, does provide ages, revealing that in this year all but one of the correctional inmates at the Toribios were between the ages of 14 and 22; the only other was a lone 28 year old.[58] Institutional patrons and administrators expressed sensitivity to age differences in determining punishments, and lengths of incarceration also depended at least partly on age. The longest, multiple-year sentences were generally restricted to the older inmates, such as the abusive husbands and fathers committed by their families and the soldiers committed for criminal offences. Youths interned by their families for insubordination were more typically committed for shorter periods, with some spending less than a day in this institution. Some young people appear not to have been confined at all, but sent there only to receive a number of lashes.[59] Early release on the orders of parents or other authorities also could curtail a stay at the Toribios. Municipal policing official (*comisario del cuartel*) Pedro de Miranda, for example, wrote to the Toribios administrator in 1824 to request that Francisco Rodríguez be freed, 'believing that the time that he has found himself a prisoner...should be sufficient for his correction and to remind him of his duties, obligations, and the behaviour that he should observe in his relations with his neighbours and family'.[60]

The Toribios in Broader Context

The Toribios was not the only old regime charitable institution that fulfilled the functions of a juvenile reformatory, but it was the chief juvenile correctional facility in Seville during its years of operation. In an earlier period, Seville's municipal orphanage for boys also had performed a comparable role. Like the Toribios, it admitted not only 'charity' cases but also boys sent there for punishment or behavioural reform, including by their own parents. One commentator observed, '[I]ts teacher instructs, corrects, and punishes [the boys], with a rigor befitting their ages, doing all that it required to set them straight and remove all their bad vices[.] Many parents take their sons there so that fear and punishment correct them and remove their bad inclinations...'.[61] By the eighteenth century, however, the municipal boys' orphanage had dwindled in size to house only a handful of residents. Moreover, the only other male orphanage operating in Seville during the eighteenth and early nineteenth centuries, a royally patronised institution which had been established to train orphans for maritime careers in the Spanish fleet, eschewed this correctional role, carefully screening applicants and even warning its residents that they could be sent to the Toribios if they misbehaved.[62] This policy had originated with an inspector's conviction that the threat of being sent to this institution 'viewed with horror' by Seville's youth would deter residents of the maritime orphanage from misbehaving or running away.[63]

Among Seville's female orphanages, none filled a comparable role of orphanage-cum-reformatory until much later in the nineteenth century. In fact, administrators of the city's female homes explicitly distinguished themselves from 'correctional institutions'. The administrators of one ordered that prospective residents 'must enter between the ages of seven and ten, since this is a house of education, not correction',[64] and the municipal girls' orphanage had a similar age stipulation and rationale.[65] There was a small institution in the city that served as a place of female 'correction' or 'reclusion', presumably including girls and adolescents; yet this institution was never as large or prominent as the Toribios.[66] Although eighteenth-century observers complained that Seville needed a female counterpart of the Toribios,[67] none of the existing female orphanages assumed this role. Families seeking to 'prevent' or 'reform' daughters' wayward behaviour may have boarded them at religious institutions, a fate to which misbehaving males - like the son-in-law of the Marquis of Gelo (noted above) - were also liable.

Outside Seville, institutions established to take in orphans and other poor young people sometimes also performed 'correctional' functions, often at the behest of parents. In many places, both male and female youths were interned. While the *prevention* of criminal or moral offences was the dominant agenda of such institutions wherever they existed, scholars have found parents and officials also interning 'delinquent' youths in institutions originally established for the poor and homeless in a variety of other European cities. Spanish scholars, for example, have found parents in early modern Murcia and Zamora placing misbehaving young people at institutions originally designed as asylums for the poor.[68] Maurice Capul has reported that in eighteenth-century Paris, juvenile criminals were sent to specially designated juvenile correctional areas of the *Hôpital Général*, while in Lille they were sent to an institution originally founded for vagrants, but which ultimately also housed minors condemned in criminal sentences and those who had disobeyed their parents.[69] Sandra Cavallo has noted that in eighteenth-century Turin, both male and female youths were interned in charitable institutions for correctional purposes.[70] Sherrill Cohen has found that early modern refuges for women (primarily former prostitutes) in Tuscany accepted young girls who had already 'fallen into trouble' and/or lost their virginity, but that administrators at explicitly 'juvenile' charitable institutions, like their counterparts in Seville, increasingly concentrated on 'educating honest girls without subjecting them to the contaminating presence of the female deviants'.[71]

In England, the internment of juvenile delinquents developed through somewhat different institutions, perhaps in part because the types of juvenile charitable institutions that elsewhere came to double as juvenile correctional facilities (orphanages, conservatories, etc.) were not as prevalent due to widespread use of parish apprenticeships and other placements for poor young people. Bridewells are better known sites for the internment of England's juvenile delinquents (apparently including young people committed by their own parents[72]) and transportation to the colonies also became a prominent feature of English practice.[73] Nonetheless, by the later eighteenth century, a variety of English philanthropic initiatives targeting children and youth - in London alone, Lambeth Asylum for girls, the Marine Society for boys, and the Philanthropic Society for young people of both sexes - increasingly accommodated both delinquent and poor young people, paralleling practices at many continental institutions.[74] As for the United States, Timothy Hacsi has noted that most orphan asylums there did *not* house juvenile delinquents;[75] but it is also important to recognise that his focus is on the 1830s through the 1930s, by which time separate juvenile reformatories were already being established.[76]

The practice of interning juvenile offenders at charitable establishments thus appears to have been common in many parts of eighteenth and early nineteenth-century continental Western Europe, at least. Yet it would be a mistake to conclude that all orphanages and other institutions for poor young people were fundamentally 'punitive'. This certainly was not the case in Seville. Not all of Seville's old regime juvenile charitable institutions filled punitive roles, and even those that did - including the Toribios - filled other roles, as well. What *was* consistent across all of Seville's eighteenth- and early nineteenth-century orphanages is that they were populated by a wide variety of young people, not just parentless children and otherwise destitute young people. Although these institutions had originally been established for orphans, many residents had surviving parents or guardians who had sent them to Seville's orphanages for educational and other purposes. Some families were economically desperate and sought the charity dispensed by orphanages so that their children could be assured basic food, shelter, and supervision. For others, somewhat better off, recourse to orphanages was part of longer-term strategies, an attractive vehicle to provide for a child's future, be that through a son's education and training for a future career in the Spanish maritime empire, or one of the dowries that would eventually enable a girl at Seville's orphanage for noble girls to join one of the city's elite convents. Some parents even paid to board children at these institutions to tap the educational services they provided.[77]

Such a diverse orphanage population was not unique to Seville. Scholars working in a variety of historical settings have found that comparable institutions commonly served a variety of young people, not all of whom were full orphans or otherwise bereft of family ties outside the institutions. Such findings suggest that charitable institutions frequently complemented rather than substituted for parents and other adult guardians.[78] They also contribute to a growing body of scholarship that expands the traditional focus on charity providers to include recipients and the ways they manoeuvred within charitable systems to pursue their own strategies - as Peter Mandler has put it, revealing the 'uses' as well as the 'purposes' of charity.[79] Other recent scholarship on policing (of juvenile delinquents, among others) similarly questions prevalent 'social control' models, emphasising instead the ways that individuals and families used institutions and interacted with authorities for their own ends.[80]

This case study of the Toribios squares well with such approaches and findings. The fact that this establishment became better known as a correctional facility for juvenile delinquents than a charitable institution for poor children is not merely an emblem of the oft-noted association among 'poverty', 'delinquency', and 'internment'. It also reflects another way that families integrated this and other charitable institutions into their own domestic and child-rearing strategies. The evolution of the Toribios' increasingly 'correctional' role is not wholly attributable to outsiders' efforts to supplant families' control over their children, but a process that families - especially parents - played a critical role in. Recognising that families incorporated this institution into their own strategies blurs artificially sharp distinctions between 'familial' and 'institutional' responses to child care and discipline and provides some insight into the development of one precedent for the residential, institutional discipline of young people prior to the establishment of juvenile reformatories. The finding that both families and other authorities used this charity home as a 'reformatory' before such institutions formally existed - even before the 'invention' of juvenile delinquency, some would contend[81] - emphasises the need to look beyond the rhetoric and labels of nineteenth-century reformers to see how both families and authorities defined dissolute or criminal young people and sought to 'correct' or 'reform' them within the legal and institutional contexts available to them.

Endnotes

The research for this article was generously supported by the Program for Cultural Co-operation between Spain's Ministry of Culture and US Universities, a Fulbright Research Grant to Spain and Indiana University's History Department, College of Arts and Sciences and University Graduate School. I also gratefully acknowledge the assistance of Helen Nader, Pam Cox, Heather Shore, Edith Schoell Tikoff, Lydia Murdoch, James Riley, Joby Gardner Felix Masud Piloto and David Reher.

N.B. All translations from Spanish-language manuscripts and printed sources are mine.

[1]   L.T. Empey, 'The Progressive Legacy and the Concept of Childhood', in *Juvenile Justice: The Progressive Legacy and Current Reforms*, ed. L.T. Empey (Charlottesville, 1979), pp. 25-26.

[2]   H. Cunningham, *Children and Childhood in Western Society since 1500* (London, 1995), pp. 145-50, quotation from p. 146.

[3]   S. Schlossman, 'Delinquent Children: The Juvenile Reform School', in *Oxford History of the Prison*, ed. N. Morris and D.J. Rothman (New York, 1995), p. 364.

[4]   See, for example, N. Zemon Davis, 'The Reasons of Misrule: Youth Groups and Charivaris in Sixteenth-Century France', in *Society and Culture in Early Modern France* (Stanford, 1975), pp. 97-123. N. Schindler, 'Guardians of Disorder: Rituals of Youthful Culture at the Dawn of the Modern Age', in *A History of Young People in the West*, ed. G. Levi and J.-C. Schmitt (Cambridge, Mass., 1997), vol. 1, pp. 241-82. J.F. Harrington, "Singing for His Supper': The Reinvention of Juvenile Streetsinging in Early Modern Nuremberg', *Social*

History* 22 (1997), pp. 27-45.

5 P. King, 'The Rise of Juvenile Delinquency in England 1780-1840: Changing Patterns of Perception and Prosecution', *Past and Present* 160 (1998), pp. 116-17.

6 F. Collantes de Terán, *Los establecimientos de caridad de Sevilla, que se consideran como particulares: Apuntes y memorias para su historia* (Seville, 1886), 159 (note 1).

7 F. Aguilar Piñal, *Temas Sevillanos*, 1st series, 2nd ed., rev. and aug. (Seville, 1992), pp. 51-57. V. de la Fuente, *Los Toribios de Sevilla. Las Adoratrices[.] Memorias leídas en la Real Academia de Ciencias Morales y Políticas* (Madrid, 1884); *Enciclopedia universal ilustrada europeo-americana* (1928), s.v. 'Toribio. Hist Los Toribios de Sevilla' and 'Tribunal Tutelar de Menores'. J.L. Morales, *El niño en la cultura española* (Madrid, 1960), vol. 1, p. 422. Collantes de Terán, pp. 151-96.

8 W.J. Callahan, *Church, Politics and Society in Spain, 1750-1874* (Cambridge, Mass., 1984), pp. 145-85, esp. pp. 178-79.

9 Archivo Municipal de Sevilla (hereafter, AMS), XI, vol. 63, docs. 23, 26. Archivo Histórico Nacional in Madrid (hereafter, AHN), Consejos, bundle 625, doc. 6. Archivo de la Diputación Provincial de Sevilla (hereafter, ADPS), Hospicio, bundle 1, doc. 18, and bundle 18, account books. G. Baca, *Los Thoribios de Sevilla: Breve noticia de la fundación de su Hospicio, su admirable principio, sus gloriosos progresos, y el infeliz estado en que al presente se halla...* (Madrid, 1766), p. 101. J. Gómez y Medina, *Modo de vida que han de observar los exercitantes, distinguidos en la nueva vivienda de la Casa Colegio de Toribios de la ciudad de Sevilla . . .* (Seville, 1792), p. 4.

10 'Asistente' is the title in Seville of the royally appointed officer more commonly known in other Spanish cities as the 'corregidor'. See Francisco Morales Padrón, *La Ciudad del quinientos*, 3d ed., rev., 'Historia de Sevilla' series, ed. F. Morales Padrón (Seville, 1989), pp. 212, 215-16.

11 Baca, pp. 102-4.

12 Baca, p. 103.

13 AHN, Consejos, bundle 831, doc. 27.

14 ADPS, Hospicio, bundle 13b, various unnumbered documents. In 1754, Seville's municipal council found that the Toribios 'appeared to be more a harsh prison for the guilty than a charitable refuge of helpless innocents'. AMS, XI, vol. 63, doc. 20.

15 AMS, Hospicio, bundle 1, doc. 58.

16 Morales, vol. 1, p. 789.

17 F. Villamazares, 'La jurisdicción especial de los tribunales tutelares de menores en el ordenamiento procesal español', in *Estudios jurídicos en homenaje al Profesor Santa Cruz Teijero* (Valencia, 1974), vol. 2, pp. 575-91.

18 M.E. Perry, *Crime and Society in Early Modern Seville* (Hanover, New Hampshire, 1980), p. 209.

19 R. Kagan, *Students and Society in Early Modern Spain* (Baltimore, 1973), p. 8.

20 Royal Decree of 14 July 1781, copy at AMS, V, vol. 293, doc. 30.

21 P. Griffiths, *Youth and Authority: Formative Experiences in England 1560-1640* (Oxford, 1996), pp. 19-34.

22 See, for example, M. Velázquez Martínez, *Desigualdad, indigencia y marginación social en la españa ilustrada: Las cinco clases de pobres de Pedro Rodríguez Campomanes* (Murcia,

1991), esp. pp. 220, 232. For an analysis of the evolution of concepts of Spanish age labels according to changing dictionary definitions, see V. Fernández Vargas and L. Lorenzo Navarro, *El niño y el joven en España (siglos XVIII-XX): Aproximación teórica y cuantitativa*, with prologue by J. Bosch-Marín (Madrid, 1989), pp. 165-67.

23 See, for example, *Gran enciclopedia Rialp* (Madrid, 1984), s.v. 'Tribunal de menores'. *Enciclopedia universal ilustrada europeo-americana*, s.v. 'Tribunal'. Morales, vol. 2, pp. 394-96.

24 A. San Vicente Pino, *El oficio de padre de huérfanos en Zaragoza* (Zaragoza, 1965). Morales, vol. 1, pp. 394-96.

25 Baca. AMS, XI, vol. 63, docs. 15-28. Principal discussions of the Toribios include those in Aguilar Piñal, *Temas sevillanos*, pp. 51-57; Collantes de Terán, pp. 151-96; de la Fuente, pp. 6-25; M. Jiménez Salas, *Historia de la asistencia social en Espana en la edad moderna* (Madrid, 1958), pp. 213-14; Morales, vol. 1, pp. 422-30; and V. Romero Muñoz, 'Vida ejemplar de Toribio de Velasco', *Archivo Hispalense* 32 (1960), pp. 195-215.

26 ADPS, Hospicio, various bundles, especially 1, 13b, 18.

27 See, for example, B. Geremek, *Poverty: A History*, trans. A. Kolakowska (Cambridge, Mass., 1994), pp. 206-29. M. Foucault, *Madness and Civilisation: A History of Insanity in the Age of Reason*, trans. R. Howard (New York, 1965), esp. 38-64. R. Jütte, *Poverty and Deviance in Early Modern Europe* (Cambridge, 1994), pp. 169-77.

28 Jütte, pp. 36, 40. For a specific example of this phenomenon, see R.M. Schwartz, *Policing the Poor in Eighteenth-Century France* (Chapel Hill, 1988), pp. 51-52, 94-99.

29 Cunningham, 147.

30 AMS, XI, vol. 63, doc. 16. See also Baca, esp. pp. 11-12. ADPS, Hospicio, bundle 1, doc. 24.

31 Perry, pp. 190-211.

32 Baca, p. 12. See also Baca, p. 62 and AHN, Consejos, bundle 625, doc. 3.

33 Baca, p. 11. See also AHN, Consejos, bundle 625, doc. 3.

34 Baca, pp. 102-3. Gómez y Medina, pp. 3-7.

35 ADPS, Hospicio, bundle 18, account books (income). The inmates of Seville's royal prison also were expected to pay for their room and board. See Perry, pp. 76-77.

36 See, for example, the case of inmate Don Francisco Ordoñez in ADPS, Hospicio, bundle 18, account book (income) for 1814.

37 ADPS, Hospicio, bundle 13b, letter from José García on behalf of Felipe Parrado, [Seville], n.d. (ca. 10 June 1830), to [José María Rodríguez, Seville].

38 ADPS, Hospicio, bundle 13b, letter from Pedro Nantet, 27 November 1831, to [José Manuel] Arjona, [Seville].

39 For example, ADPS, Hospicio, bundle 13b, letter from Antonio Fernando Sierra y Arce, Seville, 17 November 1824, to [José María Rodríguez], Seville.

40 ADPS, Hospicio, bundle 18, account books (expenses).

41 ADPS, Hospicio, bundle 13b, letter of Orocia Vertusco, n.d. (ca. 1 July 1825) to [José María Rodríguez, Seville].

42 Francisco Aguilar Piñal, *Siglo XVIII*, 3d ed., rev. , 'Historia de Sevilla' series, ed. Francisco Morales Padrón (Seville, 1989), pp. 255-56.

43 ADPS, Hospicio, bundle 18, unnumbered document labelled 'Año de 1790 Prontuario donde

se apuntan las entradas y salidas de Exercitantes . . .'.

[44] Gómez y Medina also notes that the correctional inmates at the Toribios included 'people of all classes, and all the Provinces of Spain and the Indies'. Gómez y Medina, pp. 5-6.

[45] Gómez y Medina, p. 19. ADPS, Hospicio, bundles 1 and 18, account books (income).

[46] Gómez y Medina, p. 21. ADPS, Hospicio, bundle 18, account books (expenses), e.g., for 1826.

[47] S. Woolf, 'Introduction: The Poor and Society in Western Europe', in *The Poor in Western Europe in the Eighteenth and Nineteenth Centuries* (London, 1986), p. 27.

[48] Gómez y Medina, p. 5.

[49] Ferrer's case is documented in a lengthy set of correspondence from February 1827 through August 1831. See ADPS, Hospicio, bundle 13b, especially letters from Vicente Quesada, Seville, to José María Rodríguez, [Seville].

[50] ADPS, Hospicio, bundle 13b, letter from José Manuel Arjona, Seville, 23 March 1830, to José María Rodríguez, [Seville].

[51] ADP, Hospicio, bundle 13b, letter from [José] Manuel Arjona, Seville, 10 November 1825, to José María Rodríguez, [Seville].

[52] ADPS, Hospicio, bundle 13b, letter from Francisco de Paula Nieto y Ahumado, Seville, 13 March 1824, to [illegible]. (The addressee of this letter is illegible due to water damage, but it was almost certainly Seville's *asistente*, who likely forwarded this letter to the administrator of the Toribios, José María Rodríguez.)

[53] See, for example, ADPS, Hospicio, bundle 13b, letter from Ygnacio Francisco [Ayuro?], Seville, 12 February 1830, to [José María Rodríguez, Seville] and ADPS, Hospicio, bundle 13b, letter from José Manzano, Seville, 1 September 1825, to [José María Rodríguez, Seville].

[54] ADPS, Hospicio, bundle 13b, letter from Francisco Xavier de Outon, Seville, 20 December 1825, to [José María Rodríguez, Seville]. ADPS, Hospicio, bundle 14b, letter from Vicente de [Quesada?], Seville, 15 August 1827, to José María Rodríguez, Seville.

[55] ADPS, Hospicio, bundle 13b, letter from Manuel García de la Cotersa, Seville, 21 September 1831, to [José María Rodríguez, Seville]. ADPS, Hospicio, bundle 13b, letter from Pedro Miranda, Seville, 8 June 1824, to [José María Rodríguez, Seville]. ADPS, Hospicio, bundle 13b, letter from Antonio Suárez, Badajoz, 30 August 1831, to [José María Rodríguez, Seville].

[56] ADPS, Hospicio, bundle 13b, letter from Luis Gonzago Colón, Seville, 13 October 1827, to [José María Rodríguez, Seville]. ADPS, Hospicio, bundle 18, account books (income).

[57] ADPS, Hospicio, bundle 18, account book (income) for 1823.

[58] As this 1833 count of Toribios wards was made two years after this institution came under the administrative oversight of Seville's new general poorhouse (*hospicio*), it is possible that some of the customary population of the Toribios might have been reassigned to other divisions of the poorhouse by this date. ADPS, Hospicio, bundle 1, doc. 18.

[59] In 1826, for example, Seville's royally appointed senior municipal official (*asistente*) and sheriff (*alguacil mayor*) sent several boys to the Toribios, ordering that each be given '12 lashes by way of correction'. ADPS, Hospicio, bundle 13b, letter from Josef Manfredi, Seville, 27 June 1826, to [José María Rodríguez, Seville].

[60] ADPS, Hospicio, bundle 13b, letter from Pedro Miranda, Seville, 21 June 1824, to [José

María Rodríguez, Seville].

[61] AMS, XI, vol. 32, doc. 1. See also J.I. Carmona García, *El extenso mundo de la pobreza: La otra cara de la Sevilla imperial* (Seville, 1993), pp. 98-99, and *El sistema de la hospitalidad pública en la Sevilla del antiguo régimen* (Seville, 1979), p. 52.

[62] *Ordenanzas para el Real Colegio de San Telmo de Sevilla* (Madrid, 1788), pp. 114-16, copy at Archivo General de Indias in Seville (hereafter, AGI), Indiferente General, bundle 1635.

[63] AGI, Arribadas, bundle 555, unsigned copy of a 1779 report by Antonio de Arnuero.

[64] Beaterio de la Santísimia Trinidad, Seville, uncatalogued manuscript labelled 'Copia de las Constituc[io]nes e Ynforme correspond[ien]tes al Beat[eri]o de la S[antísi]ma] Trinidad de esta Ciud[a]d de Sev[ill]a . . .,' dated 13 December 1796.

[65] AMS, IV, vol. 24, doc. 3.

[66] F. Avellá Chafer, 'Beatas y beaterios en la ciudad y arzobispado de Sevilla', *Archivo Hispalense* 65 (1982), pp. 120-21.

[67] AMS, XI, vol. 63, doc. 28.

[68] J.J. García Hourcade, 'Itenerarios de miseria. (Los pobres murcianos frente a los mecanismos asistenciales)', *Investigaciones históricas época moderna y contemporánea* (Universidad de Valladolid), 14 (1994), pp. 65-85, esp. pp. 69, 80. M.I. Galicia Pinto, *La Real Casa Hospicio de Zamora[:] Asistencia social a marginados (1798-1850)* (Zamora, 1986), p. 114.

[69] M. Capul, *Abandon et marginalité: Les enfants placés sous l'Ancien Régime*, with preface by M. Serres (Toulouse, 1989), pp. 170-71.

[70] S. Cavallo, *Charity and Power in Early Modern Italy: Benefactors and Their Motives in Turin, 1541-1789* (Cambridge, 1995), pp. 247-48.

[71] S. Cohen, *The Evolution of Women's Asylums Since 1500: From Refuges for Ex-Prostitutes to Shelters for Battered Women* (New York, 1992), pp. 63-70, 116-17, 154-55; quotation from p. 116, referring to the conservatory of Saint Francis de Sales in eighteenth-century Florence.

[72] W. Smith, *State of the Gaols in London, Westminster and Borough of Southwark* (London, 1776), as quoted in W.B. Sanders, *Juvenile Offenders for a Thousand Years: Selected Readings from Anglo-Saxon Times to 1900* (Chapel Hill, 1970), pp. 62-63.

[73] Griffiths, pp. 366-73; and I. Pinchbeck and M. Hewitt, *Children in English Society* (London, 1969-73), vol. 1, pp. 102-11.

[74] D. Andrew, *Philanthropy and Police: London Charity in the Eighteenth Century* (Princeton, 1989), pp. 109-19, 182-86.

[75] T.A. Hacsi, *Second Home: Orphan Asylums and Poor Families in America* (Cambridge, Mass., 1997), p. 118.

[76] Hacsi, pp. 1, 11-13; Schlossman, pp. 363-89.

[77] V. Tikoff, 'Assisted Transitions: Children and Adolescents in the Orphanages of Seville at the End of the Old Regime, 1681-1831' (Ph.D. diss., Indiana University, 2000), pp. 81-171, 349-52.

[78] See, for example, E. Sonnino, 'Between the home and the hospice. The plight and fate of girl orphans in seventeenth- and eighteenth-century Rome', in *Poor Women and Children in the European Past*, ed. J. Henderson and R. Wall (London, 1994), p. 99. S. Cavallo, 'Conceptions of poverty and poor-relief in Turin in the second half of the eighteenth century', in *Domestic Strategies: Work and Family in France and Italy, 1600-1800*, ed. S.

Woolf (Cambridge and Paris, 1991), pp. 148-99, esp. 174-80. T.M. Safley, *Charity and Economy in the Orphanages of Early Modern Augsburg* (Atlantic Highlands, New Jersey, 1997), p. 5. L. Murdoch, 'Imagined Orphans: Poor Families, the Home, and Child Welfare in England, 1870-1914' (Ph.D. diss., Indiana University, 2000). H. Goldstein, *The Home on Gorham Street and the Voices of its Children* (Tuscaloosa, 1996), pp. xii, 70. J.A. Dulberger, ed. '*Mother Donit fore the Best': Correspondence of a Nineteenth-Century Orphan Asylum* (Syracuse, 1996), p. 10. Hacsi, pp. 1-2, 11, 104-47. See also Pinchbeck and Hewitt, vol. 1, pp. 149-53.

[79] P. Mandler, 'Poverty and Charity in the Nineteenth-century Metropolis', in *The Uses of Charity: The Poor on Relief in the Nineteenth-Century Metropolis*, ed. P. Mandler (Philadelphia, 1990), pp. 1-2. See also the introduction by J. Barry and C. Jones to their edited volume *Medicine and Charity before the Welfare State* (London, 1991), p. 11. Recent work addressing families' (especially parents') uses of explicitly juvenile charity and public welfare or protective services includes the scholarship on orphanages in various historical contexts already cited, as well as R. Cicerchia, 'Minors, Gender, and Family: The Discourse in the Court System of Traditional Buenos Aires', *History of the Family: An International Quarterly* 2 (1997), pp. 331-46. P. Ferguson Clement, 'Families and Foster Care: Philadelphia in the Late Nineteenth Century', in *Growing Up in America: Children in Historical Perspective*, ed. N.R. Hiner and J.M. Hawes (Urbana, 1985), pp. 135-46.

[80] For example, in his analysis of 'streetsinging' - an aspect of juvenile delinquency in early modern Nuremberg - Joel Harrington has argued that the 'the still ubiquitous two-tiered model of elite/popular 'cultures' suggests a false dichotomy of interests and especially of power'. Harrington, p. 28.

[81] A.M.Platt, *The Child-Savers: The Invention of Delinquency* (Chicago, 1969). S. Margarey, 'The Invention of Juvenile Delinquency in Early Nineteenth-Century England', *Labour History* 34 (1978). M. May, 'Innocence and Experience: The Evolution of the Concept of Juvenile Delinquency in the Mid-Nineteenth Century', *Victorian Studies* 17 (1973), pp. 7-29. See also Schlossman, pp. 363-65.

Chapter 4

'Crimes inexplicables': Murderous Children and the Discourse of Monstrosity in Romantic-Era France

Cat Nilan

In 1838, François Bourillon, a ten year old shepherd, was put on trial for the sexual assault and murder of a four year old girl.[1] Coverage of his trial in the popular legal journal the *Gazette des Tribunaux* expressed both shock and dismay at the spectacle presented by a young child 'accused of two crimes that seem far removed from the character and habits of that age'. The reporter's pencil-portrait of the defendant sought to explain the crime through the child's appearance and demeanour:

> Bourillon withstood the ordeal of the solemn occasion of a criminal court session with a self-assurance beyond his years. This young child, whose outward appearance would suggest that he has not yet reached his real age, has a gentle enough face when he is at rest. But as soon as he is addressed, his expression darkens and his face takes on a hue that does not belie the acts of cruelty to which he abandoned himself.

The most disturbing thing about this child was his mental acuity:

> One trembles to think of the awful future prepared for him by his so criminal inclinations, inclinations which, in this case, showed themselves to be accompanied by all the signs of an intelligence one would desire not to encounter in this defendant.[2]

The *Gazette des Tribunaux* was a professional journal for lawyers, but it enjoyed a far wider readership due to its detailed and sometimes lurid accounts of criminal and civil trials. As in so many other cases of this sort, which were reported in its pages, a murderous child's behaviour was explained in terms of his failure to adhere to a prescribed model of innocent childhood. Instead of gentleness, cruelty and criminal inclinations; instead of what one social reform activist identified as 'sacred ignorance', a too acute intelligence; instead of dependency, self-assurance.[3] Thus the murderous child was constructed as 'unnatural' or 'monstrous'.

Throughout the first half of the nineteenth century, the child who committed an 'atrocious' crime such as murder was perceived by many French commentators as an affront to the only recently consolidated model of innocent childhood.[4] The 'precocious perversity' of the child murderer seemed to open up a breech in dominant cultural constructions of childhood, eliciting what were often panicked responses from French social critics and cultural arbiters.[5] What follows is an examination of some of the discursive strategies employed by journalists, legal professionals, and social reformers in their efforts to describe and explain children who had committed criminal acts which overstepped the bounds of the culturally conceivable. Beginning with some general arguments about the cultural construction of the child criminal, it will then focus on press coverage of the trials of several murderous children.

In *The Melodramatic Imagination* Peter Brooks argues that, following the Revolution of 1789, French society was desperate for moral absolutes. This was a desire that found its most telling expression in the turn-of-the-century melodrama.[6] In the wake of the turmoil and ambiguities of the revolutionary era, theatre audiences were drawn to dramatic stagings of a conflict between good and evil, in which patent innocence suffered but eventually triumphed over the most blatant villainy. However hackneyed much of this literature may appear to the modern reader, it provided a ritualised expression of the reassertion of social order, both in its affirmation of a black and white morality stripped of ambiguities and in its sentimentalised portrayal of social and familial relations.

The cultural construct of childhood innocence, which had already begun to emerge in the eighteenth-century as an outgrowth of Enlightenment attitudes toward nature and education, was reinforced and reshaped by this post-Revolutionary movement. Through the medium of the melodrama the child was written into the public drama of the early nineteenth century as an unsullied embodiment of innocence:

> Especially when the heroine is herself beyond adolescence, a child may be introduced as the bearer of the sign of innocence. ... For children, as living representations of innocence and purity, serve as catalysts for virtuous or vicious actions. Through their very definition as unfallen humanity, they can guide virtue through perils and upset the machinations of evil, in ways denied to the more worldly.[7]

No longer merely the Rousseauean or Wordsworthian link between the alienated adult and the world of nature, the innocent child also became the lynchpin of the domestic sphere, the symbolic repository of peace, harmony, and stability sheltered from the discord, violence, and aggressive competition of the public sphere. Yet the construct of innocence was, from its inception, inherently unstable, indeed untenable. As James Kincaid has argued in his controversial but extremely important *Child Loving: The Erotic Child and Victorian Culture*, the desire for innocence was so strong and pervasive in the nineteenth century that many cultural commentators were able to insist, often against the most explicit evidence, that children were essentially innocent beings.[8]

In the French legal arena, this re-conceptualisation of childhood came into its own at a time when the criminal code was being substantially re-worked. While children had long enjoyed a certain legal dispensation from the full penalties for criminal acts (a tradition stretching back to Roman law and revived on the continent in the middle ages), the French Revolution formalised this exculpation and the Napoleonic Code gave it an enduring expression in French law. Sixteen had been set as the age of criminal responsibility and juvenile delinquents acquired a new legal status distinct from adult offenders.[9] Mechanisms were set in place to take account of children's lesser 'discretion' and punishment was replaced, at least in theory, by a gentler 'correction' suited to what was perceived as the child criminal's greater innocence and educability.

However, the desire to provide legal recognition of all children's innate innocence inevitably came into conflict with the desire to impose harsh deterrent penalties on all criminals. French society had been wracked by political and economic unrest since 1789 and the French ruling elites were intensely concerned about maintaining social order through an expansion of the policing mechanisms of the state.[10] Two strong cultural imperatives - the desire to actively construct the child as innocent and the desire to reaffirm social order through the stigmatisation of the personally responsible criminal actor - necessarily clashed when they were confronted by the criminal child. In point of fact, a very substantial percentage of children arrested in France during the first half of the nineteenth century had committed offences that were not conceptually incompatible with conceptions of childhood innocence. In Paris, roughly 40% of child prisoners in the 1830s and 40s had been arrested for vagrancy and 15% for begging.[11] While these children were often incarcerated, most often for lack of any adult guardian willing to claim them, they were readily conceived of as 'victims' who, although they might have had incipient criminal tendencies, could still be considered children in need of firm but kind adult guidance. The fiction that they were being 'corrected', not punished, by detention, glossed over the conceptual difficulties raised by the existence of what were, in reality, juvenile prisons. Of the remaining 45% of Parisian child offenders, 40% had been arrested for theft.[12] Most of these young thieves had committed the pettiest of crimes, often stealing bread or sweets. They too could readily be construed as childlike in their behaviour - as desperately hungry or naughty gluttons, not cunning burglars or threatening muggers.

However, a small core group of children could not be written off as fundamentally innocent - these were the 'precociously perverse'. They included those vagrants, beggars, and thieves whose behaviour was perceived as violating the model of childhood innocence. Key indicators might be behaviour exhibited during the prosecution process, for example failure to cry at their trial.[13] However, also included were children who had intentionally committed acts of violence: a very small percentage of the French juvenile delinquent population - less than 2% in Paris - but noteworthy because they seemed to provide such a provocative violation of the rule of innate childhood innocence.[14] Of this sub-population of violent offenders, children who murdered or attempted to murder others were clearly out-liers - they represent an infinitesimal percentage of all legal cases. However, if murder cases involving children were rare, they were for that very reason given considerable media attention. Much of the commentary on murderous children from the 1820s through the 1840s expresses intense anxiety about these children, an anxiety that is over-determined and excessive in light of the rarity of these cases. Insofar as newspaper coverage of the trials of child murderers was shaped by the effort to reconcile conflicting cultural impulses about childhood and crime, it tells us much about the cultural faultlines revealed in responses to the criminal child.

Like the two-headed calf, the murderous child exercised a fascination that was based on his or her status as a perceived anomaly. Where the 'normal' innocent child was a creature of the family, the murderous child was an atomised individual, acting upon personal impulse and not subservient to parental control. The innocent child was natural, the murderous child was primitive and atavistic - a notion abhorrent to most Romantic-era commentators. The innocent child was naturally good, washed clean of original sin and intuitively connected with the things of the spirit; the murderous child was wilfully and explicitly evil. The innocent child was gentle, peaceable, and kind; the murderous child was violent, aggressive, and cruel. The innocent child was educable, a soft wax, a pliant sapling, ready and willing to take the shape and form lent it by adult guidance; the murderous child was an autodidact of evil, wilful, self-directed, and already hardened in vice. The innocent child was sexually immature, feminine in appearance, and lacking in all sexual knowledge; the murderous child was sexually precocious, prematurely (or unnaturally) masculine, and too knowing about the adult mysteries. The innocent child was, for all of these reasons, irresponsible - '*sans discernement*'; the murderous child was discerning, and therefore fully responsible for cunning and cold-blooded crimes.

Crimes Inexplicables: the Murderous Child on Trial

As Peter Brooks has noted, 'it is the rare melodrama that does not have a villain'.[15] And melodramatic villains are usually tall, dark, strangers moved by brutal passions, not little boys and girls. Yet, in the real-life drama of the courtroom, the 'conveyor of evil' sometimes overturned theatrical convention and appeared in virtue's form.[16] When a child committed a depraved and intentional act of violence, the proverbial innocent was revealed as a villain, shaking to their foundations the very ethical certainties the melodramatic world-view was designed to promote and uphold. How can one explain a crime that is, by its very nature, 'inexplicable', as one report on a 15 year old girl who attempted to poison her master and his entire family insisted?[17] For the reporters of the *Gazette des Tribunaux*, as for other criminal justice and social reform specialists, this was a vexing question and one that could rarely be answered to their entire satisfaction.

The *Gazette*'s writers, usually so eager to fill their accounts with florid prose, frequently claimed to be struck speechless by the enormity of assaults, rapes, and murders committed by children. Commenting on the trial of a 14 year old boy who had 'subjected his mother to unheard of assaults', the reporter deliberately (and titillatingly) withheld a full account of the boy's actions: 'My pen refuses to set down this story'.[18] The case was a 'scandal' - not only because of the physical violence involved, but also because it too graphically demonstrated the depravity of at least one child and thereby threatened the prevailing conceptual categories of age-appropriate behaviour. Moreover, this particular case forcibly subverted the ideal of tender familial relations so closely related to the innocent childhood construct. Other accounts involving children charged with especially heinous crimes emphasised the *inconceivability* of these children's actions:

> ...We have received the following communication, the contents of which offer an example of a very precocious perversity, and which one may find difficult to comprehend...We reported...the arrest of two young children who had committed the most inconceivable outrages against their two sisters...[19]

What is significant here is not whether reporters were truly horrified, but that they felt the need to make use of 'too horrible for words' as a rhetorical device. This act of self-censorship highlights the existence of an 'unspeakable', of realities beyond the range of acceptable public discourse (and which themselves serve as boundary markers). But being incapable of or unwilling to talk about these crimes does not provide satisfactory explanations - or readable columns of newsprint. Reporters clearly felt compelled to provide some sort of analysis of the aetiology of these crimes, and they resorted to a grab-bag of explanatory models. As self-consciously modern commentators with a largely secularised worldview, they were especially drawn to the models provided by the emerging criminological sciences and pseudo-sciences.

Explaining the Murderous Child Through Science

In 1833, a nine year old boy living in a village near Limoges forced a five year old girl into a fire and held her there when she tried to escape.[20] The girl died a few hours later, but not before having named Jean Penny as her murderer. This 'unheard of act of cruelty' produced 'consternation' in the village - and Penny's neighbours began to recall other instances of cruelty on his part. The child's behaviour caused the judge to suspect that Penny might be insane - 'atteint de démence' - and the courts asked two doctors to examine him, 'in order that they might acquire, through the most rational means, a knowledge of his penchants and his tastes, in a word, of his moral state'.[21]

There is a certain sense here, as in similar cases, that a child who would engage in acts of violence must, by definition, be mentally ill. The doctors, however, found Penny fit to stand trial, even though his behaviour during his pre-trial incarceration seemed to provide new indications of abnormality. The *Gazette's* report notes that Penny failed to express any emotion during his detention, but acted with considerable 'guile', a word often used to condemn the precocious cunning of criminal children. In addition, a local newspaper even claimed that Penny had been caught strewing the prisoners' recreation yard with broken glass. At the trial, the phrenological theories of Franz-Joseph Gall, which were enjoying a considerable mode at this time, were called upon to explain Penny's behaviour: the child was said to have cranial protuberances that indicated a 'penchant for murder'.[22] However, one of the doctors who was called to testify - presumably for the prosecution - quickly discounted this suggestion, noting that Gall's theories were still being studied and could not be considered proven. In any case, the phrenological system could not be applied to Penny because, '[he] is far from having reached the age at which all of his organs will have reached their full development'. The prosecuting attorney offered an even more forceful rejection of phrenology:

> ...to maintain, in effect, that bumps of theft or murder force the unfortunate possessor of such a skull to commit murder or theft is to judge man on the material level, it is to deny him his divine origin, it is to rob him of that intelligence which makes him superior to other creatures, and which gives him the power to control his evil inclinations.[23]

Anxious not to provide defendants with a means of escaping personal responsibility for their crimes, the prosecution rejected determinism, but begged the question of whether or not a child could be considered as fully responsible as an adult for their criminal actions.

Science had clearly failed here. With the doctors unable to provide any conclusive and rational reasons for Penny's behaviour, the reporters' initial physiognomic description of Jean Penny is left to stand as the only, if clearly insufficient, explanation for his crime:

> At first sight, this child appears to have beautiful eyes, but when he is attentively examined, his gaze is almost always equivocal, and sometimes one would be inclined, despite oneself, to recognise in his eyes and in his smile a certain appearance of ferocity.[24]

The Inexplicable Monster

The Penny case is cited here because it is typical of the coverage of many cases involving murderous children during this period. Gestures are inevitably made toward scientific and medical explanatory models, but these models almost invariably fail, leaving behind only uncertainty and an uncomfortable sense of the inability of human reason to confront and explain a child's wilful violence. When all else failed, reporters attempting to explain the violent actions of certain children, threw up their hands and, like Samuel Taylor Coleridge in his analysis of Shakespeare's villainous Iago, brought in a verdict of 'motiveless malignity - how awful!'.[25] The case of Honorine Pellois, an 11 year old tried for having murdered two toddlers by pushing them into a well, can further serve as an illustration of the problems confronted by journalists in their accounts of murderous children.[26] The two reports on Honorine's crimes consist of a virtual compendium of possible pseudo-scientific explanations for violence. It was noted that the girl had a history of 'cruel' behaviour; she suffered from a 'frightening monomania for murder'.[27] Phrenologists would find new support for their theories in her precocious perversity - and, perhaps most damning of all, 'Certain parts of her body, which presented something imperfect and extraordinary, indicated shameful habits'.[28]

Nevertheless none of these explanations seemed sufficient, and the language used in the description of the girl's trial quickly left science behind. Honorine ceased to be human, let alone a little girl: she was 'a little monster', an 'infernal creature'; she 'gnash[ed] her teeth like a monkey', she 'burst out laughing like a demon'.[29] But at bottom the reporter insisted, this murderous child went so far beyond conceivable and acceptable categories of childlike behaviour that nothing could explain her 'prodigiously monstrous' behaviour, which must needs 'upset all of the moralist's ideas'. The existence of a child such as Honorine again remains a great mystery:

> ...when one has observed Honorine Pellois's attitude when confronted by her judges; when one has seen her dry eyes and the smile on her face in the midst of the rending emotions of the proceedings; when, above all, one has heard her candidly recount her crimes with a horrible naivete, it is unfortunately difficult not to believe that the human species contains undefinable beings who seem to find instinctual pleasure in evil, and who are almost predestined to become the terror of other men.[30]

The attempt to replace the monstrous with the pathological, superstition with reason, had failed and nothing could be done except to lock away the child-monster for the longest possible time, in this case 20 years.

Explication in Search of a Crime: A Case of Parricidal Monomania

Honorine Pellois had done something horrible. However, what is most interesting in the coverage of her case - and in similar cases - is the patent unwillingness of adult commentators to entertain the idea that a child could do something horrible and still be, in a certain sense, 'innocent', thus still be a child. Once a child had done something horrible it was almost as if all of their childlike traits were replaced by monstrousness - their precocious perversity was all-embracing and manifested in all of their behaviour.

It is not enough that Honorine is cruel: she must also be too smart for her age, sexually deviant, monomaniacal, and so on. This extreme reaction to the wilfully murderous child suggests an instability in the idea of childhood itself, an anxiety that innocent childhood is in fact a more fragile construction than adults would like it to be.

A final peculiar but, arguably, significant case demonstrates this instability very clearly. In 1832, Parent-Duchâtelet, already known for his pioneering work on urban sanitation and prostitution, published an article entitled 'Vicious and Criminal Inclinations Observed in a Young Girl' in the thirteenth issue of a new and influential forensics journal, the *Annals of Public Hygiene and Legal Medicine*.[31] The article consisted almost entirely of a transcript of police reports, with a brief commentary by Parent-Duchâtelet. It was almost immediately reprinted in its entirety in the *Gazette des Tribunaux*, whose editor explained that he had hastened to publish it because it could be of the 'greatest interest' to readers. The *Gazette*, less scholarly in its tone, changed the article's title to the rather more dramatic 'Parricidal Monomania in a Young Girl'.[32] The bizarre contradiction of this case was that no crime, whether violent or not, was ever committed by the young 'parricidal monomaniac' involved. In 1825, an eight year old girl, who had been begging in the street and who claimed to have been abandoned, was taken to a Parisian police station by a passerby. When the child's mother arrived at the station to claim her daughter, the mother proceeded to tell the police officer a long and complex tale about her child's perverse inclinations. The mother insisted that her daughter had repeatedly expressed the desire to kill both of her parents by slicing their throats with a knife, that she had engaged in sexual play with young boys and wanted to do so with adult men, and that she could not be stopped from masturbating. The parents had done everything they could to correct their daughter, but she persisted in her murderous threats:

> ...[my husband] tried to correct her ...; he whipped her with a riding crop; another time, he tied her to the foot of the bed for half an hour with a strip of leather; none of that did any good; my little girl didn't shed a tear, and coldly replied to her father: *hitting me won't do anything, you can cut my throat, and I won't change*, ... I've already said that this very extraordinary child never cries, never laughs, and doesn't amuse herself by or with anything; she just sits on a very little chair, her hands crossed, and as soon as I turn my back, she touches herself; I teach her to read, I make her sew and knit, but since this is all in spite of her, it doesn't produce any results.[33]

It is not necessary to read very far into this account to see a rather troubled family. It is important to note that the child had only recently come to live in her parents' home, having spent her infancy with a wetnurse and her early childhood with grandparents in the countryside. One possible explanation for the intense hostilities expressed in the mother's account is that the child's parents were simply unprepared to deal with an active and perhaps troubled little girl and there is a strong suggestion that the child's father wished to abandon the girl to a foundling home. That the child expressed the active desire to kill her parents seems fairly well-established by the police reports, but that she had been fed these ideas by adults - and quickly learned that she could attract considerable attention by expressing them - also seems evident.

However the modern reader interprets the details of this narrative, and whatever the 'true' facts in the case, the police took the mother's story seriously. The messy ambiguities in the case were stripped away and the child's expressed interest in murder and sex was explained in the very language of criminal pathology promoted by journals like the *Annals of Public Hygiene and Legal Medicine*. Thus, the investigating officer found.

That the young *** has a harmful proclivity for onanism, which must be destroyed if the ravages it has already wrought in this child are not to be augmented. That this harmful habit by itself could have unsettled the intellectual organs of this child, and caused the horrible *monomania* that she has been struck by; that if one can with reason think that this obsession with killing her mother is the result of a mental derangement, one can fear that if the cause subsists, then that idea, strengthening with age, may make it easier for the child to put it into execution.[34]

He concluded that, if the child could not be cured, she must be put under surveillance and sequestered from society. The child's parents turned her over to the state, and local authorities paid for her to be placed in a convent school. She was eventually apprenticed out to a jeweller. Although, at the age of 14, she appeared outwardly obedient and well behaved, she remained an unnatural child, 'sad and taciturn', incapable of playing or amusing herself. Parent-Duchâtelet ends the article with the ominous observation that the girl's mother believed that she had never broken her dangerous habit of masturbation.[35]

Here the child has become a monster in the absence of any actual monstrous behaviour. An expressed interest in murder - which all parties, including the child herself, acknowledged would have been impossible for the child to execute at the tender age of eight - is taken as evidence of a severe and probably irreparable mental derangement necessitating constant supervision within an institutional setting. The problem is not that acts of violence committed by children are inexplicable - it is, of course, usually the case that a careful examination of specific circumstances will allow the articulation of persuasive narratives of causation, even in horrible and extreme cases. The problem in the cases which have been examined here is that explication is not permissible because the combination of violence and childhood was not tolerable, given both the terms of the prevailing model of childhood and of the model of criminal causation. A child murderer is especially awful only when a society insists that children are qualitatively different from adults in their behaviours and motivations. A child murderer becomes monstrous - and not merely tragically human - when children can remain human only by adhering to a stereotyped model of behaviour not applied to adults.

Endnotes

[1]   'Bouches-du-Rhone (Aix). Enfant de dix ans accusé d'attentat à la pudeur et de meurtre', *Gazette des Tribunaux* [henceforth GdT] 2824 (7 September 1834), p. 1038. Bourillon was found guilty, but was acquitted under the terms of article 66 of the *Code pénal*, which allowed judges to find that children under the age of 16 had acted 'without discretion' and to sentence them to a term in a juvenile facility (a 'house of correction for young detainees') not to exceed their twenty-first year. In this case, Bourillon was to remain incarcerated until he turned 18.

[2]   Ibid.

[3]   L. Bernard, *Conseils aux jeunes détenus* (Paris, 1839), p. 4.

[4]   Drawing their precedent from Roman law, French jurists of the eighteenth century designated as *crimina atrocissima* ('the most atrocious crimes') high treason, parricide, premeditated murder, blasphemy or sacrilege, and highway robbery, as well as other especially 'atrocious' crimes. Even when these crimes were committed by a minor, they drew heavy retribution and full legal penalties.

[5]   A key term in the juvenile delinquency discourse of the period. This concept is analysed extensively in my own 'Precocious Perversity: Childhood, Crime, and the Prison in July Monarchy France', the book manuscript from which this paper is derived.

[6]   P. Brooks, *The Melodramatic Imagination: Balzac, Henry James, Melodrama, and the Mode of Excess* (New York, 1985 [orig. ed. 1975]).

[7]   Brooks, p. 34.

[8]   J. Kincaid, *Child Loving: The Erotic Child and Victorian Culture* (New York and London, 1992).

[9]   Until 1912, when a family court system was instituted, juvenile delinquents' special legal status was reflected in sentencing and punishment procedures, but not in the judicial process itself. For a discussion of the 1912 legislation, see: R. Badinter, *La Prison républicaine (1871-1914)* (Paris, 1992).

[10] The most tendentious presentation of this argument first appeared in Michel Foucault's *Discipline and Punish: The Birth of the Prison* (New York, 1979) and an enormous amount of ink has since been spilled in response to that book's analysis of modern trends in policing and social control. J-G. Petit's *Ces peines obscures: La prison pénale en France (1780-1875)* (Paris, 1990) presents a more nuanced version of Foucault's key arguments and serves as a good jumping-off point for further exploration of this historical question.

[11] These statistics are derived from the booking records *(régistres d'écrou)* of juveniles held in three Parisian prisons, Sainte-Pélagie, the Madelonnettes, and the Petite Roquette, c. 1830-1849 (Archives Départementales de la Seine et de la Ville de Paris, DY 2-3, 7-8). A detailed analysis of these records appears in the sixth chapter of my book manuscript, 'A Demographic Profile of the Parisian Boy Prisoner, 1830-1848'. While substantial regional variation is reflected in juvenile crime statistics, the Paris figures are broadly representative of those of other urban areas.

[12] Ibid.

[13] For a detailed discussion of contemporary responses to emotionally impassive children, see

my article, 'Hapless Innocence and Precocious Perversity in the Courtroom Melodrama: Representations of Child Criminals in a Paris Legal Journal, 1830-1848', *Journal of Family History* 22 (1997), pp. 251-85.

[14] See note 11. The percentage of children arrested for violent crimes was likely to be higher outside of Paris, but that is only because so few children were arrested for any crime in the provinces. The provincial figures can be gleaned from: Ministère de la Justice, *Compte général de l'administration de la justice criminelle en France* (Paris, 1825-1850).

[15] Brooks, p. 32.

[16] Ibid., p. 33.

[17] 'Cour d'assises, Hérault: Empoisonnement d'une famille entière commis par une jeune fille de 15 ans. - Crime inexplicable', *GdT* 3572 (20/21 February 1837). See also: *GdT* 3578 (27/28 February 1837).

[18] *GdT* 1902 (17 September 1831), p. 1084.

[19] *GdT* 2260 (10 November 1832); GdT 4511 (22 February 1840), p. 397.

[20] The case was reported as it unfolded in three separate articles, *GdT* 2465 (10 July 1833), p. 895; GdT 2580 (21 November 1833), p. 67; GdT 2593 (6 December 1833), p. 122.

[21] *GdT* 2465 (10 July 1833), p. 895.

[22] *GdT* 2593 (6 December 1833), p. 122. Franz Joseph Gall's most important work, *Anatomie et physiologie du système nerveux en général, et du cerveau en particulier*, was published in Paris in four volumes between 1810 and 1819. Although Gall died in 1828, his work remained widely influential (and widely disparaged) throughout the 1830s and 1840s.

[23] Although phrenology is mentioned fairly frequently in the *Gazette des Tribunaux*, reporters tended to mark their distance from this theory by ascribing phrenological analysis to others and by gently deriding their findings (e.g.: 'his skull ... offers all of the signs from which the grand-priest of phrenology would recognise an inclination to cruelty ...' [*GdT* 4563 (23 April 1840), p. 605]).

[24] *GdT* 2580 (21 November 1833), p. 67.

[25] R.A. Foakes ed., *Coleridge on Shakespeare: The Text of the Lectures of 1811-1812* (Charlottesville, VA, 1971).

[26] *GdT* 2791 (28/29 July 1834), p. 907; 'Effrayante monomanie pour le meurtre', *GdT* 2890 (22 November 1834), p. 79.

[27] Other murderous children were also said to have demonstrated an inclination toward cruelty prior to the commission of their crimes. See for example: *GdT* 2043 (1 March 1832), p. 455 ('It would appear that Martin Saubelet, of such tender years, had already given proof of the most perverse inclinations'.). Attempts to make this a clinical category are apparent in Leuret's 'Observations médico-légales sur l'ivrognerie et la méchanceté, considérés dans leurs rapports avec la folie', *Annales d'hygiène publique et de médecine* légale 24 (1840), pp. 372-401), which argues that some individuals are incapable of controlling their vicious inclinations and that 'their vices of the heart are carried so far as to constitute a veritable monstrosity' (p. 398). Leuret discusses a case involving a child under the title 'Cinquième observation. -- Méchanceté native; penchant à la destruction de toutes sortes d'objets; tentatives d'homicide et d'incendie observées chez une jeune fille' (pp. 397-401).

[28] *GdT* 2890 (22 November 1834), p. 79.

[29] Ibid.

30   Ibid.
31   Parent-Duchâtelet, 'Penchants vicieux et criminels observés chez une petite fille', *Annales d'hygiene publique et de médecine légale* 7 (1832), pp. 173-94.
32   *GdT*, 'Monomanie parricide chez une jeune fille' 2022 (5 February 1832), pp. 374-6.
33   Parent-Duchâtelet, p. 180.
34   Ibid., p. 189.
35   Ibid., p. 194.

Chapter 5

Testing the Limits: Redefining Resistance in a Belgian Boys' Prison, 1895-1905

Jenneke Christiaens

Historical research on nineteenth century prisons has focused mainly on the mechanisms of control that accompanied the rise of imprisonment as a modern form of punishment. It has analysed prison as an institutional system and has tended to examine the production of order through, for example, its regulation of labour, silence and activities, its educational programmes and its architecture. This approach has resulted in a historiography from which the experiences of prisoners themselves have been largely absent. The same is also true of historical studies of nineteenth century special prisons and re-educational institutions for young offenders. The absence of young inmates within their own history is striking. The ways in which juvenile delinquents experienced, and the extent to which they submitted to, or resisted, penitentiary discipline remains an open question.

By using a more qualitative approach this chapter aims to tackle precisely this question of submission and resistance. It is based on a case study of 'incorrigible' Belgian boys imprisoned in the special disciplinary section of the famous *maison de force* in Gent at the end of the nineteenth century.[1] In an attempt to counter the passive and subordinate (historical) image of the juvenile delinquent, I will focus particularly on juvenile prisoners' ways of dealing with the discipline and punishment that constituted their 're-education'.

Resistance in the Study of Crime and Punishment

The rise of the modern prison can no longer, if indeed it ever could, be presented as a linear success story. One reason for this is that recent investigations of the daily resistance that the penal system had to face have made it possible to offer a new approach to the history of (crime and) punishment. Understanding this resistance can allow us a certain insight into the system from the perspective of prisoners.[2]

This approach developed over time from the work of British social historians.[3] With the use of concepts such as 'social crime', 'criminalisation processes' and 'survival strategies' another history of crime *from below* has been made possible, precisely because such concepts acknowledge and incorporate 'the thoughts and feelings of those people whose behaviour [they] seeks to explain'.[4] Resistance - defined in the very broad sense of not behaving as one is supposed to behave rather than in the more familiar if more narrow sense of organised or politicised dissent - stands at the centre of this perspective on crime. However, despite this rich social historiographic tradition, histories of punishment and especially histories of prisons have been disappointingly poor in this respect, with the exception of some important work on the French penal system.[5]

By contrast, criminological (or penological) research on prisons has paid much attention to prisoners and their perspective on prison life and to the effects of long-term imprisonment upon them.[6] As a result of contemporary prisoners' protests and insurrections, recent criminological research has reflected a renewed interest in problems of prison order.[7] As Scraton et al have argued, this criminological research *from below* has allowed the inclusion of inmates' perspectives on prison coercion and punishment. It has also challenged official diagnoses of 'problems' in prison by suggesting alternative explanations, and made it possible to change the perception of what punishment can or should be.[8] This kind of criminological research is based on a specific empirical source: the views of prisoners. Historians in general work with rather more silent sources and, in this particular field, with a much reduced range of biographical and ego-documents. The difficulty of finding personal accounts written by or about prisoners and especially juvenile delinquents is well known to historians in this area. Given these difficulties, what kinds of sources might show something of the perspectives of young prisoners in the nineteenth century? To answer this question we have to take a closer look at how we might conceive the resistance of prisoners.

Resistance Within Prison Walls

How, then, should resistance be defined in the prison context? Should definitions be restricted to the more evident, and therefore more apparently *conscious* manifestations of resistance, such as prisoner protests and uprisings? What is the relationship between protest on the one hand and adaptation to prison life on the other?[9] In the wake of Foucault's claims as to the close relationship between power and resistance, we have to adopt a far broader and more open concept of resistance[10]. If resistance is contemporary to power and if there is always a possibility to resist, then even the apparent acceptance of prison rules can be read as a form of resistance, albeit masked or disguised.

J.C. Scott's research on political domination and subordination led him to the influential conclusion that relations of dominance and resistance always have two faces: one public and one hidden.[11] Scott therefore distinguishes between different forms of resistance on the basis of their public or hidden character. He describes the public interaction of power (and resistance) relations as the 'public transcript'.[12] This public transcript embodies the apparent (political and social) consensus sustaining both the complete or partial subordination of some and the practices of dominance of others. In this sense, public forms of resistance can be seen as a part of this consensus (a consensus enacted in most liberal democracies).

The concept of the public transcript can be applied to the (nineteenth century) prison context where material forms of dominance take easily recognisable forms: every aspect of material life within prison walls, from food to work to clothing, is (meant to be) part of this material dominance. The same can also be said about symbolic or status-based dominance: a complete subordination of the inmate is required and is clearly illustrated by the image of bowed head and by displays of respect, obedience and compliance. Last but not least, an absolute and unquestionable dominance at the ideological level becomes possible. This hegemonic dominance is justified through the offenders' (established) guilt and the socially and legally sanctioned nature of their punishment. Within criminological literature, especially that shaped by Goffman's concept of 'total institutions', much attention has been paid to this kind of hegemonic domination within prisons and psychiatric institutions. Taken together, these different forms of domination (material, symbolic and ideological) would seem to create a kind of 'totalitarian' power within institutions that makes resistance almost impossible. However, even in such extreme situations, resistance has been (and continues to be) possible.

But limiting the analysis of dominance and resistance to their overt, public forms reduces prisoners to passive subordinates, who only occasionally react in an exceptional and mostly explosive way: for example, through prison riots. These exceptional moments of resistance are commonly explained by what Scott describes as the safety-valve model: systematic domination and submission produce pressure and frustration, because they induce a desire to speak out or hit back. If nothing is done to reduce this pressure it can lead to inevitable explosions of resistance.[13] Significantly, this build-up of pressure and desire to resist are sources of a disguised and hidden way of dealing with dominance: in Scott's words, they constitute the 'hidden transcript'. The hidden transcript consists of a more backstage story, played out in the hidden interactions and spaces where subordinate (as well as dominant) groups and individuals can privately formulate their resentment of and resistance to the public transcript and its practices of dominance.[14] But this must not just be understood as an articulated and spoken, albeit whispered, defiance. The hidden transcript must also be seen to encompass small, ordinary and everyday forms of resistance, because, as Scott says, 'it is impossible to separate veiled symbolic resistance to the ideas of domination from practical struggles to thwart or mitigate exploitation'.[15]

These *infrapolitics of the weak*, such as foot dragging, feigned ignorance or false compliance, are well known. Defining all these actions as forms of resistance makes it possible to understand what happens in the periods between (prison) revolts.[16] This perspective depends upon the recognition of the existence of a 'basic antagonism of goals between dominant and subordinates that is held in check by relations of discipline and punishment'.[17] Dominance and resistance must therefore be seen as part of a dynamic relation that is constantly being tested. This testing of the limits becomes visible where explicit mechanisms of punishment and reward are active. It is precisely by examining the testing of the limits that the more precise ways in which subordinates (*in casu* prisoners) submit to and resist dominance can be detected. In this sense, documents such as punishment registers as well as individual discipline reports offer invaluable historical traces of the daily testing of the limits within the prison. These historical sources provide a glimpse of everyday forms of resistance. They begin to make it possible to open up the world of compliance and defiance of, in this case, the young prisoner or juvenile delinquent.

The Gent Prison for Incorrigible Delinquent Boys, 1887-1920

Social and institutional historical research has traced a pedagogical evolution within the nineteenth century punishment of juvenile delinquents in Western Europe: a move from punishment to re-education. This *pedagogisation* of penal practice in Belgium is clearly reflected in the changing names and functions of its nineteenth century juvenile institutions. The first Belgian juvenile prison opened its doors in 1844 in St. Hubert. In this early period it was called a '*maison pénitentiaire pour jeunes délinquants*' (a penitentiary house for delinquent boys). By 1867 it had been renamed, becoming a '*maison pénitentiaire et de réforme*': a new name which made a new and explicit reference to the goal of reform rather than mere punishment. More than a decade later, in 1881, it was made into a '*maison spéciale de réforme*', a name which discarded all reference to the penitentiary. By the end of the century, any allusion to the penal character of these institutions was avoided and even banned: from 1890 it was known, together with five others, as an *école de bienfaisance* (welfare school).[18] The gradual re-naming of this institution illustrates very sharply the gradual redefinition of nineteenth century Belgian discourses and institutional practices around juvenile delinquents: prisons were becoming schools and prisoners were becoming pupils. This shift, which occurred at the same time in many parts of western Europe, was fundamental to the 'birth' of the modern juvenile delinquent.

What these new names meant in terms of daily institutional practice and the life experiences of young delinquents needs to be more fully investigated. However, this changing language suggests that many aspects of juvenile justice policy, from sentencing to reform, were beginning to be shaped by a new pedagogical logic rather than an older classical penal logic. Nineteenth-century Belgian criminal and penitentiary policy was clearly developing around the perceived needs of a particular group of young delinquents: those who were judged to be 'innocent', even if they had committed an offence, and, as such, sent for long periods of correction or re-education.[19] Thus, by law, the 'innocent' juvenile delinquent was not being punished but re-educated, even though he or she was often sent to the same penitentiaries as those considered guilty. In the second half of the nineteenth century, then, institutional correction became more generally applied and can be considered as a forerunner of Garland's 'welfare sanction'.[20] A number of other practical changes in late nineteenth century Belgian penitentiary policy further serve to demonstrate the gradual pedagogisation of juvenile punishment.[21]

In 1887 a central disciplinary section for boys was opened within the existing *maison de force* (male prison) in Gent. It was intended for 'incorrigible' boys from the *écoles de bienfaisance* and prisons. The category 'incorrigible' was presented as a new pedagogical label that made it possible to segregate 'bad' elements within the re-educational setting and thereby to effectively exclude them from the welfare sanction. The use of this category was a further evidence of the shift from classical penal logic (founded on responsibility or guilt) towards a pedagogical or social logic (based on individual abnormality or dangerousness). The 'incorrigible' delinquents can be seen as the residue of the re-educational project. Incorrigibility was a flexible pedagogical black box that could be made to hold a whole range of bad apples.

The juvenile disciplinary section in Gent's *maison de force* was the only Belgian institution for incorrigible boys. Incorrigible girls were sent to a similar section in the women's prison in Brugge. Between 1887 and 1920 (the disciplinary section was closed down in 1921) more than 3,000 'bad' boys were transferred to Gent. With an average age of 17, this group can be considered as the 'older brothers' of the innocent younger delinquents in the *écoles de bienfaisance*.[22] Most of them had a long penitentiary case-history and had spent some time either in an *école de bienfaisance* or in prison before being transferred to Gent. In 1895 approximately 63% of the incorrigible boys entering the disciplinary section had already spent more than one year in another institution. 44% of them had spent more than two-and-a-half years in such places. This category of incorrigibles was, notably, not composed of *serious* juvenile delinquents who had committed serious crimes. The majority of the boys had been originally prosecuted for petty property offences (68% of Gent inmates in 1895) or vagrancy (20% in 1895).[23] This further shows the category 'incorrigible' to have been a product of the new pedagogical, rather than the classical penal, approach to juvenile delinquency.

In general, four 'pedagogical' reasons were used to justify these transfers: boys could be transferred if they misbehaved in an *école de bienfaisance*; misbehaved during licensed release from such a school; misbehaved while placed in a family or in a work scheme; or were found guilty of a further offence (recidivism). The transfer option can be easily identified as an obvious means of punishment management used by the *écoles de bienfaisance*. Besides 'innocent' juvenile delinquents, the Gent disciplinary facility was also meant to receive 'guilty', and thus already-punished juveniles after they had served their generally short prison sentences. As a result of an 1891 legislative reform of the sentencing of young offenders,[24] all 'guilty' juvenile delinquents (those judged to have acted with discernment and convicted of an offence) were automatically 'put at the disposition of the government'. This meant that all guilty juvenile delinquents were transferred, after a short stay in prison, to the Gent disciplinary facility until they reached the age of majority or even until they reached the age of 21. Thus, from 1891 onwards, both innocent but incorrigible juvenile delinquents, as well as guilty juvenile delinquents were sent to the disciplinary section in Gent.

The Gent boys' prison was severe. Harsh discipline formed the core of its regime. 'Soft' re-education methods were thought to be insufficient to reform those incorrigible inmates sent there from 1887 onwards. Instead, they were subjected to an old remedy: prison discipline. The fact that large numbers of adult male prisoners were also housed there was not considered to be a major obstacle to effective juvenile reform. The Minister of Justice's preference for the old Gent institution was closely linked to its typical penitentiary character. Gent seemed to offer the best penitentiary means of securing strict discipline via its spatial arrangements of cellular sections for solitary confinement, dormitories, large workshops and indoor *promenades* or walks.[25] Besides its typical architectural dimensions, penitentiary coercion was delivered by the strict organisation of activities in time and space. The internal house code was a product of this coercion, with its detailed regulation of the rhythm of everyday life. In Gent, the regime of the *écoles de bienfaisance* was to be applied in a more strict and severe way.[26] Daily activities consisted of work, education and military exercises - all combined with a strong dose of moralisation. In this respect, apart from the cellular prison setting, the regime was not that different from that of an *école de bienfaisance* although it certainly was more restricted: incorrigible boys were not allowed walks outside the building; visits were allowed only once a month and only then as reward for good behaviour; and letters to parents were allowed to be written twice a month. Contact with the outside world was restricted to a minimum. Good behaviour was rewarded, bad behaviour punished. Bad boys could be required to spend time in solitary confinement in one of the isolation cells. Institution rules required punished inmates to be visited daily by the director, doctor, teacher and chaplain, to counter the potential dangers of such confinement.[27]

During their confinement young incorrigibles were supposed to be subjected to 'total' coercion and prison discipline. Nineteenth-century prison regimes, with their aim of securing complete subordination, sought to eliminate every form and sign of resistance. This was especially the case where the disciplining of these incorrigible juveniles was concerned. Of course, the moral improvement of the young inmates was one of its goals, but above all it was intended to break the wilfulness of incorrigible boys.

Infrapolitics of Young Delinquents: Practices of Resistance

The remainder of this chapter focuses, however, on the resistance of this group of boys. It is based on the individual files and internal punishment registers of the Gent juvenile section.[28] These sources help to unlock the infrapolitics of everyday forms of hidden resistance. Reading instances of so-called bad behaviour as forms of defiance allows the specific character of resistance in this specific penal setting to be explored more fully

This perspective brings together two aspects of punishment within prison. On the one hand, every recorded transgression of the rules was viewed by staff as 'bad' behaviour and as resistance. On the other hand, such transgressions were viewed by inmates as a creative way of 'testing the limits'. The boundaries of penitentiary coercion were thus tested every day in various overt and covert ways. To continually and simultaneously interpret inmate actions in these two ways is to expose the fundamental contradiction between the position of the inmates and the position of prison staff - between those subject to the regime and those upholding it.

Punishment registers disclose a whole range of very obvious and simple forms of everyday resistance because they were directly concerned to document the daily responses of inmates to prison life. Alleged challenges to and breaches of the rules were registered on an individual basis. Each dated entry contained a brief account of the incident, a summary of the punishment imposed and the name of the staff member who had made the report. In addition, these offences were also recorded in individual prisoners' files. This research is based on Gent's punishment registers and personal files between 1895 and 1905. During that period 1,530 individuals were punished for breaking the prison rules (see table 1).

These sources are limited in the sense that they do not record every challenge to prison rules: rather, the incidents that they document should be seen as only the tip of the iceberg since many episodes were dealt with informally.

Around 43% of reported incidents concerned bad behaviour, disobedience or lack of discipline. In most cases, this lack of discipline took the form of everyday disobedience during routine activities such as the promenade, classes or work: refusal to enter classes or workshops, refusal to recite prayers, encouraging others to misbehave, and so on. For example, on 16 January 1907, Julien caused trouble in the workshop by hiding tools and encouraging friends to do the same.[29] He was sent to solitary confinement for one day on a diet of bread and water.

Prison labour routines and the prison workshop were common settings for juvenile resistance. Between 1895 and 1905 more than 10% of internal punishments were linked to poor work performance which was variously described as refusing to work, working slowly, working badly, being idle or indifferent or showing ill will. These observed and recorded conflicts at workshop level show just how difficult it was for the authorities to secure the total submission of juveniles to the labour regime. They are more obvious forms of hidden resistance. As such they are classic examples of everyday workplace resistance in the world *outside* the prison as documented by many labour historians.

Table 1. Registered breaches of domestic rules 1895-1905[30]

	1895-1900	1901-1905
Possession of goods	29	88
Communication	45	144
Misbehaviour	106	146
Discipline	229	61
Disobedience	35	78
Destruction	57	55
Disturbance	35	76
Confronting guards	27	59
Violence with co-inmates	21	32
Refusal to work	97	69
Escape attempt or conspiracy	9	9
Collective resistance	0	16
Self-mutilation	4	3
Totals	**694**	**836**

However, prison order could be more openly resisted in a more overt way. The rule of silence was one of the obsessions of nineteenth century prison authorities. In the evening and during the night complete silence was expected from the Gent boys. However, some dared to infringe this basic rule: some by yelling and screaming, others by whistling or singing or by making a general noise in their cells. Clearly, this was not allowed: prisoners were not supposed to sing their way through their detention. Singing was taken as an open provocation of the system and its representatives (in this case, the guards). In 1905, two boys were punished for singing obscene songs during their transfer from prison to court. Earlier, in November 1902, Joseph had been locked up in a solitary cell after a disturbance. Undeterred, he dared to yell and sing, further disturbing the silence of the solitary section.[31] Provocative, obscene and above all, joyful, songs clearly flouted the re-moralisation upon which the boys' re-education apparently depended. Joseph was given a further day of bread, water and solitary confinement.

Any unauthorised contact or communication between the boys was banned. Hence, every attempt at communication was punished. Between 1895 and 1910 more than 12% of punished offences concerned some form of forbidden communication. As outlined above, audible forms of communication such as singing, yelling or chatting in the cells, in the refectory or during the walk were outlawed. But so were less overt forms. The punishment registers also reveal the far more silent, clandestine and inventive ways by which inmates tried to maintain contact with each other and, notably, with the outside world. These incidents foreground the coercion of silence that confounded an obviously strong need to communicate. Such contact was established in different ways in different situations: boys could pass messages to each other in the toilets, in the refectory, in the workshop, during mass or classes or walking from workshop to cell via looks, glances, tapping on water pipes, writing on windows or by writing notes and letters.

Many guards intercepted illicit letters ('billet suspect'). This detected correspondence - a very risky but very common form of communication - represents only a fraction of what must have been a constant exchange between inmates. These writings point to the existence of a certain autonomous social space created by and belonging to these young prisoners. On 13 October 1897, Jan was caught trying to pass a small note to another boy.[32] He was punished with five days of solitary confinement. The note was hidden in a very small envelope and read as follows:

> Beloved friend, I already knew what you told me because yesterday van tomelen had already told me himself but I didn't dare to say it because of the fight because I already knew for 4 days that Jef gave him that many kisses and if you don't want to believe it ask den kankelerie for it is he who told it to me, but you don't have to think that I told jef that it was finished between you and the small one (...) It is too much for me to speak to him. See here your friend JJ Janssens, answer me.[33]

These few words shed light on a prison underground, a world of alliances, arguments and gossip. It shows that despite the severe regime, boys did more than pass written messages to one another and that very close friendships and emotional (and very possibly homosexual) relationships were established and maintained.

Joseph had more than 15 discipline reports in his file. At least eight of these concerned prohibited written and verbal communication. He was found shouting from his window to others walking on the yard, and was even caught climbing the wall trying to talk to adult prisoners on the other side. In June 1905 a message written by him was intercepted. It was written on the back page of his bible and was meant for his friend, Felix.

> Hello dear Felix, Felix here is a little song and poem (...), Felix some more weeks and then we will see our work when you go to Brussels with the girls. My dear Felix send me some words to know how you're doing. Put it by the prison wall and I will pick it up. Your friend...[34]

Joseph's poem for Felix, which earnt him two days solitary confinement with the usual bread and water, was called 'Les filles' (The girls), and as such further challenged the prison's moral code.[35] It read as follows:

The girl is only fifteen
And she leaves already her parents
The girls

Only to run after the young people
Poor she forgets her good parents
The girls

Late in the evening, on the boulevard
You can see them run, late very late
The girls

Communication was not only restricted between prisoners, but also between them and the outside world. Contact with family members was minimal and subject to strict control. Every letter leaving or entering the prison was checked. Family visits were considered to be a privilege not a right and were only granted to those who behaved well. On the other hand, these visits also represented a potential threat to the regime as they made it possible to get letters to the outside. In December 1907 Julien was caught, having agreed to pass a letter from a fellow inmate to his visitor.[36] The visits also made it possible to smuggle scarce or prohibited goods into the prison, especially tobacco for which there was much demand. On 5 April 1905, Emile was caught with tobacco during a post-visit body search.[37] The smuggling of goods can be easily seen as a form of material resistance. Prisoners could react violently when illicit tobacco or other goods were discovered on them. Emile, for one, fought the guards as he tried to escape them.[38] The report on the incident stated that the guards had to knock him down in order to control him. The punishment he received was severe: no visits for two months and three days of solitary confinement on bread and water.

Goods such as tobacco and food were not only smuggled into prison for personal and immediate use. Rather, such trafficking points to the existence of what could be called a black market. In 8% of the recorded disciplinary episodes between 1895 and 1905, young prisoners were caught in possession of goods, including home-made keys and knives. Through this illicit traffic young prisoners could create new ways of subverting the regime. While this should not be overstated or romanticised, it was nevertheless an essential element of everyday resistance.

Small forms of resistance reveal another side of penitentiary dominance and coercion: a hidden world where submission was by-passed and opposed in ways that imply a certain subcultural cohesion. Indications of the existence of such a subculture within the Gent institution can indeed be traced. Punishment registers reveal that some inmates were disciplined because of attempts to tattoo themselves on their hand or forearm. According to nineteenth century criminological literature these prisoners' tattoos were considered not only to be external signs of their inner criminal nature, but also signs of their group cohesion or culture.[39] Tension between inmates, which was quite often expressed through violence and fights, can also be seen as a product of this sense of subculture. Group cohesion or subculture does not (and did not in these instances) produce only peaceful relations. The registers report a daily environment of verbal violence, yelling and insults. Fights broke out in the refectory, in the workshops and in the corridors. Albert, for example, was punished more than once during the summer of 1907 because of quarrels and fights with other prisoners.[40] One of these incidents, a night-time fight, created general chaos and resulted in Albert being locked in his cell, from where he insulted and shouted at the guards. Finally, he was ordered to undergo three days solitary confinement. Such examples of inter-prisoner violence and conflict suggest that inmate subculture operated according to its own social control mechanisms. Describing this phenomenon, Scott argues that 'members of a dissident subordinate subculture can act informally to foster a high degree of conformity to standards that violate dominant norms', that '[s]olidarity among subordinates, if it is achieved at all, is thus achieved, paradoxically, only by means of a degree of conflict', and that '[c]ertain forms of social strife, far from constituting evidence of disunity and weakness, may well be the signs of an active, aggressive social surveillance that preserves unity'.[41]

The subordination of young inmates to the guards and prison rules placed them under constant pressure. Some simply broke down, and are recorded as crying, screaming and destroying their cell furniture as well as books, clothes and other meagre possessions. However, destructive behaviour must not only be understood as an act of despair. It could also be intended to directly disrupt prison order. Julien was punished on 19 August 1906 for smashing a window as part of a collective attempt to break out of the workshop.[42] Sometimes these infrapolitics took a more dramatic personal turn. Almost nothing is known about suicides among juvenile delinquents in nineteenth century Belgian prisons and reformatories. Penitentiary documents are silent on the issue. However, disciplinary registers shed some light on the problem of self-mutilation among the Gent boys. Between 1895 and 1905, three cases of self-mutilation were reported. Leopold was punished at the end of April 1902 because he voluntarily harmed himself.[43] How and why he did this was not reported. This kind of behaviour might be explained, of course, in existential terms, but might also be read as a more instrumental form of resistance.[44] Those who self-harmed might, after all, be transferred to the medical service or declared unfit for heavy prison labour.

Plans and actual attempts to escape are part of what can be described as typical prison folklore, a folklore dominated by those few 'heroes' who managed to succeed. The foiling of escape plans indicates again the existence of a secure and relatively *free* social space where these things could be planned, discussed or dreamt about over long periods of time. Escape attempts accounted for a very small minority (only 1%) of entries in the Gent disciplinary registers. In December 1895 Camille attempted to climb the prison wall.[45] His motives, however, are not clear. Did he want to simply escape (and if so, from what aspect of prison life), or did he merely want to take a look at the surrounding city? Whatever the motive, escape attempts attracted a very harsh punishment: Camille's solitary confinement with the usual bread and water lasted for 14 days rather than two or three.

For all its covert and more hidden forms, resistance could sometimes very suddenly take an overt and open form. This could be directed not only against coercion *per se*, but against its representatives: the prison guard, teacher, director and so on. Quite a number of inmates dared to revolt openly against their re-educators. Between 1895 and 1905, 86 young incorrigibles blatantly resisted them in ways ranging from simple answering back to direct threats and physical intimidation. Violence against guards was rare, but tended to erupt when they intervened to re-establish order after a disturbance. More often, prisoners talked back to guards when they were challenged for breaking a rule. During the summer of 1905 Joseph was reprimanded for shouting at other prisoners.[46] Joseph's answer to the guard was quick and sharp: 'I don't care about you or your report!', then, 'Go to hell troublemaker!' Three days of solitary confinement followed. During the walk on 20 September 1907, Julien was similarly reprimanded for shouting in the courtyard. His response went further, with a threat to beat the guard concerned.[47] Six days of solitary confinement followed. Sometimes, young prisoners could answer back without actually speaking. Emile, for example, first refused to obey the guard who asked him to return to his workshop, then stepped up this resistance by threatening him with an iron bar.[48] He was rewarded with three days of isolation.

These more individual forms of resistance have a well-known collective counterpart: prison revolt. These events are comparable to other forms of extra-institutional public resistance, such as strikes, insurrections and even revolutions.[49] One such collective uprising was reported in the disciplinary registers. In April 1905 a group of 25 juvenile delinquents were locked up for an indefinite period in solitary confinement and were not allowed visits for three months. According to the report, they had caused large scale disorder, refusing to work, disobeying instructions, damaging cell doors and furniture and inciting others to 'indiscipline'.[50]

Conclusions

Conflicts in nineteenth century prisons were generally explained either in terms of the momentary failings of otherwise well-managed penitentiary regimes or in terms of the innate criminality of the prisoners themselves. Frequent anthropological-style investigations of the use of *argot* (prison slang) and the practice of tattooing by inmates are very significant in this sense. However, the wide range of smaller conflicts, such as those presented above, show that conflict was produced to a large extent by everyday tensions in the relationship between inmates and the regime. Further, it is clear that young delinquents played an active role in creating and sustaining this tension. The infrapolitics of resistance were very much a part of everyday practices of re-education and punishment in Gent and in other nineteenth century juvenile justice institutions. Efforts to analyse the treatment of juvenile delinquents in the nineteenth century (or any other period of time) require not only an understanding of the specific penal policy towards juvenile delinquents, with its special institutions and tailored regimes. It also requires a more precise understanding of the role that these young people themselves performed. The figure of the juvenile delinquent cannot be understood solely as the product of power, social control and normalisation, as a passive figure submitting to coercion, punishment and re-education. On the contrary, the juvenile delinquent was very much a product of resistance, a resistance itself framed in the language of power. The everyday forms of resistance detailed here are crucial expressions of the juvenile delinquent's own history.

Endnotes

1 This chapter is based on my PhD research: J. Christiaens, *De geboorte van de jeugddelinquent (België, 1830-1930)*, (Brussel, 1999).

2 See M. Perrot, 'Délinquance et système pénitentiaire en France au XIXe siècle', *Annales E.S.C.* (1975), pp. 69.

3 J. Humphries, 'Enclosures, common rights, and women: The proletarianisation of families in the late eighteenth and early nineteenth centuries', *Journal of Economic History* (1990), pp.17-42; P. King, 'Gleaners, farmers and the failure of legal sanctions in England 1750-1850', *Past and Present* 125 (1989), pp.116-50; J.M. Neeson, *Commoners: common right, enclosure and social change in England, 1700-1820*, (Cambridge, 1996); B. Bushaway, *By Rite. Custom, ceremony and community in England 1700-1880*, (London, 1982); J.G. Rule, 'Social crime in the rural south in the eighteenth and early nineteenth centuries', *Southern History*, 1 (1979), pp. 135-53; S. Humphries, 'Steal to survive: the social crime of working class children 1890-1940', *Oral History Journal* 9 (1981), pp. 24-33.

4 S. Humphries, *Steal to survive*, 24. See for a criminological revival of this concept in: J. Lea, 'Social crime revisited', *Theoretical criminology* 3 (1999), pp. 307-25.

5 Exceptions are: M. Perrot, 'Délinquance et système pénitentiaire' pp. 68-69; M. Perrot, '1848. Révolutions et prisons', *Annales Historiques de la Révolution Française* (1977), pp. 306-38; P. O'Brien, *The promise of punishment. Prisons in nineteenth-century France*, (Princeton, 1982).

6 See for example: S. Cohen, and L. Taylor, *Psychological survival: the experience of long-term imprisonment*, (Harmondsworth, 1972), p. 216; L.H. Bowker, *Prisoner subcultures*, (London, 1977).

7 R. Sparks, A. Bottoms and W. Hay eds. *Prisons and the problem of order*, (Oxford, 1996); P. Scraton, J. Sim and P. Skidmore, 'Through the barricades: prisoner protest and penal policy in Scotland', *Journal of law and society* 15 (1988), pp. 247-62; P. Scraton, J. Sim and P. Skidmore, Prisons under protest, (Philadelphia, 1991), p. 181. For research on the Belgian situation see: B. Bulthe and C.H. Janssen, *Les prisons et la contestation*, (Bruxelles, 1984).

8   P. Scraton, J. Sim and P. Skidmore, *Through the barricades*, 247.

9   O'Brien describes this spectrum as follows: 'prisoners did not leave their identities and roles (...) outside the prison gates. (...) Those experiences were in turn transformed and adapted to the penal environment and became the basis of an informal system within the institution. (...) (T)aken together, individual and collective protests constituted only a minority of the responses of prisoners to their institutional setting. The large majority of prisoners adapted and adjusted, but not without creating new subcultural forms in process', P. O'Brien, 76-77.

10 M. Foucault, 'Entretien', in: B.H. Levy, *Les aventures de la liberté. Une histoire subjective des intellectuels*, (Paris, 1991), pp. 380-1. See also: M. Foucault, 'La poussière et le nuage' in *L'impossible prison*, ed. M. Perrot, (Paris, 1980), pp. 35.

11 J.C. Scott, *Dominance and the arts of resistance. Hidden transcripts*, (London, 1990).

12 Scott explains this in the following terms: 'I mean the public performance required of those subject to elaborate and systematic forms of social subordination: the worker to the boss, (...) the slave to the master, (...). I shall use the term public transcript as a shorthand way of describing the open interaction between subordinates and those who dominate'; and: 'The public transcript is, to put it crudely, the *self*-portrait of dominant elites as they would have themselves seen. (...) It is designed to be impressive, to affirm and naturalize the power of dominant elites, and to conceal or euphemize the dirty linen of their rule', J.C. Scott, 2 and 18.

13 J.C. Scott, *Dominance*, 186.

14 J.C. Scott, *Dominance*, 4-5.

15 J.C. Scott, *Dominance*, 188.

16 J.C. Scott, *Weapons of the weak. Everyday forms of peasant resistance*, (London, 1985), 29.

17 J.C. Scott, *Dominance*, 193.

18 In 1890 Belgium had four *écoles de bienfaisance* for delinquent and vagrant boys (St. Hubert, Ruislede, Namur, Rekem) as well as a special disciplinary section in the old *maison de force* of Gent. At the end of 1890 (31 December) more than 1,500 boys resided in these institutions. At the same point in time, 299 girls were confined in the two *écoles de bienfaisance* (Beernem and Namur) for delinquent girls. See in: J. Christiaens, *De geboorte*, 425.

19 Two categories of juvenile delinquents - the innocent and the guilty - were defined in article 66 (article 72 from 1867) of the 1810 penal code. The principle of discernment was crucial here. The courts had to acquit minors younger than 16, even if they were guilty of an offence, if they were judged to lack normal discernment (because of their young age). These innocent juvenile delinquents could be simply sent back home or could be placed in correction for a determined period until their majority. If, however, the court considered that the young person did have the required discernment (even if they were younger than 16), he or she was declared guilty and sentenced. Between 1844 and 1871 those innocent juvenile delinquents who were sent to correction by the courts were placed in an *école de bienfaisance*, usually for several years. During the same period, guilty delinquents could also be sent to an *école de bienfaisance* although usually for a shorter time (3-6 months); however, some could still be sent to prison. After 1871, guilty young offenders were excluded from the *écoles de bienfaisance* and sent (back) to the adult prisons. A reform in 1891 made further changes: after this, a guilty juvenile offender could be transferred - once they had served their short prison sentence - to the Gent disciplinary section or to an *école de bienfaisance* until they reached the age of majority. For a more detailed discussion, see: J. Christiaens, 'A history of Belgium's Child Protection Act of 1912: the redefinition of the juvenile offender and his punishment', *European Journal of Crime, Criminal Law and Criminal Justice* 7 (1999), 5-21. On the discovery of the innocent juvenile delinquent in the Netherlands in the second half of the nineteenth century, see C.H. Leonards, *De ontdekking van het onschuldige criminele kind. Bestraffing en opvoeding van criminele kinderen in jeugdgevangenis en opvoedingsgesticht, 1833-1886*, (Hilversum, 1995).

20 Garland defines this as 'a sanction which takes as its object not a citizen but a client, activated not by guilt but by abnormality, establishing a relation which is not punitive but normalising', D. Garland, 'The birth of the welfare sanction', *British Journal of Law and Society* 8 (1981), pp. 40.

21 For an overview of this process, see: J. Christiaens, 'A history of Belgium's Child Protection Act of 1912'.

22 J. Christiaens, *De geboorte*, 198-205.

23 J. Christiaens, *De geboorte*, 427.

24 Loi du 27 novembre 1891 sur la répression du vagabondage et de la mendicité, *Pasinomie* (1891), pp. 439-59.

25 Arrêté ministériel du 21 mars 1887 - règlement concernant la création et l'organisation du quartier de discipline à la maison spéciale de réforme à Gand, *Pasinomie* (1887), pp. 7-58.

26 Artikel 3, Arrêté ministériel du 21 mars 1887, *Pasinomie*, 57-58.

27 Arrêté ministériel du 21 mars 1887 - règlement concernant la création et l'organisation du quartier de discipline à la maison spéciale de réforme à Gand, *Pasinomie* (1887), pp. 58 (in footnote).

28 Disciplinary registers (1895-1905) and individual files (100 files - population of disciplinary section Gent), General Archives Beveren, Prison Gent, VIII.2.2.196-8.

29 Julien was 17 and convicted for theft *avec effraction et escalade*. He was punished with an imprisonment of six months and *put at the disposition of the government* until his twenty-first birthday. Prisoners file nr. 3742.

30 The categorisation of the data in this table is adapted from more detailed descriptions of offences in the discipline registers. Categories do not therefore always correspond to the offences established in prison rules.

31 Joseph was almost 21 years old. He was convicted in 1901 for several correctional offences, such as theft, abuse (breach) of confidence and forgery. Prisoners file nr. 3596.

32 Jan was 18 and was convicted in 1895 for (simple) theft. He received a short prison sentence (15 days) and was afterwards transferred to Gent. Prisoners file nr. 2240.

33 Prisoners file nr. 2240.

34 Prisoners file nr. 3596.

35 Prisoners file nr. 3596.

36 Julien was 20 and was convicted in 1905 for violence. Prisoners file nr. 3750.

37 Emile was almost 18. He was convicted in 1900 for fraud. At the time he was less than 16 and the judge considered that he lacked discernment. He was placed in correction, and ended up in the disciplinary section at Gent. He was released almost a month after the reported incident, and five years after his conviction. Prisoners file nr. 3424.

[38] Prisoners file nr. 3424.
[39] A. Lacassagne, *Les tatouages, étude anthropologique et médico-légale*, (Paris, 1881); C.
      Lombroso, *Le crime: causes et remèdes*, (Paris, 1899); G. Tarde, *La criminalité comparée*,
      (Paris, 1890); L. Vervaeck, *Le tatouage en Belgique*, (Bruxelles, 1906).
[40] Albert was 19, convicted for vagrancy and *put at the disposition of the government* until his
      twenty-first birthday. Prisoners file nr. 4064.
[41] J.C. Scott, *Dominance*, 129-31.
[42] Julien was 17 and convicted for theft with *effraction and escalade*. Prisoners file nr. 3742.
[43] General Archives Beveren, Gevangenis Gent, VIII.2.2.197.
[44] See also M. Perrot, 'Délinquance et système pénitentiaire', 69.
[45] General Archives Beveren, Gevangenis Gent, VIII.2.2.196, (1895 - n° 45).
[46] Prisoners file nr. 3596.
[47] Prisoners file nr. 3750.
[48] Prisoners file nr. 3424.
[49] See for example M. Perrot, 'Révolutions et prisons', 306-38.
[50] One of those involved, Alphonse, was 18 and had been convicted for theft in 1902. The
      judge considered that he lacked discernment and he was placed in correction until his twenty-
      first birthday. He was released in September 1907, having spent more than three years in
      Gent. Prisoners file nr. 3590.

Chapter 6

Border Crossings: Care and the 'Criminal Child' in Nineteenth Century European Penal Congresses

Chris Leonards

In the late spring of 1848 Willem Hendrik Suringar, chair of the Dutch Society for the Moral Improvement of Prisoners (*Nederlands Genootschap tot Zedelijke Verbetering der Gevangen*, referred to here as the Dutch Prison Society), was very concerned about the social and political upheavals occurring across several European cities and the part that criminals in particular might be playing in this. He feared that in Amsterdam, 'released prisoners could play a pernicious role and could threaten and endanger the tranquillity, possessions, health, - yes, the very lives of many in municipality or town'. In France, where released prisoners allegedly numbered between 30 and 40 thousand, he thought it likely that large numbers of them had been involved in the Paris uprisings where, 'assisted by wives, concubines and children, [they had] formed a strong army that, *having nothing to lose*, had no thought of respect or fear whatsoever'.[1]

Suringar's international view of criminality and delinquency may seem striking given that he was addressing a national annual meeting of his Society. However, his internationalism was no doubt shaped by what he had heard and experienced at the international penal congresses he had recently attended in Frankfurt and Brussels where he had debated matters of prison organisation and after-care with fellow philanthropists and renowned discussants such as Ducpétiaux from Belgium, Crawford from Britain, Mittermaier from Germany, David from Denmark and Moreau-Christophe from France.[2] These groups - forerunners in the fields of social, penal and philanthropic policy - were very aware of what was going on in the streets and used their meetings to share hopes and fears inspired by the revolutionary spectre that seemed to be haunting Europe.[3]

In this chapter I will show how several significant penal developments, from special juvenile confinement to the after-care of released minors, which have been presented as if they originated in ways specific to particular European countries, were in fact conceived at and through a series of international penal congresses held in major European cities across the nineteenth century. These congresses gradually became battlefields where governmental and non-governmental agencies, or effectively, public and private enterprises, clashed over the question of how best to deal with issues of welfare and social order. They were also, in a sense, international markets where transnational opinions on the meaning and management of social order were both formed and broken. Ultimately, they served not only as centres of information and debate for visitors, but also grew in importance as authoritative institutions in their own right, strongly influencing national decision making.

Here, I will suggest how the congresses' discussions and decisions led to an important shift in the treatment of juveniles in which practical attention moved away from 'hard core criminal children' to the much broader category of 'endangered children', thereby contributing to what I have called the discovery of 'the innocent criminal child'.[4] I will do this first by outlining the broad agenda of the congresses in the nineteenth century. Secondly, I will examine in more detail some of the discussions on juveniles and juvenile care that took place at congresses held in the 1840s, 70s and 90s. Thirdly, I will compare these supra-national ideas and resolutions with policy-making and implementation at the national level by looking at developments in the Netherlands.

The Congresses

European integration and communication is not just a twentieth century phenomenon. From 1846 onwards, congresses of various kinds took place in major European cities. As well as the penal congresses discussed here (and detailed in Table 1), which focused on subjects such as prison reform, penal law, juvenile care, ex-prisoners and general welfare provision, there were others which centred on medicine, poor relief, statistics, philology, law and women's rights. The penal congresses acted as key nodes in a wider network of philanthropists, prison directors and inspectors, lawyers, government officials, architects and other 'moral entrepreneurs', with delegates attending from many European and even some American states.

Table 1. Persons and countries present at the international penal congresses, 1846-1950

year	place	persons	countries
1846	Frankfurt a./M.	75	11
1847	Brussels	196	16
1857	Frankfurt a./M.	-	-
1872	London	341	21
1878	Stockholm	297	26
1885	Rome	234	25
1890	St. Petersburg	740	26
1895	Paris	817	24
1900	Brussels	395	29
1905	Budapest	450	28
1910	Washington	-	33
1925	London	-	-
1930	Prague	-	-
1935	Berlin	-	-
1950	The Hague	-	-

Starting in the 1840s as casual debating conventions, by the 1870s they had become much larger, more formally organised and more influential. In this, they were typical of the development of what might be called 'congress culture'. Fifteen of these congresses were held between 1846 and 1950, mostly at five year intervals (with the exception of the 1860s and 1940s). As Table 1 also shows, delegate numbers grew from 75 at the first congress in Frankfurt in 1846, to 341 at the fourth in London in 1872, to 817 at the eighth in Paris in 1895. The numbers of countries represented grew from 11 to 21 to 24 respectively.

The nature of their proceedings changed over the course of the century as the meetings became longer and their agenda more weighty. Despite these changes, reports of congress proceedings retained a broadly similar form, and typically included an agenda, or day order, followed by a fuller transcription of debates, questions and answers, and ending with a summary of the conclusions reached and resolutions passed whether unanimously or by a majority. These published printed reports must have been widely circulated, given that they can still be found in many national and prison-related libraries.[5] This circulation was an important feature of the congresses, especially the early ones, since as unofficial bodies, their members' main means of disseminating information was by publishing the proceedings themselves, reporting back to national organisations, giving lectures, writing newspaper articles and so on. Another important means of doing this was to invite official government representatives to attend, which congress organisers did from the start, in the hope that this would impact more directly upon national decision making processes.[6]

In the 1850s, congress agenda were usually prepared by congress organisers: for example, organisers M.G. Varrentrapp and E. Ducpétiaux put together the agenda for the first and second events in Frankfurt and Brussels respectively, with the apparent agreement of prospective delegates. From the mid-1870s, agenda were produced more formally by a special committee, the International Penitentiary Commission, set up under the initial chairmanship of E.C. Wines after the 1872 London congress following consultation with several penal experts.[7] Often, issues left unresolved from the previous congress were discussed at the next.

Until the Paris meeting of 1895, congress deliberations were organised into three broad sections: 'penal legislation', 'penitentiary establishments' and 'preventive means'. Thereafter, a fourth section was introduced, devoted to 'children and minors'.[8] This development signalled a wider shift in the focus of these international discussions. The relative importance of questions linked to 'penal legislation' and 'penitentiary establishments' diminished over time, while that of questions related to 'preventive means' and 'children and minors' increased (see Figure 1). Although juveniles had featured in almost every discussion of crime and crime prevention and had been included on the agenda of every congress, there was a marked increase in interest in them from the 1870s onwards, culminating in the Paris meeting of 1895. The next section explores this shift further by considering three moments in these European discussions of juvenile care, crime and correction: the Frankfurt and Brussels congresses of 1846 and 1847; the London congress of 1872 and the Paris congress of 1895.

Criminal Children and Congressional Discourses

Debates at the first two congresses, held in Frankfurt in 1846 and in Brussels the following year, were dominated by the question of confinement, and, in particular, the desirability of solitary confinement as a way of dealing with both adults and juveniles. In the two preceding decades, experiments in special residential care for criminal juveniles had been set up in a number of European states. In Britain, separate juvenile prisons were established at Millbank in 1823 and Parkhurst in 1838.[9] In the Netherlands, a juvenile prison was opened in 1833 in Rotterdam,[10] while in France a cellular prison for children, La Petite Roquette, was set up in Paris in 1836,[11] and in Belgium, Saint Hubert prison was set up in the Ardennes in 1840.[12] Alongside these juvenile prisons other institutions aimed explicitly to resocialise the young through special education and intensive prolonged periods of care. The Raue Haus near Hamburg in Hanover - started in 1833 by Johann Hinrich Wichern - is seen as *the* model for several other European initiatives of this kind, such as France's famous

Figure 1. Questions tabled at international penal congresses, 1846-1910

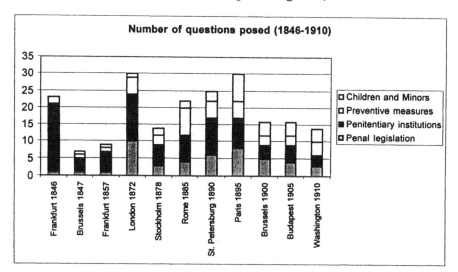

Mettray set up by F.A. Démetz in 1840; Britain's Red Hill set up in Surrey by S. Turner in 1841; Belgium's Ruisselede and Beernem set up by Ducpétiaux in 1849 and 1852.[13] Despite these significant institutional developments, any discussion of the apparent value of investing in the long-term resocialisation of criminal children was eclipsed in the early congresses which were instead dominated by discussions of the prison system in general.

Delegates at the Frankfurt and Brussels congresses generally saw solitary confinement as the most effective form of confinement for all adult prisoners.[14] Although the issue of after-care societies and juvenile asylums had been put on the formal Frankfurt agenda, discussions of different kinds of solitary confinement had taken up all the congress time.[15] As congress transcriptions show, the chair of the Dutch Prison Society, W.H. Suringar, played a very important role at this gathering. After a remarkable change of mind a few years earlier,[16] he had become a zealous supporter of solitary confinement, or, as his Dutch opponents put it, a 'cellomaniac'. At the Brussels congress, the question of after-care, framed by its supporters as an indispensable part of penitentiary reform, and the question of how solitary confinement should be applied to juveniles, were explicitly put to the delegates. The congress formally resolved that special houses of educational correction should be erected for juveniles with regimes which would satisfy both these demands by combining solitary confinement with outplacement in agricultural colonies or apprenticeships with farmers, artisans or industrial workshops. This resolution might be taken to imply that there was a broad agreement among delegates as to the use of diverse methods of reform. However, transcriptions of the proceedings show that this compromise was the product of bitter disagreements between 'cellomaniacs', commanded by W.H. Suringar, and 'agrarian colonists', led not by Démetz, the famous director of the Mettray colony, as one might expect, but by a relative outsider, Wolowski, a French professor of 'industrial legislation', who condemned the solitary cell by comparing it to a coffin: if a coffin was a 'chemise de bois' (wooden shirt), then the cell was a 'chemise de pierre' (stone shirt).

. The 'cellomaniac' case for the solitary confinement of juveniles was saved by a supporter of Suringar named Von Baumhauer who persuaded delegates that this would only be applied to a certain proportion of young offenders, namely those who had acted with discernment and who had chosen to break the law. The proper treatment of 'innocent' children, which he argued was not the question facing them at that moment, should be placed on the agenda of the next congress.[17] Another argument that proved pervasive if also highly dubious was that solitary confinement, or 'bonne compagnie' (good company) as supporters sometimes referred to it, was supported by the well-known British penal reformer, Elizabeth Fry. Suringar confided to the congress that Fry had told him herself that she saw the value of solitary confinement, even for women. This view was immediately refuted by Lord Pearson, a London-based solicitor and member of the British parliament, who read aloud from a letter written by Fry shortly before her death in which she clearly stated her opposition to solitary confinement. This farce was concluded by Mollet, a Dutch delegate, who told the congress that he had spent a whole day discussing prison systems with Fry some six weeks before her death but while 'she was still in good health' and, by implication, of sound judgment. According to Mollet, when he told her that solitary confinement would not mean total confinement and that a prisoner's solitude would be broken by regular communication, Fry had expressed her wholehearted approval for it.[18]

Some 20 years later the continuing need and demand for reformatory treatment as distinct from punishment or confinement was reflected in the full official name of the 1872 London congress which met as the 'International Congress on the Prevention and Repression of Crime, including Penal and Reformatory Treatment'.[19]

In practice few real *innovations* had occurred within European juvenile justice since the introduction of the famous model institutions of the first part of the century, although the number of specialist juvenile institutions had increased considerably. In Belgium 'Écoles de Réforme' were set up in Ruiselede and Beernem in 1848. In the Netherlands separate reformatories for delinquent boys and girls were opened in 1857 and 1859.[20] In Britain new reformatory and industrial schools were established in the 1850s. In France, some 18 new agricultural colonies had been set up by 1860, along with several naval and industrial colonies and 'ouvroirs' (workshops) for girls in the 1870s.

The London congress did not take the opportunity, however, to assess this institutional growth or to reflect on the broader changes it represented within the field of juvenile justice. Rather, it might best be seen as the start of a more general Western prison reform movement, a movement clearly influenced by north American ideas and practices. No fewer than 82 American delegates attended the London congress (compared with just nine delegates from the Netherlands[21] and even fewer from France and Prussia). They represented a variety of states and organisations, notably the influential American Prison Association. The programme was organised by E.C. Wines, secretary of the American Prison Association and a US federal government commissioner, who aimed to run the congresses on a more official basis, with greater government representation and more formalised proceedings.[22] One motive for this re-organisation may have been to scale down the exhausting and often circular discussions of solitary confinement which had dominated previous congresses and which were at odds with the views of many American reformers; the greater influence of official government delegates may have been another.[23]

This fresh start meant that the London congress enjoyed much more space for critical contemplation. In the sessions devoted to children and juveniles many of the discussants took the opportunity of describing those correctional schools with which they were familiar or outlining those which they saw as representing good practice. The programmes of certain French, American and British schools - Mettray, the Ohio Industrial School, the Wisconsin Reform School, Feltham Reformatory and others - were praised in these discussions. As a means of addressing the set congress question, 'What is the treatment likely to be most effective for the reformation of juvenile offenders?', British delegate and veteran juvenile justice campaigner Mary Carpenter offered a long statement on 'English Reformatories and Certified Industrial Schools', and New York delegate Charles Loring Brace read a paper on 'The Prevention of Juvenile Crime in Large Cities'. The fact that the deliberation of this question was extended in a second sectional meeting on the last day of the congress indicates something of the new importance attached by these gatherings to children and juveniles. Thus, notwithstanding that the only resolution reached by this section was a rather superficial one - 'that large congregate schools were to be deplored and that schools on the cottage or family plan were highly desirable' - and that, according to some, these discussions took up altogether too much congress time,[24] it seems clear that a substantial shift had taken place in relation to 'the juvenile question' since the mid-century congresses: the question of solitary confinement for minors had been displaced by considerations of a much wider range of possible treatments, focused firmly on reform and re-education.

These new views were expressed even more powerfully and effectively at subsequent congresses in Stockholm in 1878, Rome in 1885 and St. Petersburg in 1890. The 'preventive' session of the Stockholm congress for instance addressed a question that had been neglected since the Brussels meeting of 1847; how to make institutional provision for those delinquent children who had acted without discernment as well as those who were in need of care such as the homeless and abandoned. According to an official resolution reached concerning this group of 'innocent' children,

> it [was] not a question of executing a penalty or chastisement, but of giving an education, whose aim [was] to place [them] in a condition where they can gain an honest living and be useful to society instead of injuring it.[25]

While this emphasis on re-education had already begun to appear in many European countries, the Stockholm congress may be taken as representative of a wider overall shift away from simple punishment in juvenile justice practices.

Central to this shift were two particular notions of the family. First, there were calls for family-style penal institutions. A clear model emerged from the Stockholm discussions: institutions should be small, should promote mutual responsibility and, above all, should correspond to 'the conditions in which the working classes live[d]' by offering 'scholastic instruction on a level with that of elementary schools; the greatest simplicity in the food, clothing and lodging of the children; and above all, labor'.[26] Later, the importance of the idea of the family was taken one step further with a new focus on parents' responsibility for their children's delinquency. While idealised institutional families were looked to as a solution to the problem of delinquency, real families were identified as a key cause of that problem. A lengthy debate on this issue at the 1885 Rome congress framed the 'innocence' of certain groups of delinquent children in terms of the responsibility of their parents, with bad parenting held up as a principle cause of delinquency. Despite the difficulty of being seen to undermine parents' (or, more accurately, fathers') rights over their children, the 1885 congress passed a resolution advising that,

> one of the methods to be recommended is to authorise the courts to declare, for a determined period, whole or part of the parental rights forfeited when there is sufficient evidence of a responsibility on the part of the parents.[27]

The 1890 St. Petersburg congress took this matter further by repeating calls for the courts to be able to challenge parental authority in certain cases and by recommending that courts should be allowed to demand that children committed to correctional establishments or to public or private welfare institutions should remain there until they reached the age of majority, which usually was 21.[28] In connection with this, the 1895 Paris congress advised that the upper age limit of a juvenile in legal terms should be extended to 18 at least, the age at which boys became eligible for military service in many European states.

The Paris congress - presided over by the Dutch law professor, Pols - also marked a significant move towards what might be called 'product diversification' in the realm of juvenile care. The question as to whether a series of different institutions should be set up under different names for different classes of minors was positively answered by a resolution supporting the idea that institutions might be public or private, might house children for long or short periods and might have regimes that varied according to the age of the juvenile, the nature of their offence, their degree of discernment and their perceived need for correction or treatment.[29] Gender differences, or the need for distinct regimes for boys and girls, were not mentioned but simply taken for granted. In this and other senses, then, the congresses' framing of 'the children question' had matured.

In summary, the care, correction and re-education of criminal juveniles had been part of the congresses agenda from the outset, or at least from the second meeting onwards. The differences drawn between children who had acted with moral discernment and those who had acted without allowed for a certain diversification of judicial options. Discussions of juvenile solitary confinement which had dominated the early congresses were gradually eclipsed by a new focus on re-education in purpose-designed children's colonies and other specialist children's institutions. The congresses were also run on increasingly formal lines, especially after 1872 and, partly as a result, saw increasing rivalry between delegates from public and private bodies. As the next part of this chapter shows Dutch representatives, notably Suringar, Von Baumhauer, Domela Nieuwenhuis and Pols (all members of the Dutch Prison Society except the latter), played a particularly active role in these gatherings.

The Dutch Experience

Over the course of the nineteenth century, the Netherlands - like several other European countries - established special prisons and reformatories for juvenile offenders.[30] These new institutions were first established by members of the middle class and privately organised Dutch Prison Society. Founded in 1823, this organisation was a major instigator of new ideological and practical approaches to the (moral) treatment of criminals in general and juveniles in particular between the 1820s and the 1850s. Through their activities, which included prison visiting, primary and vocational teaching in institutions, public lecturing and circulating of reform literature, the members brought new values to the penal realm. However, many were active beyond the penal realm and were engaged in other social projects from the reform of public education and pawnbrokers shops to visiting the poor and building public bath houses.[31] Most were motivated by a general liberalism, although for many this was very much connected to their Protestant faith. Significant numbers were, like some of their counterparts in similar North American penal associations, actively involved in non-conformist minority denominations such as the Quakers and the Remonstrant Church. While they did not expect dramatic results from their work with adult criminals, they had much higher hopes for their work with criminal children who were more receptive to reform and, more simply, could be subjected to longer periods of reform than adults.

During the first half of the nineteenth century the Dutch Prison Society focused almost exclusively on the care of criminal children. In 1833 it set up a juvenile prison in Rotterdam - the first in the Netherlands and one of the first in Europe as a whole. This dark, damp building in the centre of the city initially admitted both boys and girls, although a separate girls' prison was opened three years later in Amsterdam.[32] Managerial responsibilities were divided between the Society and the Dutch government. The government undertook to maintain the building and arrange for the employment of staff, while the Society took a much more active role in the daily running of the prison, using it as a place to develop a special regime for juvenile inmates that focused heavily on their moral education. Since children were committed to the prison by the courts, their general maintenance costs were met by the government. However, the Prison Society covered all 'extra' expenses, such as the appointment of a school teacher.

Life in these early juvenile prisons was not structured around the practice of solitary confinement as it was in Paris' Petite Roquette but through a combination of two types of control: first, classification by age and morals, and second, a system of silence, known as 'the Auburn System' after the U.S prison that had pioneered it.[33] In practical terms, this meant that young inmates were divided into three classes each with distinct privileges, uniforms, seating arrangements and permissions to speak: children in the lowest class were forbidden to speak at all except during short periods spent in the small prison courtyard and were required to take their meals apart from the other classes with their faces turned to the dining room walls. By contrast, children in the highest class were only forbidden to speak during meals and during the night, and could receive fortnightly visits from their parents and relatives.[34] As with all these institutions, however, the effectiveness of the Rotterdam regime cannot be reliably proven. Recidivism rates, a readily available if disputable indicator of success, did not paint a favourable picture. During the prison's existence in Rotterdam (up to the 1860s), the proportion of recidivists rose dramatically from 5% of the inmate intake in the 1830s to 35% in the 1860s.

Dutch national juvenile justice strategies helped to shape, and were in turn shaped by, ideas circulating at the transnational European penal congresses. Suringar, chair of the Dutch Prison Society, was, for example, influenced by advocates of solitary confinement and periodically advocated that it be introduced into juvenile institutions.[35] However, after his visit to Mettray in 1847 he seemed more ready to accept that solitary confinement should be limited to adults, while more diverse methods should be used to reform criminal children.[36] The congressses' gradual drawing of more precise distinctions between children who had acted with moral discernment and those who had acted without encouraged the Dutch Prison Society and other Dutch moral entrepreneurs to explore new methods, particularly in the field of re-education. Children judged to have acted with discernment and subsequently convicted were generally sentenced to short periods of detention of up to a few months, while those judged to have acted without discernment and sent for re-education were generally required to remain in the same penal institutions until their eighteenth birthday. Congressional debates and visits to other countries' juvenile institutions seem to have directly influenced Suringar, and by extension, the Dutch juvenile justice in the direction of diversification. His experiences at the Frankfurt and Brussels congresses and his visit to Mettray in 1847 led him to investigate the possibility of establishing a 'Dutch Mottray' for criminal children requiring longer periods of re-education. Unlike the regular youth prison, the proposed institution would be a rural agricultural colony run on family lines, where 'the soil would be made better by the children and the children by the soil'.[37]

The 1850s were a crucial period in the development of the Dutch juvenile justice system. Two distinct yet intertwined branches developed on the reformatory tree. First, special re-educational institutions *were* established for innocent juveniles who had acted without discernment but these *were not* established as any logical progression of existing private initiatives of the Dutch Prison Society. Second, a Dutch Mettray was set up, but not for young *delinquents*.

When Suringar first proposed a Dutch rural colony he imagined it as an institution primarily for younger delinquent boys and older boys who had acted without moral discernment - a group that promised to be more responsive to re-education than those admitted to existing youth prisons with their high rates of recidivism. However, this plan was undermined from the start by the scheme's main financial backer - an Amsterdam based, Protestant benefactor - who insisted that no boy who had had any prior contact with the police or the courts should be admitted. As a result, the Dutch Mettray project was re-orientated towards the residential rescue of so-called endangered children. Since there was much overlap between this and the correction of criminal children and given the climate of general support for greater diversity in the prevention and reform of delinquency, this re-orientation was broadly acceptable to Suringar and most of his fellow-philanthropists. The opening of Dutch Mettray in 1852 prompted the opening of many other privately managed institutions for vulnerable and endangered children. By the end of the nineteenth century, 80 such institutions had been established which housed up to 12,500 children - ten times the number that could be accommodated in the six institutions then run by the juvenile justice system.[38] Indeed, in the early twentieth century the Dutch government increasingly passed the care of criminal children over to the private philanthropic sector not least because their track record seemed more successful than that of state-run juvenile penal institutions.

Meanwhile a second change was taking place. The Dutch government began to expand its penal responsibilities by itself establishing new institutions for those juveniles who had committed a crime without moral discernment. The government's actions here were shaped by a number of factors: its increasingly prominent role in the emerging international penitentiary community and its support for the view of this community that the reform of juveniles should be diversified; its handling of domestic parliamentary battles over the future shape of the Dutch prison system[39]; and its desire to curb the expansion and influence of the privately organised Dutch Prison Society.[40] In this sense, the expansion of government penal responsibilities must also be viewed as a logical outcome of Dutch state building and expanding governance in the second half of the nineteenth century.[41]

In 1857, with the support of newly appointed general prison inspector Alstorphius Grevelink, a new state reformatory for boys was opened in the city of Alkmaar.[42] Here, new educational practices were combined with older moral treatment regimes of the existing youth prisons. The boys entering the reformatory were of a somewhat different nature to those admitted to the Rotterdam prison. They tended to be younger and were required to undergo longer periods of reform lasting up to their eighteenth birthday. They were treated as children first and as criminals second. In court, as well as in the reformatory itself, increasing attention was paid to their perceived mental, physical, intellectual and familial disadvantages. Also, increasing emphasis was placed on the need to strengthen their will. This combination of older and newer approaches seemed to produce good results - as far as government reports on the behaviour of discharged children can be trusted[43] - and began to shape the treatment of criminal children more generally. In short, the number of children judged to have acted without moral discernment (and therefore eligible for long term reform in such institutions) steadily increased after the late-1850s when new institutions were opened. By contrast, from the mid-1870s onwards, the number of criminal children convicted of offences (and therefore not eligible for such places) diminished considerably in the Netherlands.[44]

These developments were formally documented in the new Dutch penal code of 1886 which further blurred the boundaries between the criminal and endangered child. As a result of the code, the treatment of criminal children within the judicial system was to resemble even more closely the treatment of children in the private philanthropic re-educational institutions. The numbers of children passing through the judicial system remained small, as did the number of places available to accommodate them. Between 1833 and 1915, the number of places grew from a mere 100 to around 1,200, and just 12,000 children had occupied these places across this whole period. After 1850, the majority of these children were those who had acted without moral discernment.[45]

Juvenile justice developments in the Netherlands might thus be summarised in terms of three major shifts: first, a shift away from the punishment of criminal children; second, a shift towards re-educating criminal children; third, a shift to the preventive educating of endangered children. Within this, the relationship between often rival public and private bodies also changed considerably. In the 1850s, the early lead taken by private philanthropic bodies was re-taken to an extent by the state. Private bodies remained central to juvenile institutional provision, however, and the penal realm continued to be characterised by public-private partnership as more criminal children were entrusted to private bodies by the turn of the century. Overall, penal discourses moved from emphasising the guilt of the criminal child to emphasising their innocence (a construction which increasingly rested on the assumed responsibility and culpability of their parents). This crucial reconstruction of the criminal child was not simply the result of moral conviction. It was also strategic in that it allowed both public and private agencies to intervene in social life in ever more thorough and permanent ways.

Conclusions

In view of the sustained involvement of Dutch experts like Suringar, Von Baumhauer, Pols and others in the congresses, one would perhaps have expected to see more innovative and pioneering penitentiary practices in the Netherlands. As this was not the case, further research could ask why Dutch practices tended to be imitative rather than innovative. Part of the answer to this question would seem to lie in the ever-present tension between the public and private realms in nineteenth century Dutch society. After 1850 this constant rivalry led to an alienation between the Dutch Prison Society and Dutch government representatives both at the national level in debates on preferred penitentiary systems, and on the European level in debates at the penal congresses. At home, together with the growth of new innovative agencies active in the non-penal care of endangered children, this led to a certain stagnation of the Dutch Prison Society. Abroad, it meant that government officials and Prison Society members increasingly took turns to represent Dutch opinion at the congresses.

Between the 1830s and 1890s, there was a considerable change in the way that criminal children were conceptualised and treated. In penal discourses and public commentaries they were broadly transformed from pernicious wrongdoers needing punishment into vulnerable victims needing care. But it was not just conceptions of these children that changed: the whole penitentiary and reformatory system, and the whole range of 'forces of organised virtue' involved in it, changed as well.[46] By the late nineteenth century, this had become an all-encompassing system offering care to all dangerous and endangered juveniles and jointly maintained by public and private organisations. This expansion of responsibilities and this interplay of public and private influences in the Dutch case were representative of broader shifts at the European level as reflected in the deliberations of international penal congresses and in other trans-European practices.

Endnotes

1   W.H. Suringar, 'Aanspraak van den voorzitter, ter opening der Algemeene Vergadering', in
     Jaarverslag van het Nederlandsch Genootschap tot Zedelijke Verbetering der Gevangenen
     over 1847, pp. 61-62 in C.G.T.M. Leonards, *De ontdekking van het onschuldige criminele
     kind; bestraffing en opvoeding van criminele kinderen in jeugdgevangenis en
     opvoedingsgesticht, 1833-1886* [*The Discovery of the Innocent Criminal Child; Punishment
     and Education of Criminal Children in Youth Prison and Reformatory, 1833-1886*]
     (Hilversum, 1995), p. 165 [author's emphasis].

2   H.B. verLoren van Themaat, *Zorg voor den Veroordeelde in het bijzonder na zijne
     invrijheidsstelling* (Utrecht, 1910/11), p. 320.

3   *Débats du Congrès pénitentiaire de Bruxelles: session de 1847, seances des 20, 21, 22, et 23
     Septembre*, ed. E. Ducpétiaux (Bruxelles, 1847); *Débats du Congrès pénitentiaire de
     Francfort-sur le-Mein, 28, 29 et 30 septembre 1846*, ed. M.L. Moreau Christophe (Paris,
     1847); W.H. Suringar, 'Adviezen op het eerste Frankfortse Poenitentiair Congres in 1846
     uitgebragt', *Dagblad van Overijssel 1847*; J. Varrentrapp, *Verhandlungen der ersten
     Versammlung für Gefängnisreform, zusammengetreten im September 1846 in Frankfurt am
     Main*. (Frankfurt a.M., 1847); M.M. Von Baumhauer, *Verslag der beraadslagingen op het
     poenitentiair congres gehouden te Frankfort a/M. 28, 29 en 30 september 1846*. (s.l., 1846).

4   Leonards, p. i.

5   For example, Bibliotheek van het Vredespaleis, the Hague; Bibliothèque Ste-Geneviève,
     Paris; British Library, London; Bibliothèque des Advocates, Brussels.

6   The numbers in fig. 1 come from a variety of sources, notably: *Actes du Congrès
     pénitentiaire international de Paris 1-9 juillet 1895*. (Melun, 1895); *Débats du Congrès
     pénitentiaire de Bruxelles: session de 1847, seances des 20, 21, 22, et 23 Septembre*, ed. E.
     Ducpétiaux (Bruxelles, 1847); *Le Congrès pénitentiaire international de Stockholm , 15-26
     aout 1878; Actes du 2me Congrès*, ed. L. Guillaume. (Stockholm, 1879); *Actes du Congrès
     pénitentiaire international de Saint-Petersbourg 1890*, ed. L. Guillaume. (Saint-Petersbourg,
     1890-1892); *Actes du Congres penitentiaire international de Bruxelles août 1900*, ed. L.
     Guillaume & C. Didion (Berne, 1901); *Débats du Congrès pénitentiaire de Francfort-sur le-
     Mein, 28, 29 et 30 septembre 1846*, ed. M.L. Moreau Christophe (Paris, 1847); *Prisons and
     Reformatories at Home and abroad, being the Transactions of the International Penitentiary
     Congress held in London, July 3-13, 1872*, ed. E. Pears (London, 1872); *Actes du Congrès
     pénitentiaire international de Rome novembre 1885 / publ. par les soins du Commission
     executif* (Rome,1887-1889); *Prison reform at home and abroad: a short history of the
     international movement since the London congress, 1872*, ed. E. Ruggles-Brise. (London,
     1924); W.H. Suringar, 'Adviezen op het eerste Frankfortse Poenitentiair Congres in 1846
     uitgebragt', *Dagblad van Overijssel*. (Zwolle, 1847); W.H. Suringar & J.A. Jolles.*Oordeel
     van het congres te Frankfort in september 1857 over het stelsel van afzonderlijke opsluiting.*
     (s.l., 1857); N.K. Teeters, *Deliberations of the International Penal and Penitentiary
     Congresses; Questions and Answers: 1872-1935*. (Philadelphia, 1949); H.B. verLoren van
     Themaat. *Zorg voor den Veroordeelde in het bijzonder na zijne invrijheidsstelling*. (Utrecht,
     1910/11); M.M. Von Baumhauer, *Verslag der beraadslagingen op het poenitentiair congres
     gehouden te Frankfort a/M. 28, 29 en 30 september 1846*, (s.l., 1846).

7   verLoren van Themaat, p. 381.

⁸   See fig. 2 for absolute and relative numbers by these categories of questions posed. The series could be made compatible over time by isolating the questions on children and minors from the third category 'preventive means' in the period before 1895. Sources: see note 6.

⁹   D.J. Bosley, 'The Problem of the Young Offender - an Ideal Solution? Agricultural Reformatories in England and France: the Nonage 1800-1854' in *History of Juvenile Delinquency. A collection of essays on crime committed by young offenders, in history and in selected countries*, ed. A. G. Hess & P. F. Clement. (Vol. 1, pp. 289-325). (Aalen, 1990); P. King & J. Noel, 'The origins of the 'problem of juvenile delinquency': the growth of juvenile prosecutions in London in late eighteenth and early nineteenth centuries', *Criminal Justice History. An international Journal, 14*, (1993), pp. 17-41.

¹⁰   Leonards, pp. 113-6.

¹¹   M. Perrot, 'Les Enfants de la Petite-Roquette'. *L'Histoire, 100*, (1987), pp. 30-38.

¹²   J. Christiaens, *De geboorte van de jeugddelinquent (België, 1830-1930)*. (Vol. 1). (Brussel, 1999); M-S. Dupont-Bouchat, *De la prison a l'école; les pénitenciers pour enfants en Belgique au XIXe siècle (1840-1914)*. (Heule, 1996).

¹³   Bosley, pp. 289-325; Christiaens, pp. 123-92; H. Gaillac, *Les Maisons de Correction. 1830-1945*. (Paris, 1971); King & Noel, pp. 17-41; Leonards, pp. 16-19.

¹⁴   Ducpétiaux, passim; Moreau Christophe, passim.

¹⁵   Von Baumhauer, *Verslag der beraadslagingen*, pp. 75-79.

¹⁶   W.H. Suringar, *Gedachten over de eenzame opsluiting der gevangenen*. (2 ed.). (Leeuwarden, 1843), p. 3.

¹⁷   Ducpétiaux, pp. 58-60. Just two years before this, Von Baumhauer and Suringar had visited French Mettray and had given enthusiastic reports on the benefits for juveniles of the agrarian colony model. Von Baumhauer even delivered his book on the visit to the Brussels' congresses secretary Ducpétiaux: M.M. Von Baumhauer, *De landbouwkolonie te Mettray (in Frankrijk), een voorbeeld voor Nederland*. (Leeuwarden, 1847). [The agrarian colony at Mettray (in France), an example for the Netherlands]. Nevertheless he now seemed to favour solitary confinement even for certain categories of juveniles.

¹⁸   Ducpétiaux, pp. 89-90.

¹⁹   J. Domela Nieuwenhuis & D.I. Mackay, *Verslag aan het Hoofdbestuur van het Nederlandsch Genootschap tot Zedelijke Verbetering der Gevangenen van het Internationaal Congres over het Gevangeniswezen te Londen*. (Amsterdam, 1873), pp. 33-40; E. Pears, passim.

²⁰   Bosley, pp. 289-325; R.G. Fuchs, 'Juvenile Delinquency in Nineteenth-Century France' in *History of Juvenile Delinquency. A collection of essays on crime committed by young offenders, in history and in selected countries*, ed. A.G. Hess & P.F. Clement (Aalen, 1990), pp. 265-88; Gaillac, Ch. 2.; Leonards, pp. 199-253; M. May, 'Innocence and Experience: The evolution of the concept of juvenile delinquency in the mid-nineteenth century'. *Victorian Studies: a quarterly journal of the humanities, arts and sciences, 17*, (1973), pp. 7-29; E. Meuwissen & J.D. van Gasse, 'Quelques aspects du sort réservé aux jeunes délinquants en Belgique au XIXe siècle' in Hess & Clement ed. pp. 625-35.

²¹   The Dutch delegation included two government representatives, B.J. Ploos van Amstel and M.S. Pols, and two members of the Dutch Prison Society, D.I. Mackay and J. Domela Nieuwenhuis. W.H. Suringar did not attend, and in fact died in September 1872, two months after the congress.

²²   verLoren van Themaat, p. 334.

²³   Although all preceding congresses had advocated solitary confinement as the only effective

system, it had not been implemented on a wide scale. Instead, from the 1850s a growing number of voices could be heard against the exclusive idea of the cell, and in favour of intermediate or progressive systems like the Irish system: verLoren van Themaat, pp. 337-8.

[24] Teeters, pp. 34-35.

[25] Guillaume , *Le Congrès pénitentiaire international de Stockholm*, passim; Teeters. p. 47.

[26] Teeters, p. 47.

[27] Teeters, p. 54.

[28] Guillaume, *Actes du Congrès pénitentiaire international de Saint-Petersbourg 1890*, passim.

[29] *Actes du Congrès pénitentiaire international de Paris 1-9 juillet 1895*; Teeters, p. 98.

[30] Leonards, pp. 56-66.

[31] P.N. Helsloot, 'Een geschiedenis van 200 jaar volksontwikkeling' in *Om het Algemeen Volksgeluk. Twee eeuwen Particulier Initiatief. Gedenkboek ter gelegenheid van het tweehonderdjarig bestaan van de Maatschappij tot Nut van 't Algemeen*, ed. W.W. Mijnhardt & A.J. Wichers (Edam, 1984); B. Kruithof, 'De deugdzame natie. Het burgerlijk beschavingsoffensief van de Maatschappij tot Nut van 't Algemeen tussen 1784 en 1860'. *Symposion, Tijdschrift voor maatschappijwetenschap, 2*(1) (1980), pp. 22-37.

[32] The Dutch Prison Society had wanted to locate both of these prisons in Amsterdam where they could manage them from their headquarters which were located there. On the other hand the Dutch government successfully argued that the first youth prison should be in Rotterdam, because vacant penitentiary buildings dating back to the 1660s could be adapted for this purpose.

[33] Up to the 1840s the Dutch parliament favoured the Auburn system of separation at night and absolute silence during communal day time, whereas the majority of the Prison Society still favoured the classification system, until 1843 when Suringar began to support solitary confinement (W.H. Suringar, *Gedachten over de eenzame opsluiting der gevangenen*. (2 ed.). Leeuwarden, 1843).

[34] Leonards, *De ontdekking van het onschuldige criminele kind*, pp. 141-2.

[35] Suringar, *Gedachten over de eenzame opsluiting*, pp. 8-9.

[36] W. H. Suringar, 'Mijn bezoek aan Mettray' in Von Baumhauer, pp. I-XXXII.

[37] J.J.H. Dekker, *Straffen, redden en opvoeden; Het ontstaan en de ontwikkeling van de residentiële heropvoeding in West-Europa, 1814-1914, met bijzondere aandacht voor Nederlandsch Mettray* (Assen/Maastricht, 1985), pp. 175-9.

[38] Dekker, pp. 330-44; J.J.H. Dekker, J.J. Dankers & C.G.T.M. Leonards, 'III. Van de Bataafse Republiek tot de Kiderwetten. Wezen, boefjes en verwaarloosde kinderen, ca. 1795-1905'in *Wezen en Boefjes; zes eeuwen zorg in wees- en kinderhuizen*, ed. S. Groenveld, J.J.H. Dekker & T.R.M. Willemse, T. R. M. (Hilversum, 1997), pp. 255-339; Leonards, pp. 113-65, 199-253.

[39] H. Franke, *The emancipation of prisoners : a socio-historical analysis of the Dutch prison experience* (Edinburgh, 1995).

[40] This is reflected in the way in which a further Dutch Prison Society residential experiment was eventually thwarted by the government. The Leiden based 'Refuge for Released Criminal Boys' had to be closed down within less than ten years because of lack of government cooperation in employing boys in the Dutch navy and army. C. Leonards, *The Leiden' Refuge for Boys, 1857-1865; Residential After Care for 'Morally and Physically Disabled' Criminals in the Netherlands*. Paper presented at the European Social Science History Conference (Amsterdam, 2000)

[41] A. de Swaan, *In the care of the state: health care, education and welfare in Europe and the USA in the modern era* (Cambridge, 1990).

[42] In 1859 another opened for girls in Montfoort: Leonards, pp. 57-58.

[43] Leonards, pp. 246-47. Some 75% of the boys were reported as behaving 'well' in the first years after leave. The behaviour of only 8% was reported 'moderate'. The category 'bad' did not exist. The rest had either died, or had been institutionalised again.

[44] Leonards, pp. 61, 278. The number of convicted versus 'innocent' children was 421 - 47 in 1855, 283 - 248 in 1875 and 24 - 783 in 1895.

[45] Leonards, p. 59.

[46] This concept is taken from C. Lasch, *Haven in a Heartless World: the family besieged* (New York, 1979) p. 169. It can be used to refer to the whole range of feminists, temperance advocates, educational reformers, liberal ministers, penologists, doctors, bureaucrats and others involved in this kind of nineteenth century social and moral reform.

Chapter 7

Gender, After-care and Reform
in Inter-war Norway

Astri Andresen

This chapter deals with a group of people who had one experience in common: they spent part of their childhood in reform schools (*skolehjem*). They shared this experience with many others in countries where industrialisation and urbanisation were considered to have created specific problems around childhood and youth which could not be solved through traditional means; parental and social control, prison or, in some countries, charitable institutions. Other means were called for, and, in the nineteenth century, reform schools were developed in several states to counter delinquency, protect society and construct new kinds of childhood.[1]

In Norway reformatories were recommended by the 1896 Child Welfare Act (*vergerådsloven*) as instruments to turn the most deviant and delinquent children into 'normal' children, and thereby to protect society.[2] The 1896 Act helped to establish child welfare as a separate field and made three key changes to existing institutional reformatory practices. First, the new reformatories were to be managed by the state. Second, all delinquent children under the age of 15 were to be sent to them rather than to prison, regardless of their offence. Finally, reformatories were also established for girls as well as for boys.[3]

Since histories of European reform schools are now reasonably well established, this chapter will focus on their longer term impact upon individual children and their families. Drawing on sources relating to 85 girls and 328 boys discharged on probation from the schools between 1918 and 1950 and returned to the town of Bergen, it examines the experiences of children following their release.[4] It focuses on the years between the end of the First World War and the outbreak of the Second, since the impact of war on the relationship between gender and delinquency is too complex a field to be dealt with here.

According to the theories of Michel Foucault, reformatories, like prisons, were likely to promote criminal careers.[5] However, I will not concentrate upon the criminal records of those discharged since I am concerned to investigate the experiences of girls rather than boys. In Norway, as across Europe and North America, criminal offences did not play a prominent role either in their pre- or post-reformatory careers.[6] Nevertheless, girls did resist dominant ideas as to how they should behave and, as a result, some became inmates of reform schools. Although small in number, they serve to illustrate the wider social expectations of, and fears about, young working class women growing up in the inter-war period. Their resistance as well as their compliance will be discussed first in terms of gender relations and second in terms of the broader relations between youths, their families and local child welfare agencies. Three key questions will be addressed. What effect did the reform school experience have on children's later options and life chances? Did the experience carry the same meanings for girls as it did for boys? What role did parents and the local child welfare board play in the lives of those discharged on probation?

The children in question were mainly working class.[7] They were judged as successes or failures by those adults concerned to monitor them, depending upon how 'well' - according to dominant cultural standards - they adjusted to society. In this chapter they will be discussed in these terms - as conformists or rebels - but also as young people trying to negotiate given rules in order to make sense of their own lives. Humphries has argued that children in similar situations should be regarded as rebels. According to him, deviant behaviour among working class children and youth was a conscious and often family-supported protest against the dominant bourgeois ideals of childhood and disciplined working class life.[8] Even if one cannot directly compare England and Norway, this argument deserves critical attention. Is it possible to determine the targets of these children's acts and, further, to establish what level of family support they may have had in this? If so, it might be possible to indicate how far social beliefs and values were held in common by children and their families. However, in opposition to the idea that deviant children had their families' support, it must be noted that the respectable working class shared many of the values of the dominant classes where the behaviour of young people was concerned.[9] Further, among casual workers and the poor, a certain lack of order and discipline could obviously be explained as a result of limited means rather than deliberate choice.

Children, Law and Local Society

On their discharge from reform schools, located hundreds of kilometres away in mid- or eastern Norway, young girls were returned to Bergen, a shipping and trading city situated in the west of the country. At the turn of the century Bergen was in the midst of industrialisation but never grew into a fully industrial city. It was, however, the second largest in Norway, with a population rising from approximately 72,000 in 1900 to 107,000 in 1939.[10] Despite that fact that it was a small city by European standards, Bergen was considered to have its full share of urban problems especially when it came to housing and unemployment. The housing problem was at its worst at the beginning of the period considered here due to a huge fire in 1916, while unemployment, a result of the international economic crisis, was especially high in the late 1920s and 1930s. For young women, however, the labour market was somewhat less strained than for men, due to a fairly constant demand for female servants.[11] The problem of poverty in general was serious: poor relief was claimed by approximately 12% of the population in 1928 and by every sixth person in 1935.[12]

Most of the children sent to reform schools came from the densely populated inner-city areas in Bergen. They were sent there by the local child welfare board, a partly elected, partly appointed and predominantly middle class body. Typically in this period, the board might consist of a judge, a priest, a doctor and a teacher, but only one worker. It was also male dominated, with just one or two women among its seven representatives. The children dealt with by the board were treated as children, under a law concerning children, but, according to the norms and practices of Norwegian society, the majority were older youths on the verge of adulthood. The average age at which girls and boys entered reformatories was around 14.5 and 14 years respectively.[13] Not all of them had committed a criminal offence; the fear that they might do so was enough, under the 1896 Act, to justify their committal to the schools. If they *had* committed an offence, they would not have been prosecuted unless they were 15 or older. Decisions to remove them from their homes would have been made not by a court but by local child welfare boards which had been given extensive powers by the 1896 Act.[14]

Children stayed at the reform schools for approximately three years on average. At the time of discharge, therefore, girls were normally between 17 and 18 years old and boys around 17.[15] What they needed most - a job and a place to live - was very scarce given the city's housing and unemployment problems. What mechanisms were in place to help them find these things? First, the 1896 Act allowed for those who misbehaved while on probation to be returned to the institution. Secondly, the Act stated that reformatory managers were responsible for 'keeping informed' about and 'inspecting' them until they were finally discharged, and then for finding employment that protected them against 'demoralising influence' (paragraphs 33 and 36). This system soon became over-stretched as it was very difficult for school managers to monitor and assist children from all over the country. As a result the 1915 Child Welfare Committee (*barnevernskomiteen*) argued that a more formal after-care system should be established that would use detailed information about the young people to provide close and continuous support by extending help and control as necessary.[16] The Committee's call was not implemented, primarily because of the economic strains of the inter-war period, and after-care continued to be a rather neglected area of child welfare.[17] In the larger towns, however, the child welfare boards did include after-care in their duties. In Bergen the male secretary of the child welfare board was responsible for discharged boys and a female inspector for the girls.

Information on the young people was gathered mainly through home visits approximately every three months, but since there were no guidelines as to how inspectors were to perform their duties they had a large amount of freedom in this respect. They also held power as their reports and proposals very much influenced decision-making in the Bergen child welfare board. Until a 1930 revision of the 1896 Act there were no rules as to how long this inspection of the discharged group should continue. Those considered to be adjusting well to life outside the reformatory were the first to be 'released' from inspection. In a few cases inspection ended when the individual reached the age of 18. However in the majority of cases it continued until they were 20 or 21 and in some instances until they were 23 or 24. From 1930, all were to be monitored at least until they reached 21. The length of the after-care period therefore varied considerably, a variation which is reflected in this study: I have followed most of these cases for between two and four years after discharge and others for longer.

413 young people were discharged and returned to Bergen between 1918 and 1940. Fluctuations in reform school admission rates and inter-war economic strains meant that discharges were not distributed evenly across the period. 193 (48%) were discharged in the 1920s, 76 (25%) in the 1930s, and 81 (27%) in the 1940s.[18] However, within this, girls' discharge rates were more stable. 27 (35%) were discharged in the 1920s (most in the first half), 22 (29%) in the 1930s and 28 (36%) in the 1940s (the majority in the latter half). These numbers indicate that the 'delinquent girl' was a more stable concept than the 'delinquent boy'.[19] On a national level the percentage of girls confined in reform schools rose from 20% in 1920 to 36% in 1945.

Defining the Need for Reform

Before the different discharge experiences of boys and girls can be considered it must be noted that they were sent to reform schools for very different reasons in the first place. Boys were most commonly committed for theft, often combined with truancy and sometimes with violence.[20] All these cases, apart from truancy, had generally been investigated by the police. Girls were also committed for theft and truancy and were sometimes accused of being violent. However, in Norway as in many other European countries, the majority were sent to the schools because they were suspected of sexual immorality or considered to be in danger of becoming immoral.[21]

Girls' cases were seldom dealt with by the police but by the local child welfare board which based its judgment on information gathered from a range of sources such as their own investigations, and medical reports as well as hearsay. The nature of cases varied but ranged from girls who were considered insufficiently domesticated to girls who had established relationships with boys of their age or who had contact with older men, to girls who were possibly selling sex and girls who had been sexually abused. They were not all necessarily sexually active but variously thought to be 'wanton', 'vain', 'flirtatious' and 'idle' and thereby, in the eyes of professional social observers, to be taking dangerous steps towards prostitution.[22] They were also thought to pose longer term social threats in the form of the spread of sexual disease, rising numbers of illegitimate children and rising claims for poor relief. These cases often met with demands for immediate action, with calls for 'the girl (...) to be removed from town as quickly as possible'.[23]

Most of the children called to appear before the child welfare board were given a warning, punished at school or at home, or sent to foster homes, orphanages or truancy schools (*tvangsskole*). There is a popular view that the children sent to reform schools were the 'worst cases' seen by the board, but the sources strongly suggest that this was not necessarily so. Patterns of selection for reform school are far from clear, and the group was made up of quite 'serious' and quite 'ordinary' cases. The fact that all kinds of children were sent to the schools became a major point of criticism in the inter-war years, prompting calls by politicians, social workers and psychiatrists for a system of separating the 'worst' children from the 'unlucky' and the 'unhappy'.

Some of the children had certainly had a largely joyless childhood and the reform schools did little to change this. The children were heavily disciplined as were many outside these institutions; the difference was that children inside institutions could not easily escape this.[24] Some conformed while others resisted. However, the overall impact of reform school experiences upon their later careers is hard to evaluate. For example, the group of girls who refused to 'behave' when discharged had generally spent the same amount of time in the schools as more compliant groups. Neither was there a significant difference in the discharge experiences of those who had been confined at the earlier age of 10 or 12 and those who had been confined in their teens.[25] Thus, no clear unambiguous relationship can be drawn between pre- and post-reformatory behaviour although more research is needed in this respect.

When the girls arrived back in Bergen they were met by the child welfare board's inspector, and often by parents or other relatives. Of the Bergen girls 55 (65%) were returned to their parents and nine (11%) to other relatives. If they did not have relatives who could offer them a *suitable* home, the welfare board normally made arrangements for them to enter domestic service (11, or 13%) or to be placed in foster homes, orphanages or other institutions (9, or 11%).[26]

The reform schools made an effort to send the girls back into the community in 'good shape', dressed in new clothes and carrying a small amount of money. Inspectors often noted their appearance on arrival, variously describing them as looking 'hearty and brave', 'kind and quiet' or 'hearty and well-dressed'.[27] Only a few 'still looked defiant and stubborn'.[28] Inspectors hoping that girls had turned from bad to good clearly found 'goodness' a visible quality. Significantly, boys' appearance when they first met with the members of the child welfare board was never commented upon.

Successful Reform: 'Normal' Girls

For the local child welfare board, and society in general, a working class girl could 'succeed' in two ways: by getting married or managing a steady job. Only marriage promised permanent success; a job was only a temporary stop on the way.[29]

Not all jobs were considered suitable for these girls, however. The board preferred the young women to become domestic servants instead of factory workers, since servants lived under more strict personal controls and the women who hired reformed girls often cooperated closely with the board, reporting on their skills, manners and behaviour. If the girl's own home was judged to be bad, it was thought especially important to get her into service. But in this sense the child welfare board was working against profound changes in patterns of female employment: domestic service virtually disappeared during the period in question.[30] Because of this, and wider changes in the girls' education, the board eventually came to play a more active role in supporting the girls. They tried to convince parents or other relatives to pay for the girls to attend further education, generally at local business schools. Only a few girls were given this chance in the inter-war period, although the 1940s saw more reformed girls in further education than previous decades.

By the end of their probation periods, 31 (36%) of the girls had found fairly steady positions as servants, sales girls or factory girls, or seemed otherwise to have settled.[31] 18 girls (21%) were married; the ultimate sign of success. Their husbands were not necessarily ideal, however; some were unemployed, others heavy drinkers, and most newly-wed couples had housing problems. Some lived on poor relief. But none of these things were uncommon in Bergen in the inter-war years, and from the point of view of the welfare board what counted was that the threat of sexual immorality seemed to be contained.

Clearly, an ordinary working class life was within reach for 'reformed' girls, and more than half of them (57%) seemed to follow a 'normal' career in this sense. They did the same things as most working class girls in the period, and probably gained the same sort of status as other young women in similar positions. Their low marriage age (around 20) illustrates their enthusiasm to be married.[32] This is not surprising, since marriage not only symbolised love, but also security, a degree of social status and a degree of independence - things which these girls may have longed for more than others. Marriage also meant that the child welfare board no longer interfered in their lives.

Many of these girls, then, wanted a 'normal' life and knew what this implied and how to achieve it. Many were fortunate in finding with good employers, in finding a husband and in maintaining good relations with families and foster-families. Some met both respect and generosity. One foster-mother wrote: 'The preacher honoured her by placing her in the front (...) She was the nicest among the candidates for confirmation; she is such a pretty and kind girl'.[33] And another: '(...) her manners are very attractive, and it is so important to us to have a pleasant person around'.[34]

Challenging Reform: 'Rebellious' Girls

But what about those who were less 'successful'? By the end of the probation period, two of the girls (2%) had died, and two others (another 2%) were in mental hospitals. Nine girls (11%) had illegitimate babies and no prospects of getting married to the baby's father, 7 (8%) were described as prostitutes, but it is hard to say with what accuracy. 14 (17%) were in more general terms described as 'difficult', or had difficulties in managing their daily lives, while two girls (2%) were in touch with the police for theft.[35]

Do these cases signal rebellion? If rebellion is defined as the refusal of accepted norms of female behaviour, some of these girls could obviously be described as rebels. The most common accusation made against them by child welfare inspectors was that they were not sufficiently domesticated and wanted to stay out late in male company: 'She is a kind girl, but wants to stay out at night (...). She is keeping company with men'.[36] Second, they did not perform their duties, be it at home or in paid work: 'She does not want to be a servant (...). She is suffering from megalomania, and is seeking bad company'.[37] Other girls simply seemed to be strong minded: 'She is a wild and difficult girl'.[38] 'She is very stubborn and difficult'.[39] 'Disobedient at home'.[40] And some girls rebelled against every rule: 'She is wild and careless, wants to stay out at night. Is not attending her work at the factory. Does not want to help her mother. Big-mouthed'.[41] The same things had often been said about the girls before they entered the whole reform process, except, now, criticisms centred on their performance at work rather than at school.

A study of girls at a reformatory in the 1950s described them as 'girls (...) longing to be on the go - girls who want to be 'where the action is'. 'Action' most often involved men, and sometimes alcohol.[42] How far can this description be applied to discharged girls in the inter-war period? Some were obviously looking for action wherever action was to be found, and in this may very well have been consciously rejecting the more 'wholesome' activities offered to them. But refusal to work as directed or being 'big-mouthed' or stubborn could not be obviously equated with a desire to be 'on the go'. Most girls simply resisted the order, obedience and monotony to which they were subjected as well the restrictions on what they should do, how they should look, and where they should go and with whom. As such, they could be seen as rebelling against rules that aimed to govern their sexual behaviour but that, in fact, influenced much of the rest of their lives.

What did these girls want instead? They did not necessarily have a common short-term goal, except perhaps trying to attain 'something else', something other than what was offered. They did seem, however, to share a long-term goal with the majority of workirlg class girls in the period: they wanted to get married. Several of the girls who eventually married had previously been described as both 'difficult' and 'indecent'; they had run away, left their jobs and antagonised both their parents and the child welfare board in a number of other ways. But they had found a spouse, and thus 'succeeded'. Thus, the label 'difficult' was not some kind of life-sentence, but could, as this evidence suggests, be cast off through marriage.

However, child welfare board sources show that some girls suffered even when they tried to succeed in these terms. They entered situations where they were ultimately disadvantaged because the rules were broken even while they were pursuing the goals of the dominant culture. Engagements were broken off, boyfriends left, parents would not allow their sons to marry them and so on, all of which could result in illegitimate pregnancy. This serves to illustrate a major point where the reform of girls was concerned: the same acts could lead to integration into society through marriage as well as to marginalisation through the conception of an illegitimate child. To some extent what happened was accidental; it was not an easy task for the girls to anticipate the most likely outcome of their choices. Some girls' stories, such as the one below, are presented as a sad mixture of misfortune and despair:

> 1.10.1923. She is in town, working as servant (...). 15.2.1924. At home, is expecting a child medio April. 10.6.1924. Has given birth to a boy (...). She is not going to marry. Her mother died, she is at home. 14.8.1924. Her child was brought to *Welanderhjemmet* [a home for syphilitic children], where it died (...). She took a hand-wagon and brought her belongings to a room in Geble Pederssens St., where she intends to live. 4.11.1924. Working at nights, sleeping during the day. 15.1.1925. Homeless. Now and again with her grandparents. 15.3.1925. Servant at a farm in the eastern parts of Norway. 28.3.1925. Back in Bergen. A prostitute. Under police control. 15.9.1925. Convicted. (...). 30.4.1926. Living with her father and brother. Fine streetgirl.[43]

This girl, and several others like her, may for a short period of time have considered herself a 'success', having apparently achieved exactly what was expected of her: a relationship with a steady boyfriend who would hopefully become a husband.

Some girls did become prostitutes, but no traces have been found in the sources to suggest that they chose prostitution as a way of gaining, in Humphries' words, 'money, freedom and independence'.[44] Rather, girls seemed to turn to prostitution only when more positive solutions were not available to them. Certainly, girls who were continually labelled as 'fallen', 'immoral' or 'indecent' could find that their options became very restricted. Dignity, self-respect and pride must have been very hard for them to achieve.

Family-Supported Rebellion?

Did the girls find any support at home for their unruly behaviour - for staying out late, refusing to work, being with (the wrong kind of) boys? Are we, as Humphries suggests, witnessing a conscious, family-supported rebellion against dominant ideas of childhood and disciplined working class life?

A small group of rebellious discharged girls could be said to have had such family support. In this sense, they may have rebelled against dominant ideals of femininity, but in doing so did not rebel against their families; on the contrary, their lifestyles were very much part of their family's own involvement in (petty) criminal subcultures.[45] Some of the discharged boys also seem to have returned to similar households, although, contrary to Humphries' claims, there are very few examples of boys clearly stealing to support their families.[46] Home-supported rebellion is thus evident only in a small minority of the working class families that had dealings with the Bergen child welfare board.

In cases where the sources give information on parents' reactions towards girls who flouted discharge rules, few traces of support have been found. While it is unlikely that those mothers or fathers who acquiesced in or encouraged their daughters' rebellion would have notified the board, there are few examples of parents actively defending their children or demanding that inspectors leave them alone. Some rare incidents could be interpreted in this way, such as when parents refused to inform the inspector of their daughter's address. This refusal was taken as proof such girls had something to hide and merely resulted in further investigation. However, most parents supported the board and apparently agreed that their daughters were 'wild' and required control. Mothers, aunts or grandmothers quite often complained about the girls' behaviour, especially during the late 1930s and during the Second World War when they feared that their daughters would mix with German soldiers. These fears and complaints were expressed in various ways, as extracts from inspectors' reports show. 'During her first months home, she was a nice girl. Now she is staying out late, and she does not want to help her mother. She is not attending her work. Her mother regrets she applied to have her home so soon'.[47] 'She is not behaving very well at home. Her mother is worried about her'.[48] 'She is difficult (...) and is staying out at nights, there is no use her step-mother talking to her'.[49] 'Her aunt has no say over her, she is strong-minded and careless (...) Wants to stay out late'.[50] Clearly then, these girls' actions were not supported by their families. These parents and relatives wanted their girls to be obedient, domesticated and respectable and were prepared to seek support from the child welfare board to manage those who behaved otherwise.

This is not very surprising, given that norms of female behaviour had a very real function in working class family life. First, grown-up girls were either supposed to earn their own living or help the family to maintain itself through their unpaid work; poor parents could not afford to support 'lazy' daughters (or sons). Second, even if parents did not fear that their daughters might be drawn to prostitution, they wanted to avoid illegitimate pregnancies for reasons of morality, economy and social mobility - having such a child was feared greatly to reduce a girl's chances of marrying a 'decent' man.

However, not all familial complaints about these girls should be taken as proof of shared values between families and the authorities. In other cases, girls were rejected by relatives because they simply did not 'fit in'. As inspectors' noted of some girls, 'Her grandmother does not want her, they do not get along very well'.[51] 'Her aunt does not want her'.[52] This may not be surprising, considering that the girls had been away from Bergen for a long time during which several changes may have occurred within their families. Kinship notwithstanding, there was a limit to the willingness of relatives to take responsibility for girls known to be 'difficult'. Some girls came to resemble parcels in search of recipients; letters were written to family members in distant corners of the country trying to find someone willing to 'take' them. The response was often negative, and the girls were more or less left to themselves to manage as best they could; either by breaking the rules or working terribly hard to keep to them. In these cases, the child welfare board had little to offer.

Parents and relatives also reported discharged young men to the board but not as frequently, partly because many of them became sailors and therefore lived away from their family homes. Like girls, boys were reported for the same reasons which had taken them to reform school and some parents, such as the father who asked for his son to be taken 'as far away as possible, to complete strangers', were very willing to ask the board to take firm action.[53] On the whole, fathers contacted the board regarding boys and mothers or other female relatives regarding girls, although women tended to report boys who had been involved in violence. There is much more that might be said here regarding gendered child rearing. However, the key point is that delinquent sons did not enjoy any more support from parents and relatives than delinquent daughters.

Around 11% of the discharged boys were returned to reform school (and a certain number sent to prison), mostly for having committed criminal offences.[54] Few girls followed this route. Their social and sexual misdemeanours may have drawn them to the attention of the child welfare board but since they had not broken the law (and were almost all over the age of 15) they could not be returned to reform school.

Gender Differences and the Child Welfare Board

Finally, how did the child welfare board's treatment of discharged boys and girls compare? First, the board devoted more energy to helping boys, rather than girls, to find work. As a rule, a job - usually an apprenticeship or a place at the vocational school - had already been arranged for a young man by the time he arrived back in Bergen. If these placements proved unsuccessful, the board would try to find alternatives, although their efforts in this regard were shaped by the broader labour market. In the most difficult years of the 1930s even the board gave up and the young men often had to make do with relief work. On the whole, however, there is no evidence that these boys experienced more difficulties in the labour market than others. This may have been helped by the fact that a large proportion (50%) of the boys claimed that they wanted to become, or were in any case apprenticed out as, sailors in the Norwegian merchant fleet.[55] As for girls, the board's efforts to find them work were limited to attempts to place them in domestic service and these placements were rarely arranged in advance of their arrival in Bergen.

Second, young men seem to have received more practical help in other fields as well; in finding a place to stay, in obtaining clothes, and in arranging financial support in the form of pocket-money, or poor relief. The few young women who sought similar practical support from the board if they became unemployed, homeless, broke or pregnant risked being put under even more strict surveillance or even being placed in a home for 'fallen' women or a girls' rescue home. One board report illustrates the logic at work here: 'Is expecting a child. Frivolous. Taken to a maternal home. Had a son several months ago, cannot be kept at the maternal home. Ready for the Women's Home'.[56] Girls in trouble primarily received more control. By contrast, boys only seemed to be subject to further control if they had committed a criminal offence.

Third, the board tended to handle the past histories of discharged boys with more discretion than those of girls. Boys were more often allowed to report to the child welfare office themselves and, moreover, to speak for themselves. Girls' stories, by contrast, more commonly reached the board via inspectors' interviews with neighbours, employers, families and friends. Again, this was partly a function of the fact that many boys were away at sea and thus beyond the everyday reach of the board. Continual attention from the board made it not simply difficult but almost impossible for girls to conceal the fact that they had been at a reform school which did little to help them make a new start. Not surprisingly, some of them expressed their anger and resentment to inspectors: 'B. grew very angry when she saw me. She said she was going to apply for factory work, but I said it would be better if she became a servant and lived with her employers. She said she would do nothing if I were to control her, - but I said I would'.[57]

Where young men were concerned, the board focused on work, wages and criminal offences. There is no evidence that the board scrutinised their private lives, or at least inspectors did not report it if they did. The 'support' of young women, however, absolutely depended upon continued scrutiny of their private lives and the board thought it only proper to report what they saw as relevant details: did the girl seek male company, did she stay out at night, did she wear make-up, who were her female friends, did she obey her parents? Such questions were endless.

This gendered treatment reflected the wider gender system, especially divisions of labour. While girls became women through domesticity, boys became men by gaining steady, paid work and preparing for a life of breadwinning.[58] In this context, the child welfare board's prioritising of young men's need for work is more understandable. However, differences within the treatment of this group were connected to the fact that boys and girls were brought into the reform system itself for different reasons, and that those reasons themselves carried different meanings. Boys' delinquency was more often interpreted by the board as the product of unchecked or excessive 'boyishness'. Although some were seen as potentially serious thieves or embezzlers, most were thought able to be reformed through the stabilising effect of work. This view extended beyond the board; in some cases employers took back into their service boys who had served prison sentences. There was even a tendency to romanticise and celebrate boys' delinquency. In a 1908 parliamentary debate, one speaker conjured the injustice of the reformatory system by comparing the ordinary reform school boy to a great national war hero: 'I fear a boy like Peter Tordenskjold would surely have been placed in reform school, had such a thing been available in his time'.[59] This is not to say that boys were not affected or concerned by their reform school experiences, but that their potential for improvement was continually stressed. In other words, their potential was not seen to be seriously disabled by moral defect.

Unless their subsequent conduct was irreproachable, young women who had been to reform school were seen as having transgressed the normal boundaries of girlhood to the point where many were viewed as potential prostitutes. Research into girls' delinquency in contemporary Europe by Hudson and others has reached similar conclusions: '(...) once an opinion had been formed, it was easy for the label of 'promiscuity' or 'being on the game' to stick (...)'.[60] In public debates no strong-willed or unruly heroine was ever invoked to illustrate any injustice performed upon them. In after-care programmes continual moral rescue, achieved through regulation and control, remained a priority. Holding a job was never enough, even if certain kinds of jobs made that regulation more easy to effect. Troublesome boys were certainly subject to regulation, but were rarely considered to be morally deviant. By contrast, troublesome girls were assumed to be morally deviant unless they could clearly prove otherwise. Obviously, such a task was not easy.

One of the unlooked-for outcomes of the board's policy was that girls experiencing real problems were often left to themselves to manage as best as they could since they tried to avoid contact with the child welfare services. Thus, they were not able to use these services for their own means. This is not to say that the board did not help any of the reformed girls; but those who received most support were those who were considered to have adapted well and therefore to have demonstrated that they shared the same values as the board. In contrast, even those young men whose behaviour challenged after-care guidelines still felt able to contact the board and ask for help, and must, to a certain extent, have felt that they could rely on its support.

Conclusions: 'Being Reformed'

Girls' reform schools aimed to inculcate idealised female behaviour. They thereby aimed to contain two major threats: prostitution and illegitimacy; but also sought to regulate girls' lives more generally.

From the state's point of view, the girls' reformatories could have been more successful despite the fact that more than half of the girls who passed through them eventually 'normalised', in the sense of finding work, marrying, keeping within the confines of proper femininity and generally leading a stable law-abiding life. Even though reform school constituted a specific experience, it did not turn the girls into a homogeneous group. They remained different in at least one key respect - some lived their lives in line with dominant values while others did not. Perhaps most importantly, the road to success, or marriage, was on the whole the same as the road to marginalisation. Thus, chance played a role in defining them as successes or failures. The answer, then, to the first question posed in this chapter as to the longer term effect of reform school experience is that the experience could point young people in more than one direction.

Another question concerned the role played by the child welfare board and parents in shaping young people's decisions whether to accept or reject wider social norms. The child welfare board has to be seen as an agent that was important to, and actively used by, families. Upon their discharge the board sought to place girls in an environment offering optimum possibilities for regulation and control. Two major aspects of its philosophy and practice stand out. First, every discharged girl was ultimately seen as a potential single mother or as a potential prostitute. Those who adapted quickly were able to shed this image; in time they were considered to be neither threatened nor threatening. But those who, even in minor ways, challenged feminine norms and those who experienced serious material and emotional problems, found their options to be very limited. In this sense, the policies of the child welfare board had a profoundly marginalising effect. Second, marginalisation had a particular effect on girls. Boys certainly suffered through the marginalisation of the reform process but seemed to be able to move in and out of mainstream society more smoothly than girls. Girls, on the other hand, needed to clearly demonstrate their new reformed status before they could move back into the mainstream: they had to marry. Marriage seemed to be the only reliable way of containing the threats of prostitution and unmarried motherhood. For young men, it did not represent such a major transition point.

Most of the families studied here upheld dominant definitions of femininity and many cooperated with the child welfare board and heeded its advice. If they themselves rejected the girl, they often tried to make the child welfare board assume responsibility for her. But just as there were several motives shaping children's choices, families too had different reasons for cooperating with the board. Some wanted to protect their girls, others wanted help in solving broader family problems.

The only agent with a more unambiguous goal where girls were concerned was the child welfare board itself. Order, obedience, domesticity and chastity were to be pursued, not only to prevent the extremes of prostitution and illegitimacy, but more importantly to keep young women's behaviour within accepted limits of femininity. Traditional definitions of female behaviour were certainly challenged in the inter-war years, but this did not appear to influence either the board or its inspectors.[61] This period's economic depression, unemployment and political radicalisation did not seem to produce many drastic changes in reformatory thinking, aside from the fact that the number of children committed to reformatories fell (and remained low) due to the perceived need to reduce public spending. One reason for this stability was that, for most of the period, the same people were employed by the board as inspectors. Its traditional composition may explain the board's defence of traditional femininity. However, this stability was primarily a product of the fact that the views of the board on matters of femininity, domesticity and sexuality, as well as on the need for state intervention in family life, were widely held in Norwegian, and indeed western, society.

Endnotes

[1]
   On the relationship between juvenile delinquency and dominant constructions of childhood, see H. Hendrick, *Child Welfare. England 1872-1989* (London and New York, 1994), pp. 10, 27-9.

[2]
   T.S. Dahl, *Child Welfare and Social Defence* (Oslo, 1985). Minor revisions to the 1896 Act were made in the period considered here, but a new law was not passed until 1953.

[3]
   The first reform school in Norway was established by philanthropists in 1841. It was intended for both sexes, but after a short period of time it was turned into a boys' school. When the 1896 Act was implemented in 1900, there were four reform schools for boys, and three for girls. By the late 1930s the number had risen to a total of ten.

[4]
   The Bergen child welfare board kept diaries on discharged children from 1918 onwards. These are now kept in the Bergen City Archives (*Bergen byarkiv*, BBY) in the Bergen child welfare board (*Bergen vergeråd*, BV), collection no.295. The diary concerning the girls is referred to here as BBY. BV. 5, and the one concerning the boys as BBY. BV. 6. Each child also had its own file, containing sources dating from their first encounter with the board until their discharge from its care. These files therefore contain documents produced by a variety of institutions and private persons, including - occasionally - parents and children themselves. These files are referred to here as *Klientmapper*.

5
M. Foucault, *Discipline and punish. The birth of the prison* (New York, 1995) [*Surveiller et Punir: Naissance de la prison*. Paris, 1975], pp. 293-308. Various statistical studies completed in the inter-war years also concluded that reformatories did not necessarily succeed in effecting reform but did not explain this in Foucauldian terms. One of the most common and enduring contemporary explanations for this failure was that children were simply removed from their homes at too late a stage. According to Stephen Humphries, penal experts in Britain held the same opinion. S. Humphries, *Hooligans or Rebels? An Oral History of Working-Class Childhood and Youth 1889-1939* (Oxford, 1981), p. 237.

6
S. Schlossman and R.B. Cairns, 'Problem girls: Observations on past and present' in G.H. Elder, J. Modell and R.D. Parke eds., *Children in Time and Place. Developmental and Historical Insights* (Cambridge, 1993).

7
The total number of children featured in this study is 413. If the term 'respectable' is used to characterise skilled workers and those holding stable jobs, the parents of a fairly large proportion of the children, 162 (39%), fit this description. 83 (20%) seemed to come from unskilled or low paid working class families. 77 (19%) were children of single mothers, widows, or in some cases deceased parents. 5 (1%) belonged to the middle class. In 86 cases (21%) no information regarding parental occupation was given. Some parents permanently or periodically lived on poor relief. BBY. BV. 5 and 6.

8
Humphries pp. 150-73.

9
On values, see Ø. Bjørnson, *Arbeiderbevegelsens historie i Norge. 2. På klassekampens grunn (1900-1920)* (Oslo, 1990), pp. 121-3 and 287-97. As to the meaning of 'respectable' and 'rough' within the working-class, see A. Davin, *Growing up poor. Home, school and street in London 1870-1914* (London, 1996), pp. 69-74. M. Sundkvist has shown that even if parents protested against decisions made by the Swedish equivalent to the Norwegian child welfare board, they never did so in ways which challenged dominant constructions of childhood. M. Sundkvist, *De vanartade barnen. Mötet mellan barn, föräldrar och Norrköpings barnavårdsnämnd 1903-1925* (Linköping, 1994), p. 241.

10
A.B. Fossen and T. Grønlie, *Bergen bys historie bd. IV. Byen sprenger grensene 1929-1972* (Bergen, Oslo, Tromsø, 1985), p. 139.

11
Fossen and Grønlie pp. 118-27.

12
Fossen and Grønlie pp. 316-17.

13
BBY. BV. 5 and 6. According to the 1896 Act, children younger than six were not to be sent to reform school. In 1915 this minimum age was raised to nine. *Norsk Lovtidende* (1915), p. 285. With some exceptions, children who had reached the age of 16 (18 after 1930) were too old to be admitted to the reformatories. *Norsk Lovtidende* (1930), p. 289.

14
The decisions could be overruled if the parents appealed to the Norwegian Department of Church and Education, but child welfare board sources indicate that parents' views were seldom heard.

15
The length of time spent at reform school is known for 82 of the 85 girls. They had an average stay of 33.4 months; the shortest stay was one year, the longest almost 6.5 years.

BBY. BV. 5. See BBY. BV. 6 for information on boys. Periods of detention seemed to have been mostly determined by the age at which a child was admitted. Girls admitted between the ages of 10 and 12 stayed on average for 4.25 years.

[16] Barnevernskomiteen av 1915: 110. Ot.Prp. nr. 2 (1921).

[17] A-L. Seip, *Veiene til velferdsstaten. Norsk sosialpolitikk 1920-75* (Oslo, 1994), pp. 65-76, 273-8.

[18] The remaining 63 children were discharged before 1920. BBY. BV. 5 and 6.

[19] At a national level the number of children confined in reform schools was fairly constant; in the inter-war years between 4-500 children were at any time confined there. During the Second World War, numbers exceeded 600, but dropped to about 300 in 1950. *Norges Offisielle Statistikk (NOS), rekke V-VIII. NOS, Statistiske meddelelser 1930-1935. NOS. X. 14. NOS. X. 142. NOS. XI. 95.* In addition to economic fluctuations, a pronounced scepticism against the institutional treatment of children and the relatively low success rate also explains the low number of children sent to reformatories.

[20] BBY. BV. 6 and Klientmapper, series I and II. Also T. Rygg, *Den som er med på leiken.* Hovedoppgave ved Historisk Institutt (Bergen, 1997), p. 65.

[21] BBY. BV. Forhandlingsprotokoll V and VI. Klientmapper, series I and II. Journaler. On Sweden, see Sundkvist pp. 145-53; on Germany see E. Harvey, *Youth and the Welfare State in Weimar Germany* (Oxford, 1995), pp. 163-4/208; on Denmark, A. Løkke, *Vildfarende børn - om forsømte og kriminelle børn mellem filantropi og stat 1880 - 1920* (København, 1990), pp. 77-8.

[22] Barnevernskomiteen av 1915: 88. On the legal aspects of prostitution and contemporary debates, see K. Melby, 'Prostitusjon og kontroll', in A. Gotaas et al, *Det kriminelle kjønn.* (Oslo, 1980), pp. 81-129.

[23] BBY. BV. Forhandlingsprotokol V, p. 18.

[24] H. Thuen, 'Reformatory Schools in Norway 1840-1950', *History of Education, 1991.* Vol.20, No.1. Also Dahl 1985 pp. 159-62.

[25] BBY. BV. 5.

[26] The percentages are calculated from BBY. BV. 5.

[27] BBY. BV. 5: 3, j.nr. 820/1918, 8, j.nr. 346/1919, 58, j.nr. 1012/1937.

[28] BBY. BV. 5: 6, j.nr. 31/1918.

[29] Marriage was not open to everyone. In the first third of the twentieth century there was a large proportion of unmarried women in the population; in 1930, 43.2% of women over the age of 15 were single. I. Blom and S. Sogner eds., *Med kjønnsperspektiv på norsk historie fra vikingtid til 2000-årsskiftet* (Oslo, 1999), pp. 233-4.

[30] S. Sogner, *Far sjøl i stua og familien hans. Trekk fra norsk familiehistorie før og nå* (Oslo, 1990), p. 83.

[31] Percentages in this and the following paragraph are calculated from BBY. BV. 5.

[32] BBY. BV. 5. Between 1916 and 1950, the average age at first marriage among Norwegian

women hovered between 25.4 and 26.4. Statistisk sentralbyrå. Befolkning. Historisk statistikk. Http://www.ssb.no/.

33 BBY. BV. Klientmapper serie II (A), j.nr. 775/1918.

34 BBY. BV. Klientmapper serie II (A), j.nr. 618/1929.

35 The figures are based on BBY. BV. 5. Not all the girls continued to live in Bergen at the end of the probation period, but the child welfare board still tried to keep track of them.

36 BBY. BV. 5: 1. 1919.

37 BBY. BV. 5: 26. J.nr. 86/1925.

38 BBY. BV. 5: 1. J.nr. 379/1927.

39 BBY. BV. 5: 14. J.nr. 182/1933.

40 BBY. BV. 5: 23. J.nr. 922/1938.

41 BBY. BV. 5: 28. J.nr. 883/40.

42 K. Ericsson, *Drift og dyd. Kontrollen av jenter på femtitallet* (Oslo, 1996), p. 36.

43 BBY. BV. 5: 13. 1923.

44 Humphries p. 237.

45 See BBY. BV. Klientmapper serie II (A), j.nr. 416/18 for a case which very clearly illustrates this point. See also j.nr. 78/1917 for cases where prostitutes lived with and were protected by their families.

46 Humphries p. 155.

47 BBY. BV. 5: 28. J.nr. 883/40.

48 BBY. BV. 5: 30. J.nr. 602/41.

49 BBY. BV. 5: 32. J.nr. 367/42.

50 BBY. BV. 1: 0. 1946.

51 BBY. BV. 5: 34. 1943.

52 BBY. BV. 5: 11. J.nr. 552/1919.

53 BBY. BV. Klientmapper II (A), j.nr. 414/1918.

54 BBY. BV. 6.

55 Percentage calculated from BBY. BV. 6.

56 BBY. BV. 5: 1, j.nr. 379/27.

57 BB. BV. Klientmapper serie II (A), j.nr. 416/18. Child welfare board report dated 20.11. 1923.

58 I. Blom, *Det er forskjell på folk - nå som før. Om kjønn og andre former for sosial differensiering.* (Oslo, 1994), p. 128. The period 1900-1950 has been labelled 'the epoch of the housewife'. See Blom and Sogner eds. pp. 227-97.

59 Stortingsforhandlingene 1908, bd. 7a, Tidende S: 1573.

60 A. Hudson, "Troublesome girls': towards alternatives' in M. Cain ed., *Growing up good.*

Policing the behaviour of girls in Europe (London, Newbury Park, New Dehli, 1989), p. 207.
[61] On both challenges to and defence of the dominant definitions of the meaning of femininity, see Blom and Sogner eds. pp. 289-96.

Chapter 8

Absent Fathers and Family Breakdown: Delinquency in Vichy France

Sarah Fishman

In a recent study, Robert L. Maginnis of the conservative Family Research Council concluded, 'Children from single-parent families are more prone to commit crime'. Making a common elision (between single-parent and unmarried mother), Maginnis explains, 'This is because unmarried mothers often lack the skills to support a family or to manage a household effectively'.[1] The popular media generally accepts such conclusions as fact, despite the serious doubt much recent scholarship casts on these assertions. A 1998 *Newsweek* headline about a program directed at single mothers claimed, 'Sorry. Government Programs Can't Undo Most of the Ill Effects of Family Breakdown'.[2]

Not just in 1990s America are single mothers blamed for juvenile crime and delinquency. The voluminous literature on delinquency produced in France before and during World War II expressed with growing urgency concerns about the impact of family breakdown on children and adolescents. In a 1943 review of scholarship, Gamet concluded, 'All authors agree about the family's responsibility in the delinquency of minors'. The fact that over 50% of delinquent minors came from families 'deserted by one or both of the parents' he considered 'an essential idea to remember'.[3] The war itself intensified public concern, removing millions of fathers from their homes and witnessing a rapid increase in juvenile crime rates. Minister for Prisoners, Deportees and Refugees Henry Frenay reported in 1945, 'unfortunately, children of POWs constitute a high proportion of delinquent children'.[4] Frenay's concerns about the impact of war captivity on prisoners' children echoed widespread anxieties expressed frequently during the war, in part a reflection of the massive and unprecedented nature of French captivity during World War II.

French Prisoners of War and the Vichy Regime

According to Yves Durand's seminal work, never before had so many men been captured in such a short period of time.[5] From the start of the 'real' war on 10 May

1940 through to the Armistice of 25 June 1940, as many as 1.9 million French soldiers were captured, of whom 1,580,000 were eventually transferred to Germany in 1940. Nearly 940,000 remained in captivity at the end of 1944. Captivity cut through the heart of French society, leaving nearly 790,000 prisoners' wives, 616,200 of them with children, to fend for themselves.[6]

The absent POWs constantly preoccupied both French society as a whole, where nearly every family had a father, brother or husband in captivity, and the French government. Children going astray represented only one potentially harmful consequence of their absence. In fact, the prisoners provided one of the main justifications for the decision by leaders like Philippe Pétain and Pierre Laval, who came to power during the crisis of the Battle of France, to maintain a French government rather than going into exile and continuing the fight. Pétain and his circle believed that France had lost the war, that England would soon fall and that France's best bet was to accept defeat and try, via collaboration, to win favourable treatment for France in a German-led new European order. Getting the French prisoners of war back home was a key goal.

Vichy's Domestic Policies and the Evolution of the Juvenile Justice System

The new leaders of 1940 also had plans for reshaping France internally, beginning by destroying the Third Republic, which they blamed for France's defeat. Republicanism, in their view, bred only laziness, egotism and hedonism. In July 1940, four Constitutional Laws created a new government, called simply the French State, whose capital was, in theory only temporarily, located in the south-central spa town of Vichy. The new leaders renounced everything that the Republic stood for- democracy, individualism, egalitarianism, liberalism. To restore France to the greatness of the Old Regime, leaders at Vichy created an authoritarian government centred on the patriarchal father-figure of the Victor of Verdun, Marshal Pétain. France would be not be run democratically but led by a natural elite. French society, rather than continuing to modernise and industrialise, would instead rest on small shopkeepers and small family farms. The French people had been justly punished, via military defeat, for their sins. Through suffering and massive quantities of Vichy propaganda, they would re-learn the virtues of religion, family, fatherland, hard work and the simple life.

A conservative, authoritarian regime trumpeting the need for moral renewal might have reacted harshly to rising juvenile crime rates, cracking down on young people who failed to heed the call for a new morality. But traditional conservatives made up only the top, most visible layer of the Vichy regime. Under the surface, various players engaged in continual power struggles throughout the Occupation, with the main contenders, in addition to the traditionalists, extreme right-wing fascists, like Joseph Darnand, and technocratic and administrative experts like Admiral François

Darlan. Certain public administrators, freed from parliamentary oversight, paid little heed to Vichy's backward-looking rhetoric and worked rather for greater efficiency and rationalisation. Several administrators from the Justice Ministry and Penal Administration thus continued working with juvenile reformers outside the government who had long advocated a shift to a more therapeutic and less punitive system for France's young offenders.

Moral outrage about youth crime was also outdone by widely shared alarmist views about French depopulation that dated back nearly a century but that gained strength after World War I. Conservatives at Vichy fervently hoped to reverse the trend toward smaller families through a combination of exhortation, financial rewards, and coercion. Couples needed to have more babies to remedy depopulation, but France also needed to rescue troubled young people and make them into productive citizens. As their part in the post-defeat search for what had gone wrong, delinquency experts intensified their critique of France's existing juvenile justice system, which they argued left France unable to redeem its wayward children. Developments in the juvenile justice system thus continued in a therapeutic direction, notwithstanding the defeat, the collapse of the Republic, the rise of an ultra-conservative, authoritarian, repressive regime and galloping juvenile crime rates.

Juvenile Delinquency Reformers of the 1930s and 1940s

By 1940, experts, government administrators and lay activists formed a virtual juvenile delinquency establishment. In the 1930s, the relatively new field of paediatric neuro-psychiatry emerged as the driving force. The most prominent specialist, Georges Heuyer, practically invented paediatric neuro-psychiatry in France.[7] Heuyer trained many students, supervising doctoral theses by Georges Menut, Guy Néron, Simone Marcus-Jeisler, and Georges-Dominique Pesle. In Lyons, two doctors, Paul Girard and Pierre Mazel directed neuropsychiatric clinical work and research. Mazel trained André Gamet and Guy Rey, while Girard advised legal specialist André Perreau. In Montpellier, psychiatrist Dr. Robert Lafon ran the child mental health clinic, where he assembled an interdisciplinary team including educators, psychologists and social workers.

Outside of medicine, several of France's leading child psychologists, including Dr. Daniel Lagache, of the University of Strasbourg and René Le Senne, Professor of Educational Psychology at the Sorbonne, also wrote about delinquency.[8] In 1934 Henri Wallon, internationally renowned professor at the Collège de France, published a scathing critique of state institutions for delinquent boys.[9] Legal experts on juvenile and criminal law contributed another perspective to the field. Juvenile judges Jean Chazal, Georges Epron, Robert Chadefaux and Erwin Frey wrote about delinquency. In Paris, Henri Donnedieu de Vabres, Professor of Criminal Law at the University of

Paris, published many articles on juvenile law, served on the editorial board of the leading journal in the field, *Pour l'Enfance 'Coupable'*.[10] Another circle of lawyers concerned about juvenile justice developed at the University of Rennes Law school, particularly Henri Joubrel, his brother Fernand, and Pierre Waquet, who completed a thesis on child protection.[11]

The field of juvenile justice attracted a number of women. Attorney Hélène Campinchi regularly served as appointed defender for the Seine Children's Court, contributed articles to *Pour l'Enfance 'Coupable'* and led the team that reformed juvenile law in 1945. Social work provided women with another avenue for activism in the field and many of those who worked with troubled minors published regularly. Social worker S. Cotte published a study of her city, Marseilles, in 1945 and, together with Albert Crémieux and M. Schachter, co-authored a highly influential and widely cited macro-study.[12]

Finally, activists who did not necessarily have degrees or special training included many in the scouting movement and religious activists like Charles Péan, Major-General in the Salvation Army, and Quaker Henry Van Etten, lead editor of *Pour l'Enfance 'Coupable'*. Reflecting the paradigm shift that had taken place in religious thinking about delinquent children and adolescents, by 1940 nearly all religious activists who worked with delinquents accepted the new, social-scientific approach.[13]

The Causes of Crime

French experts hardly spoke with a single voice about the causes of delinquent behaviour. They continued the perennial debate on the relative importance of nature and nurture, heredity and environment in explaining deviance and criminal behaviour. However, in the late nineteenth-century one of France's most influential thinkers carved out a distinctly French approach. Alexandre Lacassagne, a French doctor of legal medicine, developed his ideas largely in opposition to Italian sociologist Cesar Lombroso's theories of the 'born criminal'. At the First International Congress of Criminal Anthropology in 1885, Lacassagne insisted, 'Societies have the criminals they deserve'. Lacassagne's writings provided a 'big umbrella' for France's experts, facilitating the development of large areas of consensus across the spectrum of specialities. At least four publications in the 1940s approvingly cited Lacassagne's aphorism.[14] Lyons neuro-psychiatrist André Gamet included Lacassagne's complete statement, which articulated even more clearly the French approach. 'The social milieu is crime's cultural medium, the criminal is the microbe, an element that only gains importance when it finds itself in a medium that allows it to ferment'.[15]

Thus, despite continuing disagreements, by the 1930s experts from across the spectrum shared many fundamental beliefs about why children or adolescents committed crime. French scholars rejected strict biological determinism. Rather, they insisted that a person's behaviour and character reflected an interaction of innate, biological tendencies with an environment that either suppressed or encouraged such tendencies. They debated the relative importance of each factor; experts with a medical background tended to stress heredity and biological factors, while psychiatrists and social workers focused on family and environmental factors. Neither side, however, dismissed the other.

Environmental Factors

When considering the environment, the experts did not focus on class and standard of living. Rather, they wrote in medical terms about social hygiene issues like overcrowding and sanitation. They connected urban life to juvenile crime by pointing not to poverty and the existence of an underclass, but to such unhealthy aspects of urban life as crowding, the lack of open spaces, parks and other amenities.[16] Interestingly, the specialists combined the medical language of hygiene with a morally charged vision of city life and its evils. Cities, they wrote, presented unnatural, powerful temptations for young people - cafes, dance halls and amusement parks, for example. Writers concerned about the urban environment and juvenile crime often criticised department stores for displaying luxury items in tempting fashion to the longing eyes of France's youth, and flea markets for providing easy outlets for selling stolen goods.[17]

Nearly every book or article on juvenile crime singled out one especially dangerous environmental factor: the cinema. Doctors, lawyers, social workers, and religious activists alike decried the cinema's evil influence on the minds of France's youth. Three separate French publications cited a single study published in a Portuguese journal, *Primo de Maio*, in 1938. The Portuguese authors reviewed 1,810 recent films, counted the crimes and arrived at a grand total of 4,700 crimes and misdemeanours to which avid and impressionable young film goers would have been exposed.[18]

Several authors intensified their morally charged critique of the medium's supposed glorification of criminal and immoral behaviour by noting its physical impact on the young. The very experience of attending the cinema was unhealthy. 'In the darkness of an artificial environment... the child is impregnated with the film he sees, he is defenceless against it, and, aided by the spirit of imitation, he becomes entirely enmeshed in its atmosphere'.[19] François Liévois, from the Ministry of Public Health, and neuro-psychiatrists Pesle and Gamet also worried about technical, environmental issues-the dark, unventilated room; the stimulating bright lights emanating from the screen; the candy. Gamet cited Dr. Maria Bernarbie's medical study which found that films maintained 'the nervous system in a constant state of tension'. Bernarbie demanded that the public authorities consider 'the particular fragility of the not-yet-fully developed spinal-encephalo system of the child'.[20]

As with current concerns about violence on television, sex on the internet, suicide and rock lyrics, MTV and illiteracy, the 1940s anxiety about film rested on deep fears about modern life. The mass culture of the cinema had only recently arrived in France in the 1940s. Contemporaries worried about their children being influenced by factors beyond the control of the family, churches and schools. Much of the concern, particularly about Hollywood films, manifested another widespread French preoccupation of that era, fear of the United States and the modern, mass, popular culture it propagated.[21]

Thus nearly every expert and reformer concerned about juvenile crime in France argued that both biological predispositions and general environmental factors caused delinquent behaviour. But of the environmental factors, those who wrote about juvenile delinquency in the 1940s considered nothing as critical to children and adolescents as the family.

The Family

Minister of Prisoners, Deportees and Refugees Frenay's 1945 statement connecting absent prisoner of war fathers and delinquent children reflected public and expert opinion about father absence and broken families. French experts of the 1940s devoted a large portion of their writings to the relationship between family life and delinquent behaviour by minors. A few psychologists adopted a psychoanalytical approach to the parent-child interactions.[22] Most French studies, however, favoured an empirical approach resting on statistics gleaned from a large number of case studies.

Their conclusions about the relationship between family life and crime provide an excellent example of how a few obscure, limited studies echo through the literature and eventually emerge in the popular view as gospel. One doctoral dissertation found 64% of delinquent minors came from 'abnormal families'[23] and another found over 50% from a 'broken family environment'.[24] In 1942, leading paediatric neuro-psychiatrist Georges Heuyer confirmed the importance of family. According to Heuyer's study of 400 dossiers from boys the Seine Children's Court sent to his clinic, only 12% of these boys came from a 'normally constituted family' leaving 88% from 'broken families'.[25] Heuyer's article provided essential confirmation to those who considered broken families a pathological environment for children.[26]

By 1944, most experts who wrote on juvenile crime proclaimed as fact that some 50 to 80% of juvenile delinquents came from what were variously referred to as 'broken', 'disunited' or 'divided' families.[27] I shall use the term 'broken families' as a shorthand. Albert Crémieux, S. Cotte and M. Schachter, a Marseilles research team, undertook a macro-study of nearly 3,000 dossiers from a wide variety of studies done worldwide. Averaging the results, they came up with a global figure of 46.39% of delinquent minors who came from 'abnormal households'.[28]

However, non-researchers fixated on a higher percentage. Renowned Paris juvenile judge Robert Chadefaux stated in 1946, 'This is a truth based on experience, 80% of the minors who appeared in the Seine Children's Court come from households disorganised by divorce and separation or based on free union'.[29] Chadefaux's conclusions derived from his personal, anecdotal experiences and generally accepted wisdom, verified by the studies cited above. Similarly, family law expert Hélène Campinchi wrote in 1945, 'It would almost be too easy to prove and to recall, for example, that over 80% of the misbehaviour of minors is due to a family deficiency'.[30]

The coalescence of views around the upper bound of 80% led experts to jump to what seemed an eminently logical conclusion about the rising curve of juvenile crime after France's defeat in 1940. If broken families led to delinquent behaviour by minors, then the rapid tripling of the number of minors appearing in court between 1940 and 1942 must have resulted from the sudden removal of POW fathers from hundreds of thousands of families. Social worker S. Cotte's study of minors appearing in the Marseilles Children's Court found that the number rose from about 200 a year in the 1930s to a peak of 722 in 1942. The high point, she insisted, 'coincides with the departure of fathers as prisoners of war, deportees, forced labourers in Germany'.[31] Many writers agreed with Cotte, including Henri Joubrel who insisted that the primary reason for the rising curve of juvenile crime during the war was, 'lack of paternal authority' owing to military service or captivity.[32]

But military captivity and divorce constitute qualitatively different experiences for families. While divorce is chosen by at least one of the parents, war captivity usually implies an unwanted, temporary separation resulting from military service. Divorce in the 1940s could only be obtained as a result of adultery, cruelty or abuse, or a spouse's conviction for a serious crime. Such circumstances usually entailed serious emotional trauma and fighting between parents. Furthermore, divorce was considered a sign of personal failure and immorality. Wives bore the brunt of that stigma.

Yet our scholars insisted the father's absence alone, regardless of cause, had serious repercussions on children. According to psychologist Lagache, 'the father's absence is one of the most pathogenic conditions for the child'.[33] Assumptions about natural differences between the sexes implied a certain emotional division of labour within the family regarding child rearing. Mothers played an essential role in a child's moral upbringing. Women's caring, empathetic, nurturing nature provided children with unconditional love. But when children misbehaved, men's natural authority and superior capacity for abstract moral reasoning suited fathers to handle discipline. Gamet insisted that the father's absence not only caused economic hardship for families, forcing mothers to work outside the home, but also signalled inadequate parental authority: 'the father continues to be, no matter what anyone says, the leader... with his departure goes the threat of the 'salutary smack' that makes more than one child think twice before doing something wrong'.[34] While all authors considered the mother's role important, Joubrel explained 'a mother hardly ever has over her daughters, much less over her sons, sufficient educational influence. Never can the sweetness of affection replace the firm words of a father'. Heuyer seconded Joubrel, pointing out that mothers alone owing to the military service, captivity, deportation or forced labour of their husbands, had to 'acquire the distant father's authority, replace him'. Heuyer concedes that 'as a general rule, the French woman proved herself up to the task. But she was not always able to exert enough authority over adolescents deprived of their fathers'.[35]

Years of searching uncovered only three studies of troubled minors that explicitly considered children of POWs. Gamet's study of 524 minors examined at the Lyons School of Medicine and Pharmacy between July 1940 and July 1941 only uncovered three 'POW sons'. Pierre Flot's study of juvenile delinquency in Brittany, based on two private homes for delinquent youth between 1943 and 1945, found nine out of 200 residents with POW fathers (about 5%). Lafon's 1947 study of 100 girls at an Observation Centre found that one girl's father had been a POW.[36]

While surprised by the low number of POW children, less than 1% of his sample, Gamet had an explanation. Most POWs were between the ages of 20 and 30, therefore most of their children were probably under ten, whereas delinquent behaviour usually did not manifest itself until age 13. Gamet concluded, 'POW's sons are 'potential' delinquent minors'. Only one scholar, Mazel noted cautiously, 'It would be too easy to excuse the current upsurge in juvenile delinquency by incriminating the considerable number of POWs'. Yet he too feared the future consequences 'of such a break up of the family milieu'.[37]

Gamet raised a relevant point about the age of POW children in 1940-42 but he sidestepped the logical conclusion. Given the small number of POW children in their populations, the absence of POWs could not explain the threefold increase in the number of minors appearing in juvenile courts at that very same time, between 1940 and 1942. Minors appearing in court were real people, not Gamet's 'potential' juvenile delinquents. Court statistics did not include 'potential juvenile delinquents'. Therefore the absence of POWs did not cause the rising curve of juvenile crime between 1940 and 1942.

However, 1940s experts overlooked this death blow to their theory of the connection between war captivity and juvenile delinquency for a number of reasons. Their habit of looking at the environment in terms of social hygiene rather than class or poverty, led reformers to downplay the connection between rising theft rates and the extreme material hardships nearly all families faced. Food shortages were a constant, nearly universal and exhausting feature of life in wartime France. In fact, French caloric intake during the war was the lowest in western Europe except Italy.[38] Food rationing began gradually but by October 1940, nearly everything, noodles, rice, meat, even bread, was rationed.[39] German requisitions and purchases with overvalued marks created inexorable inflationary pressures and a thriving black market that thwarted government controls. Prices rose 200% and more during the Occupation. In contrast, Vichy maintained tight control over wages and deliberately kept them low. Working class families, with wages frozen and unions banished, faced a serious wage-price gap.[40] One post-war study estimated that during the Occupation, food took up 126% of the average income for a family of four living on one salary.[41] All families faced similar hardships, with the intensity varying by region and, especially, by income level. Those with money could afford to trade on the black market. Prisoners' families had one less adult to bring in income and share the burdens, but their situation, while more intense, did not differ in kind from other families.

Rationing and shortages influenced crime statistics in several ways, not only by inspiring the perpetual search for food, but also by creating new rules to violate and new opportunities for enrichment. Not surprisingly, adult petty crime statistics rose at a rate similar to juvenile crime rates, although on a different order of magnitude. Aggregate crime statistics and information gleaned from court records from four departments across France highlight the impact of material hardship, deprivation, new regulations, the black market and vigorous policing on crime rates.

In other words, adolescents involved in petty theft or rationing infractions were, in many ways, responding logically to their world. However, juvenile delinquency experts in the 1940s avoided conclusions that assumed adolescents were rational actors responding to external factors. Across the board, juvenile reformers, whether they blamed bad families, hereditary weakness, or psychiatric conditions, deflected blame, which might have inspired a punitive crack-down, from the young people themselves.

Thus, to a certain extent, a reform agenda blinded experts on delinquency to the weakness of their analysis connecting juvenile crime to the absence of prisoners of war. Portraying delinquent minors as victims advanced the juvenile reformers' therapeutic reforms. Secondly, by linking family breakdown and juvenile crime, specialists were nudging the problem of minors who commit crime, a group that early in the century aroused public fear and loathing rather than sympathy, into a mainstream political discourse. They successfully linked the issue of delinquency to public concerns about France's presumed family and depopulation crisis that preceded the war and that the war only aggravated.[42] Focusing on family breakdown anchored juvenile delinquency to a popular cause. The breakdown of the French family was not just lowering the birthrate, it was also ruining the children who were born. Fernand and Henri Joubrel stressed the demographic importance of rehabilitating France's youth by citing Goethe. 'To save a man is good, but saving a child is like saving a multiplication table'.[43] If 50 to 80% of the children who appeared in courts came from broken families, then delinquent youth could be portrayed as victims of selfish and hedonistic parents.

Scholars made it appear that over 50% of delinquent minors were victims of faulty parents by engaging in intentional or unintentional blurring of distinctions. In particular, 1940s authors incorporated one critical factor, the death of a parent, into the broken family category with virtually no discussion. For example, Gamet's 1000 cases included 549, or over 50% who came from 'broken families'. But 258 of the 549 families, were 'broken' by one parent's death. That figure dwarfs the 44 cases of divorce or legal separation, and 81 cases of informal separation.[44] Judge Epron's study of 176 minors appearing in the Grenoble Children's Court between 1936 and 1938 found 81 minors from broken families but 44, over half, involved the death of a parent.[45]

Crémieux and his co-authors' macro-study of 2,964 delinquent minors found some 1,375 broken homes. A total of 743 minors had lost one or both parents, 53% of the broken families and one-quarter of the total sample. Compare that to 127 cases of divorce or separation, 9% of the broken families and 4% of the total sample.[46] G. Kohler and Line Thevenin reported on 294 children who had passed through the Lyons Observation Centre between November 1943 and March 1945. As they expressed it, 129 minors came from 'families having a structural defect', 35 cases involving the death of a parent, as compared to 14 separated or divorced parents and one minor from a family experiencing 'serious discord'. They conclude, 'Thus over 50% of the delinquents came from broken family environments'.[47] None of the studies stressed the fact that half of those families had been broken by death.

All the authors include the number of minors whose parents had died, but only Menut tried to control for it. He compared his population of 'emotionally disturbed' (*caractériels*) minors with a sample of 12,876 children from regular Paris elementary schools. While 71% of the general population's broken families involved death, only 56% of the emotionally disturbed children's families did.[48] However Menut did not indicate which districts the Paris students came from, so in part he may have measured a class difference in divorce rates.

Still, Menut alone addressed the difference between death and divorce. The fact that none of the other scholars or experts considered parental death a significant category worthy of separate analysis illuminates a number of critical problems. First, the object of study remains unclear. The profusion of terms, often used interchangeably, signals the definitional confusion. The most common term, 'broken families' is used by eight authors.[49] Many terms are even more explicitly normative. Cotte writes about 'irregular families', Chadefaux refers to 'disorganised families', Robin uses the term 'incomplete families', Pesle and Crémieux use 'abnormal families', and Kohler's minors came from 'families with a structural defect'. Three authors extend the category to include families in which the mother worked outside the home for a wage - which Pesle described as abnormal households with 'working mothers who abandon their children'. Gamet asked, 'How can such a household be normal?'[50]

I would argue that the term 'broken family' strongly suggested divorced or separated parents. Certainly the tone of the discussion in the 1940s, notwithstanding the information provided in small print about orphans, implied that families were 'broken' by a parent's choice of divorce, abandonment or separation. As Gamet stressed with bold faced letters, '**over 50% of delinquent minors come from a dwelling deserted by at least one of the parents**'. Having described the families as 'deserted by a parent' Gamet lists in numerical order the causes of family breakdown, starting with the 'death of one or the other parent'.[51] For most authors, death remained an invisible factor, eliciting next to no discussion. Certainly, both death and divorce entail increased financial hardship for custodial parents and both represent traumatic events in a child or adolescent's life. But they are two different traumas.

Including minors whose father or mother had died in the same category as the children of divorce and separation doubled the percentage of 'broken' families. Adding the figures may have been intentional padding, but the normative language suggests rather that writers of the 1940s were blinded to their own analytical sloppiness by the strength of their assumptions about what constituted a 'normal' family. The definition was unrelenting. A child had to have two living parents who were legally married and resided in the same household with a mother who stayed at home.

Some analyses discussed the emotional problems created for children by situations of parental conflict and divorce, but only one author, judge Georges Epron, tried to define the 'normal' family considering not just the structure but the quality of family life. Epron reports that 81 of his 167 minors came from single-parent families. But he does not use that figure to stand in for normality. Rather, in discussing normal and abnormal families, Epron looked at the reports on home life, considering such issues as parental conflict and the family's reputation. He found a reportedly normal home life for nearly 80% of the minors. In shock, Epron asks, 'Where then are the great causes of juvenile delinquency denounced in all the studies that deal with the issue?' From the contemporary perspective, the answer would have been that Epron was looking at the wrong thing, the qualitative aspect of family life rather than the match between a child's family structure and a 'normal family'.[52] If the round hole is the two-parent, married, single-bread-earner family, than any family missing one of those elements is a square peg and by definition, 'abnormal'. The category was inconsistently labelled, each study included slightly different groups, and all studies merged categories that merited separate analysis because experts fixated on family structure, either downplaying the quality of family life or assuming that if the family structure fell outside the norm, the quality of family life would necessarily also be bad.

Furthermore, the studies were biased in ways that reduce their applicability to the total population of minors who appeared in juvenile courts. For example, Heuyer's study of 400 dossiers set the upper limit of 88% from 'broken families', a figure subsequently popularised at 80%. Yet his 400 dossiers all came from boys examined at his clinic at a home for troubled boys, hardly a random sample of boys appearing in juvenile courts. Judges sent boys to this home either while the case was under investigation (preventive detention) or as a final placement. During and after the investigation, judges returned most minors to their parents, sending only a minority of boys to homes like this. Hardly a random decision, judges were more likely to send a boy to such a place in situations they took to signal trouble in the family home.[53] As sociologist Nadine Lefaucheur recently pointed out, the proper way to test the hypothesis that family breakdown caused delinquency would have been to set up a random sample of minors charged and a control sample of non-delinquent minors.[54]

The experts of the 1940s were intelligent and well-educated. Such errors of analysis resulted both from unquestioned, patriarchal assumptions about gender and family life, and from an agenda, which, in another twist, had little to do with 'family values'. While a few studies considered ways of shoring up families, stricter divorce laws for example, or requiring parent education classes, most analyses shifted gears as they moved from explaining the aetiology of delinquency to recommending remedies. The 1940s experts wanted observation centres and scientific treatment in modern institutions, where minors would be removed from their families.[55] They were engaged in the perennial struggle of building their own professional credibility, but more importantly of exploiting that credibility to gain power and authority over the population of delinquent and troubled youth. They worked hard, and succeeded to a large extent, at inserting themselves as experts into certain procedures and institutions that dealt with 'maladjusted' children, a category that they insisted included delinquents.

In France in the 1940s, blaming the family certainly deflected censure from the minors themselves: minors who broke the law were victims of bad families. While juvenile delinquency reformers in the 1940s did not advocate fixing the families, neither did they propose punishing the minors more harshly. They believed they had the technology to repair the damage.

Conclusions

The war presented both danger and opportunity to those in the juvenile delinquency establishment hoping to reform France's system. Because impressionable children and adolescents represented the best hope for reshaping national values, France's youth ranked high in Vichy's list of priorities. But young people appearing in juvenile court were at the very least ignoring the exhortations of people like Georges Lamirand and Joseph de la Porte du Theil, the traditional, Maurrassian, Catholic conservatives who controlled Vichy's youth and educational policies.

The rapidly rising juvenile crime rate could have provoked anger against delinquent youth. Both public officials and juvenile delinquency experts considered the situation by 1941 a crisis. Rey described delinquency as 'the burning question of the day'.[56] Experts, who had in fact been stressing the role of family breakdown for years, made good use of the opportunity presented by the authorities' concern about rising crime to increase their own authority and bring about change. The war and resulting captivity of 1.5 million POWs, leaving over 600,000 'fatherless' children, corresponded to an alarming rise in the juvenile crime rate. The war, in other words, seemed to prove that the experts had been right all along. As Néron explained, the war constituted 'an experience that demonstrated the importance of the father's absence in the genesis of childhood character problems'.[37] Given such power, juvenile delinquency experts had no incentive to revise their analyses after discovering only a very small percentage of POW children in their samples. Reassessing the connection between captivity and delinquency required rethinking the assumptions behind all their previous scholarship. Experts of the 1940s were blinded to the inconsistencies of their own work because they simply had to be right.

Serious work in reforming legal procedures and institutional operations began during Vichy, whose 27 July 1942 law completely overhauled the juvenile court system and recommended serious institutional reforms. While it rescinded everything Vichy had done, the postwar Provisional Government continued work on the same trajectory, resulting in the law of 2 February 1945, which remains the foundation of France's current juvenile justice system, despite challenges posed by recent events. The 1945 law introduced two hugely significant changes. First, it declared penal irresponsibility for all minors under 16, instructing judges to make all decisions on the basis of the best measure of protection. Second, the 1945 law created a new kind of judge, the Children's Judge, who functions as the linchpin of France's system. Empowered to dispose quickly of less serious cases, the Children's Judge determines which minors undergo testing, forwards difficult cases to the full Children's Court, and centralises information and access to a wide range of social services. The 1945 law represented a decisive turn on France's long road from a primarily punitive system to the extremely, perhaps excessively, therapeutic juvenile justice system of today. The Vichy years proved critical to that turnabout.

Endnotes

[1] R. Maginnis, 'Single-Parent Families Cause Crime', in A.E. Sadler, ed., *Juvenile Crime: Opposing Viewpoints* (San Diego, 1997), p. 64.

[2] R.J. Samuelson, 'Investing in Our Children', *Newsweek* 23 February 1998: 45; For an opposing view, see K.N. Wright and K.E. Wright, 'Single-Parent Families May Not Cause Juvenile Crime', from *Family Life, Delinquency, and Crime: A Policymaker's guide* (Washington, DC, 1994), in Sadler, pp. 67-74; a recently publicised study finally considered not just the presence or absence of a father from the household, but the quality of the relationship between fathers and their children, finding a link between poor father-child relationships and drug and alcohol use amongst teenagers. I. Molotsky, 'Study Links Teen-

Age Substance Abuse and Paternal Ties', *New York Times* 31 August 1999, p. A14.
3   A. Gamet, *Contribution à l'étude de l'enfance coupable: Les facteurs familiaux et sociaux* (Lyons, 1941), pp. 23, 24.
4   France, *Journal Officiel*, Assemblée Constituante Provisoire, 22 March 1945, p. 683.
5   See Y. Durand, *La Captivité: Histoire de prisonniers de guerre français 1939-1945* (Paris, 1980), pp. 20-28.
6   On prisoners' families, see S. Fishman, *We Will Wait: Wives of French Prisoners of War 1940-1945* (New Haven, CT, 1991).
7   Heuyer ran the *Clinique de neuro-psychiatrie infantile* that began operation in 1925 at Rollet's *Patronage de l'Enfance et de l'Adolescence*, but moved during the war to the *Hôpital des Enfants Malades*.
8   Lagache evacuated from Strasbourg to Clermont-Ferrand during the Occupation.
9   H. Wallon, *Une plai de la société: les bagnes d'enfants* (Bourges, 1934).
10   Henri Donnedieu de Vabres served as a judge in the Nuremberg war crimes trials after the war. His son Jean joined Charles de Gaulle in London.
11   In Toulouse, Joseph Magnol, Dean of the Law School and juvenile law expert, and Catholic Abbot Jean Plaquevent, founder of *L'Essor Occitan*, created the *Institut Pédotechnique*, a remedial institution for 'at risk' and delinquent youth.
12   A. Crémieux, M. Schachter and S. Cotte, *L'Enfant devenu délinquant*, (Marseilles, 1945). Archives Nationales F60 1677 B 2800/3, Service de la Protection des Mineurs, 2 December 1943; Mrs Guichard, director and Miss Demoisy, social worker for Safeguarding Adolescence produced case reports for the Seine Children's Court and published articles (I could not find these women's given names).
13   Abbot Philippe Rey-Herme argued that the 'progress of child psychology' required pedagogical and not punitive solutions, *Quelques aspects du progès pédagogique dans la rééducation de la jeunesse délinquante* (Paris, 1945) pp. 3-4.
14   M. Carrasco-Barrios, *Théories sur les causes de la criminalité infantile et juvénile, étude critique* (Paris, 1942), p. 151; P. Mazel, P.F. Girard, A. Gamet, 'Deux aspects du problème social de l'enfance coupable. Le recrudescence actuelle et la cartographie lyonnaisse de la délinquance juvénile', *Le Journal de Médecine de Lyon* 528 (5 January 1942), p. 48; G. Rey, *Les Mineurs délinquants récidivistes* (Lyons, 1942), p. 14; Gamet, *Les facteurs familiaux et sociaux*, p. 17.
15   Cited in Gamet, *Les facteurs familiaux et sociaux*, p. 17.
16   Gamet, *Les facteurs familiaux et sociaux*, p. 16, Mazel et al, p. 51.
17   Gamet, *Les facteurs familiaux et sociaux*, p. 66, Mazel et al, p. 45; H. Joubrel and F. Joubrel, *L'Enfance dite coupable* (Paris, 1946), p. 31.
18   F. Liévois, *La Délinquance juvénile, cure et prophylaxie* (Paris, 1946) pp. 151-2; Liévois cites as her source for the Portugese study an article by Robert Lafon, but does not include journal title or publication date, 'Le problème actuel de l'hygiène mentale des enfants et adolescents'; Crémieux et al also cite the Portugese study, p. 89.
19   P. Blancho, *Esquisse sur l'enfance après la guerre de 1940 à 1945: Etude médico-social* (Paris, 1948), p. 24.
20   Gamet, *Les facteurs familiaux et sociaux*, p. 97.
21   Fear of the evil effects of movies on young people did not merely echo Vichy's moralism

and mistrust of America; as a theme in the literature it both predated and followed the war. See C. Lhotte and E. Dupeyrat, *Le jardin flétri, Enfance délinquante et malheureuse* (Paris, 1939); P. Nobécourt and L. Babonneix, *Les enfants et les jeunes gens anormaux* (Paris, 1939); E. Le Gal, *L'Enfance moralement déficiente et coupable* (Paris, 1943) p. 31; Rey, pp. 39-40; G-D. Pesle, *L'Enfance délinquante vue d'un centre de triage* (Paris, 1945), p. 1; R. Valet, *Contribution à l'étude du traitement et de l'assistance de l'enfance anormale, le problème de l'adaptation sociale des enfants irréguliers* (Lyons, 1942); A. Perreau, *Le Mineurs pervers de constitution* (Lyons, 1942), p. 126; D. Parker, 'Influence de la presse enfantine et du cinéma sur la délinquance juvénile', in *Quinze Conférences sur les problèmes de l'enfance délinquante* (Paris, 1946); F. Liévois, 151-2; M. Le Bourdellès, 'Notes sur le cinéma et la délinquance juvénile', *Rééducation* 8 (July 1948), p. 24; C. Kohler, 'Le cinéma et les enfants', *Revue de criminologie et de police technique* 3, no. 1 (January - March 1949), pp. 48-54; G. Robin, *L'Education des enfants difficiles* (Paris, 1948); Joubrel and Joubrel, *L'Enfance dite coupable*, p. 31.

22 H. Wallon, 'Milieu familial et délinquance juvénile', *Pour l'enfance 'coupable'* (January - February 1940); R. Le Senne, 'Caractérologie et enfance délinquante', *Educateurs* Special issue (July-August 1946), pp. 264, 268.

23 Cited by Heuyer's preface to G. Menut, *La Dissociation familiale et les troubles de caractère chez l'enfant* (Paris, 1944), p. 5, Menut also cites Neron's dissertation on p. 23 but claims that 70% of the minors were from abnormal families. Néron only published his 1928 thesis as a book in 1952. Guy Néron, *L'Enfant vagabond* (Paris, 1952) p. 67.

24 Gamet, *Les facteurs familiaux et sociaux*, p. 25.

25 G. Heuyer, *Enquête sur la délinquance juvénile: Etude de 400 dossiers* (Paris, 1942).

26 Heuyer advised Menut's thesis, a study of 839 dossiers. Menut found 551 minors, or 66%, who 'come from a broken family'. Menut, p. 23. Menut's sample was drawn from Heuyer's Pediatric Neuro-psychiatric Clinic at the Paris Faculté de Médecine.

27 The terms in French are *dissocié* from the verb *se dissocier* which means to split or break up, *désagrégé*, which also means broken up, disintegrated, and *désunis* which means divided or disunited.

28 Crémieux et al, p. 22.

29 R. Chadefaux, 'Les causes sociales de la délinquance juvénile' *Educateurs* July-August 1946, p. 246.

30 H. Campinchi, 'Le statut de l'enfance délinquante et la loi du 27 juillet 1942', in *Etudes de science criminelle et de droit pénal comparé*, ed. L. Hugueney, H. Donnedieu de Vabres and M. Ancel (Paris, 1945) p. 175.

31 Crémieux et al, p. 22; S. Cotte 'Rapport sur l'Enfance délinquante et en danger moral, d'après l'experience marseillaise' *Pour l'enfance 'coupable'* 60 (July-September 1945) p. 2. That same sentence is also repeated in Crémieux et al, p. 154.

32 Joubrel and Joubrel, p. 21; Heuyer attributed rising wartime juvenile crime rates to the eight million men mobilised in 1940, 1.9 million captured, 1.6 million POWs, 220,000 deportees and 780,000 forced laborers. Here Heuyer amplifies the number of absent men by not pointing out that the 1.6 million POWs are a subset of the 1.9 million captured which is a subset of the 8 million mobilised. G. Heuyer, 'Psychopathologie de l'enfance victime de la guerre', *Sauvegarde* (17 January 1948), p. 5.

[33] Cited in Menut, p. 27.

[34] Gamet, *Les facteurs familiaux et sociaux*, p. 31.

[35] Menut, p. 27; Gamet, *Les facteurs familiaux et sociaux*, p, 31; Joubrel and Joubrel, p. 21; Heuyer, 'Psychopathologie de l'enfance', pp. 4-6.

[36] Pierre Mazel, Gamet's advisor, cited the same figures in an article on the geographic distribution of delinquency in Lyons during the war. Gamet, *Les facteurs familiaux et sociaux*, p. 27; Mazel et al, p. 48; P. Flot, *Constatations médicales et sociales relatives à la délinquance juvénile en Bretagne* (Paris, 1945), p. 21, R. Lafon 'La 'Famille coupable'' *Sauvons l'enfance* 70 (May-June 1947), p. 4.

[37] Gamet, *Les facteurs familiaux et sociaux*, p. 27; Mazel et al, p. 48.

[38] By late 1944, the German occupiers had taken 2.4 million tons of wheat, 891,000 tons of meat and 1.4 million hectoliters of milk. R. Paxton, *Vichy France: Old Guard and New Order* (New York, 1982) pp. 144, 360; Y. Durand, *La France dans la deuxième guerre mondiale* (Paris, 1989), p. 65.

[39] D. Veillon, *Vivre et Survivre en France 1939-1947* (Paris, 1995), pp. 101, 112, 116.

[40] Already in 1942, a German study noted that prices had risen 70% since 1940, but wages had only risen 30%, a gap that widened every year. Paxton, p. 376.

[41] A. Sauvy, *La Vie économique des français de 1939 à 1945* (Paris, 1978), p. 204.

[42] Demographic fears predated Vichy and were shared by republicans, who passed the Third Republic's Family Code in 1939. Vichy did not discard the Code, but made family policy more punitive and coercive, with laws limiting divorce, severely punishing abortion and restricting married women's employment. Vichy also created the first separate 'family' administration. See M. Pollard, *Reign of Virtue: Mobilizing Gender in Vichy France* (Chicago, 1998).

[43] Joubrel and Joubrel, p. 14.

[44] Gamet, *Les facteurs familiaux et sociaux*, p. 26.

[45] G. Epron, 'Reflexions au sujet de quelques enquêtes relatives à des mineurs délinquantes' *Pour l'Enfance 'coupable'* 50 (September-October 1943), p. 5.

[46] Crémieux et al, p. 23; Menut's 839 dossiers included 36% half or full orphans, 19.5% whose parents had separated or divorced, Menut, p. 26. Flot found that 37% of the girls and 30% of the boys had lost a parent, 25% of the girls and 13.7% of the boys had divorced or separated parents, Flot, p. 211.

[47] G. Kohler and L. Thevenin, 'Le Centre polyvalent d'observation de Lyon. *Sauvegarde* 11 (May 1947), p. 1; see also R. Lafon, 'La Famille Coupable' Of 100 girls at Lafon's Centre d'Observation Olivier, 35 were orphans, 24 girls had parents who were separated or divorced, p. 4.

[48] Menut, p. 26. I have corrected an error in Menut's calculation of the number of orphans.

[49] Rey, Blancho, Kohler, Marcus-Jeisler, Heuyer, Lafon, Menut and Gamet.

[50] Gamet, *Les facteurs familiaux et sociaux*, pp. 26-27; Pesle, *L'Enfance délinquante*, p. 30; Mazel et al, p. 45; 7% had mothers who worked outside the home, Gamet, *Les facteurs familiaux et sociaux*, p. 27.

[51] Gamet, *Les facteurs familiaux et sociaux*, p. 25, 26.

[52] Epron, pp. 6-7.

[53] See N. Lefaucheur, 'Dissociation familiale et délinquance juvénile ou la trompeuse

éloquence des chiffres', in M. Chauvière, P. Lenðel, E. Pierre, eds., *Protéger l'enfant: Raison juridique et pratiques socio-judiciaires XIXe - XXe siècle* (Rennes, 1996) p. 125.

[54] Lefaucheur, p. 129.

[55] Chauvière has written about the maladjusted children sector, which emerged at the same time and struggled to include delinquent minors. M. Chauvière, *Enfance inadaptée l'héritage de Vichy* (Paris, 1980), p. 55.

[56] Rey, p. 11; see also Blancho, p. 12.

[57] Neron, p. 72.

Chapter 9

Race, Delinquency and Difference in Twentieth Century Britain

Pamela Cox

British debates around difference and disorder have been dominated by two distinct bodies of writing, the first rooted in the mid-nineteenth century and the second in the late-twentieth. Urban investigators of the mid-to-late nineteenth century, writing during years when imperial power abroad contrasted sharply with urban poverty at home and when fears for national and racial decline helped to stimulate social reform, detailed the habits of the white underclass in ways which projected them as a race apart. In this genre, made most famous by the illustrated articles of London journalist Henry Mayhew and the annotated maps of London reformer Charles Booth but encompassing a wide range of other writers, the white poor of the large cities were variously featured as feckless, degenerate and potentially dangerous. Their children's future and fate raised particular concerns that did much to shape British responses to juvenile delinquency and child neglect. Texts such as Mary Carpenter's *Reformatory Schools for the Children of the Perishing and Dangerous Classes*, Dorothy Stanley's *London Street Arabs*, Arthur Morrison's *A Child of the Jago*, William Booth's 'Children of the Lost' in his *In Darkest England* - a tiny selection of similar titles - displayed a common concern to tame the wild child, but also a common fascination for its customs and territories.[1]

This interest in native poverty was also extended to immigrants and their children. The Irish occupied a particular place in this literature which cast them as beggars, labourers and street sellers who were slow-witted, superstitious, and often drunken. Irish children, like their 'native' counterparts, were removed in large numbers from such parents by child-savers, charities and religious rescue organisations, whose activities were given new legitimacy by legislation codifying neglect, cruelty and the preventive policing of juveniles. Although incoming Italians, Germans and eastern European Jews were also vilified by many, they did not attract the more wholesale disdain reserved for the Irish which was not really dislodged, if it ever was, until the post-1945 arrival of black migrants from the Caribbean, India, Pakistan, and, later, east Africa.[2]

These groups became the focus of the second broad body of British writing dealing with disorder and difference. Although drawing on earlier post-war work, this second phase was most firmly established in 1978 with the ground-breaking *Policing the Crisis* written by black British academic Stuart Hall and colleagues from Birmingham University's Centre for Contemporary Cultural Studies.[3] This book offered a radical investigation of the symbolic status of 'mugging', or racialised street robbery, within the wider crisis of authority faced by the state in the wake of serious economic recession and played out by the police chiefly among the West Indian communities of the depressed inner cities. Together with developments in radical sociology and radical criminology, it helped to generate a new literature on race, policing and prisons which has since been dominated by the figure of the young black male, excluded from school, alienated from economy and society, victimised by the police, and over-represented in youth custody, prisons and mental hospitals. In the post-war period then, discourses of delinquency, disorder and ethnic difference came to revolve around the discontent of second and third generation urban black boys, presented as 'a social time-bomb' waiting to go off.[4]

While Solomos is certainly right about this shift in political discourses of race, his (and others') emphasis on certain factors within this story has meant that other important elements have been effaced. Young men's post-war material deprivation and social disaffection remains, of course, central to the analysis of crime and policing. Yet alongside this there is, firstly, another story to be told about young white, black and 'mixed race' women and the fears raised by their personal and sexual relationships which were considered racially threatening and culturally damaging and were therefore subject to stringent social regulation.[5] Secondly, although the post-1945 period opened a new chapter in British race relations with the large scale permanent migration of West Indian and Asian workers and families, questions of ethnic, national and religious differences had been a part of debates about delinquency from at least the mid-nineteenth century. As Gilroy has argued, representations of black criminality, often presented as an 'integral element' of black culture, have a long history reflective of a long-standing linkage of immigrants and disorder.[6]

During the first half of the twentieth century discussions of child welfare and ethnicity were continued in a number of sites. Social science departments, mostly in newer universities, began to sponsor research projects in areas with established black and mixed race communities, namely the port cities of Liverpool, Cardiff and London. These local projects became very influential at a national level and played a major part in structuring race relations discourses up to the second world war. One of the earliest of these was former probation officer Muriel Fletcher's *Report on an Investigation into the Colour Problem in Liverpool and Other Ports* published in 1930 and based on research carried out on behalf of Liverpool University's School of Social Science and the local Association for the Welfare of Half-Caste Children, an organisation supported by the Liverpool University Settlement.[7] It quickly sold out, and its contents were widely reported in the national press. From the late 1940s onwards other academics and researchers, some working with emerging pressure groups, consolidated this new tradition of racialised urban investigation which set out to distance itself from nineteenth century texts and from contemporary popular racism but which nevertheless, like Fletcher's report, reproduced many elements of both. Kenneth Little sought out the experiences of *The Negro in Britain*, Michael Banton charted *The Coloured Quarter*, Sheila Patterson detailed *Dark Strangers*, and Pearl Jephcott negotiated her way around Notting Hill, *A Troubled Area.*[8]

As well as these new initiatives coming out of the universities and pressure groups, further knowledge of the 'colour issue' was produced by older agencies. Voluntary organisations and religious groups, notably including organisations funded and run by the black community and the black churches, undertook their own investigations and made their own provision for black and mixed race children and often for their mothers too. These black organisations ranged from the small and local, such as the African Churches Mission in Liverpool, to the larger and more national, such as Harold Moody's League of Coloured Peoples and the more radical Negro Welfare Association.[9] Holidays for coloured children, youth clubs for half-caste girls, nurseries for West Indian working single mothers and campaigns against the ill-treatment of black evacuees were a small but very significant part of the overall picture of British child welfare in the first half of the twentieth century. With the high profile growth in the number of 'brown babies' born during the second world war (the product of often short term affairs between white women and African-American GIs) and the post-war increase in the numbers of West Indian women migrants, this provision became all the more significant.[10]

The British voluntary sector had historically organised itself around difference. From at least the early nineteenth century, money had been raised for particular rather than universal causes. The black poor, distressed gentlefolk, Jewish incurables, respectable Catholic boys, fallen Protestant girls, Asiatic merchant seamen and abandoned Indian servants were all, in their time, served by designated charities and designated homes. This tradition of differentiation, of making particular provision for particular groups, also greatly shaped the development of British juvenile justice facilities. These facilities rested on two foundations - one philosophical and one more practical. The identification and management of social problems in the nineteenth century relied heavily on the drawing of differences between groups: the pauper lunatic, the habitual inebriate and the delinquent child were seen to require distinct and separate treatment. Beyond this, the category of the delinquent child was subdivided further: the delinquent were to be separated from the merely neglected, the vicious from the innocent, the older from the younger, the girls from the boys, those who needed a short sharp shock from those who needed longer term re-training. This philosophical segregation was both informed by, and then mapped onto, the practical segregation already operated by the voluntary sector. The statutory juvenile justice system was built upon the incorporation, from the 1850s onwards, of voluntary sector homes, staff, funds and contact networks into a loose regulatory framework subject to occasional Home Office and local authority inspection. Existing charitable homes, which provided the juvenile justice system's institutional infrastructure, its certified schools, its probation homes, its auxiliary hostels, already largely divided children along the lines outlined above and continued to do so throughout the first half of the twentieth century. Because of their predominantly religious origins, these charities also made distinct provision for children of different faiths and denominations. This meant that within the British juvenile justice system, Protestant, Catholic and Jewish children could be admitted by courts to different certified schools, or be assigned to different probation officers.[11]

Despite these divisions, public and policy discussions of race and delinquency were arguably more obviously shaped by concerns to preserve white strength. The need to secure white racial fitness, national efficiency, imperial power and industrial prowess, as well as a drive towards social democracy and equity, underpinned many British welfare initiatives in the early twentieth century. Child welfare policies, from school-based services, to infant clinics, to neglect legislation to juvenile justice reform, were particularly important in this regard, providing as they did for the future physical, moral and mental strength of the nation. Yet although these measures were introduced in the name of 'the child', the child in question was far from a unified social subject but was a deeply differentiated conceptual being. Justice, punishment and protection for 'the child' was not based upon a concept of a common right to common provision, but was instead based upon the negotiation of a number of differences. That different children could expect different things from the juvenile justice and child welfare systems helps to explain the later construction of black youth as a 'social time-bomb', a group who were seen to pose distinct dangers which needed to be contained in distinct ways.

'Mixed Race' Children

The view that the 'mixed race' or 'half-caste' child faced social, economic, cultural and psychological disadvantages was widely held in the first half of the twentieth century. Opinion was more divided as to whether these disadvantages were the product of nature or nurture. But there was a broad popular and social scientific consensus that the problems of these children could be best contained by limiting their numbers as far as possible and by actively promoting their assimilation into white culture in order to prevent their otherwise inevitable alienation from finding expression in delinquency and disorder.

Suspicion of mixed race children in this period stemmed from a deep-seated disapproval of the relationships between their (usually) white mothers and (broadly defined) non-white fathers. Working class white girls' liaisons with 'foreign' men, prompted in part by the absence of 'foreign' women, caused particular comment and concern, first in the port cities which became home to nineteenth century migrants and merchant seamen from China, southeast Asia and Africa, and later in areas housing war-time African American GIs and in post-war centres of West Indian immigration. White girls who chose 'foreign' men were not only marked out as delinquent but seen to threaten established social and racial order - this view underlaid many texts on race relations from the late-nineteenth to the mid-twentieth century and beyond. In 1896, London City Missionaries complained that young women such as 'Canton Kitty', 'Calcutta Louisa' and 'Lascar Sally' had turned parts of the city into 'perfect pest-spots' and that the 'commingling of the worst vices of East and West' had spawned 'a 'mixed population of half-castes...[who] were often utilised by men of the Fagin type to steal, or beg, or both'.[12] Muriel Fletcher's report on Liverpool in 1930 concluded that there were four types of girl who 'consorted' with coloured men: those who already had an illegitimate child, those who were mentally weak, those already working as prostitutes, and younger women who 'make contacts in a spirit of adventure and find themselves unable to break away'. The spaces where these encounters occurred were equally undesirable. Popular meeting places included pubs, cafes, 'cocoa rooms where [the girls were] employed as waitresses', 'concerts for coloured men', and 'coloured men's dances', which were 'held fairly frequently in the cellars of the houses occupied by coloured men'.[13] Wayward white girls were thought to be lured to such places, in Liverpool and elsewhere, by the attractions of 'exotic' music, dancing, drugs and sex. Dire consequences were predicted, from addiction and demoralisation to prostitution and illegitimate pregnancy.[14] The children resulting from these encounters, numbering over 1,300 in 1930s Liverpool according to Fletcher, stood to inherit 'a certain slackness' from their young white mothers and 'a happy-go-lucky attitude to life' from their black fathers.[15]

Writing 25 years after Fletcher, Michael Banton nevertheless wrote in similar terms about the 'coloured quarter' of 1950s Stepney, an area in east London. When a white woman had 'lost all status with her own people she [could] still go to a coloured man and receive a certain amount of attention'.[16] Most of the 'United Kingdom-born women in Stepney suffer[ered] from personal instability'.[17] One of his 'more perceptive' informants among the 'coloured men' listed the kinds of women in the area. At the bottom of the list were young women known as 'utilities', described as follows:

> ...women usually in their late teens or twenties who have almost always a family background of deprivation and rejection, who are personally unstable and have no settled residence. They arrive in Stepney and hang around the cafés for two or three weeks, staying perhaps for a time with a coloured man, and then run off to Cardiff or somewhere similar.

The 'utilities' were 'frequently mentally and educationally subnormal', their careers marked by 'drift and abandon'. They drew attention to themselves, lied for 'no good reason' and stole when they were 'not in need'. They were 'unable to accept that offer of a stable relationship which they want most profoundly'.[18] Sally was presented as a typical case. A former approved school girl, and 'the daughter of a prostitute in a Welsh seaport', she found a job as a waitress in a Stepney cafe 'near to the coloured quarter'. Tiring of the job 'after about nine days', she 'met a coloured man in the street who had been one of her mother's clients' and accepted his invitation to live with him.[19]

Banton argued that coloured children born and brought up in the United Kingdom 'often had such women for mothers', white women whose girlhoods were tainted by broken homes, criminality, immorality and mental illness.[20] A significant number of others were placed in private children's homes or given up for adoption. During the second world war, this group acquired the status of a new national social problem - the 'unwanted coloured child'. The British black community were at the forefront of efforts to publicise and provide for these children. In 1946, the League of Coloured Peoples published a report, 'Illegitimate children born in Britain of English mothers and Coloured Americans', and after that became active in the welfare of 'unwanted coloured children'.[21] In the late 1940s, Pastor Daniels Ekarte, the Nigerian founder of the African Churches Mission in Liverpool, raised funds to set up a home for the illegitimate children of 'coloured American soldiers, Africans, and West Indian soldiers and technicians'.[22] The plan never materialised, however, and the children already in Ekarte's care were themselves removed from the African Churches Mission in 1949 as rumours about his 'bad character' abounded and after a damning investigation into the Mission by local and Home Office child welfare inspectors.

Clearly, the problem of 'the unwanted coloured child' was an awkward one for local and national government. The Home Office were not prepared formally to sanction racially segregated children's homes, although it is clear that certain homes in certain areas had higher numbers of black children than others, and that heavily racialised practices - more fully documented for the post-war period - operated in these institutions. If placed in care, black and mixed race children were less likely to be adopted as few black families in this period were in an economic position to do this and white couples were often advised against taking them in. One adoption worker told Sheila Patterson that it was 'all very well' for white adoptive parents to 'pet a little chocolate boy doll', but questioned whether they would 'feel the same when he grows up into a husky fellow making friends with the neighbours' daughter'.[23] Black children accounted for only 15 of the 2000 adoptions arranged by the Church of England Children's Society in 1951-55, for just one of the 181 adoptions arranged by Barnardo's in 1956, and one of the 160 adoptions arranged by National Children's Homes in the same year.[24] Once in care, they were more likely to labelled as 'difficult'. Patterson also found that white staff in children's homes found 'coloured teenagers [...] a particularly difficult group, likely to present more problems than the local teenage boy or girl', and that this was due to, the earlier physiological maturity...among most of them, to their almost invariable lack of any family or outside connections, and to their growing awareness of being 'different', not only in status as institution children in the outside world, but in appearance from the rest of the group.[25]

Staff attributed this last factor to black adolescents' development of a heightened awareness of their difference, of a new consciousness of their colour, noting that 'colour consciousness seemed to strike the coloured children themselves first of all', often as a result of 'contact with the outside world or with puberty [when] all relationships seemed to become more self-conscious'.[26] These difficulties continued when staff tried to find jobs or housing for black and mixed race teenagers after they had left children's homes. In June 1960 the National Children's Home informed the British-Caribbean Association that 'it was getting more and more difficult to place young coloured men or girls either in jobs or homes'.[27] The war-time panic around the 'unwanted coloured child' therefore helped to engender a new phenomenon in modern British child welfare: the over-represented and over-demonised black child in care.

But mixed race children who lived in their own secure families were also thought to face problems. Black fathers were ascribed distinct faults of their own which 'encouraged' their children to drift into delinquency. For Fletcher, Liverpool's foreign seamen were no longer constrained by 'tribal relations' but had not yet learned 'the restraints and control of white civilisation' and therefore treated white women 'in a contemptuous manner'.[28] Even those who had long settled in the port towns and elsewhere continued to be viewed as displaced disorientated newcomers - or as one text put it, 'left as a sort of flotsam after some commercial tide'.[29] In short, black men were seen to play by their own rules, to find it hard to read their 'host' community's cultural signs. For Kenneth Little, writing of 1940s Cardiff, 'mixed blood' children's under-achievement at school and their tendency to 'run quite wild' was compounded by their fathers' 'inability' to exercise culturally consistent control. Little believed that more significant than poverty in many coloured homes in Cardiff was:

> the fact that the father not only possesses a rather inadequate knowledge of English and cultural habits somewhat different from English ones, but is barely alive to the implications of social behaviour customary in our society.

For children, this meant that a 'pattern of conflicting loyalties and resentments [was] set up' which made routines of obedience hard to establish. Forced between loyalty to their black father or to the white society, the safest option was 'filial neutrality', or the deliberate repression of 'previous emotional fixations on either parent'. This was dangerous, however, as it could 'lead in turn to a habit of detachment in other respects and in particular to a neglect of arduous emotional as well as intellectual problems'. Parents in the coloured community were 'at the very best but partially alive to the significance of these factors' and even those who were aware concluded that 'good' behaviour was 'something which can be virtually 'magicked' into their offspring in the schoolroom in the same way as reading and arithmetic'.[30]

Not surprisingly, mixed race adolescents suffered discrimination in an already racially divided labour force. Colour was viewed, even by liberals, as a physical disability. Liverpool University Settlement workers believed that 'mixed parentage is in the modern industrial world a handicap comparable to physical deformity' and that a mixed race child's 'industrial life will approach more nearly to the normal' only if they 'can be given a compensating advantage'.[31] As part of her work, Muriel Fletcher had set up an experimental training home for coloured girls in Liverpool. Her aim was to see whether they were 'capable' of being trained in handicrafts and if so to investigate the possibility of the scheme 'being developed along similar lines to those of the Schools for the Blind, thus providing an avenue of employment for half-caste children'. This initiative, in which girls were paid on a piece work basis for embroidery, failed.[32] Fletcher put this down to the low numbers of girls involved but also to the fact that they were just unsuited to the task. The girls 'had a general aptitude for the work' but could not do 'really fine work on very light coloured materials'. They 'tired easily and lacked the power of application'. They were 'slow workers, lacking in initiative and needed constant supervision'.[33] Ultimately, her heredity was against the 'half-caste' girl.

As this shows, gender differences were very significant here. One reason why Fletcher had set up the training home (as well as a 'club for coloured girls') was because mixed race girls faced more difficulties finding work than mixed race boys. While the docks, where black and mixed race men were familiar figures, offered unskilled opportunities to the boys, domestic service, factory and retail work, where white women dominated, seemed closed to the girls. Shut out from traditional young female labour markets and carrying a 'highly sexed' heredity, mixed race girls seemed especially prone to prostitution. In this sense, black girls were viewed as presenting a more serious problem than black boys. Indeed, Fletcher's initial appeals for research funding had played on these projected problems.

> The majority of Anglo-Negroid girls seem to drift inevitably into undesirable surroundings, since it is impossible for them to secure work either in domestic service or in factories...[this] undoubtedly increases the number of prostitutes and the number of illegitimate children, born with a definitely bad heredity, and exposed to a definitely bad environment. The problem regarding boys is not so acute, but even they are only too likely to complicate the situation by their actions later on in life.[34]

According to Little, Cardiff's mixed race youth faced similar problems, with girls at a greater disadvantage. Employers recruited along rigid 'colour lines':

> Apart from employment at sea the boys are lucky to find work as errand boys or page boys, or in some other 'blind alley' occupation, and for the girls the Juvenile Employment Bureau can rarely find anything outside the 'colour line'. Virtually the only outlet with any prospects

in this respect seems to be in entertainment, where both male and female youngsters can sometimes secure jobs as dancers and singers, and an occasional engagement in a film crowd.[35]

Such work was 'uncertain as well as sporadic' and in the case of young girls 'not without its 'moral' dangers', a fact which only served to re-enforce their existing construction as sexually wayward.

The mixed race child, then, was certainly viewed in this period as a 'social time-bomb' of sorts, albeit with a long fuse. Actual crime rates within this juvenile group were recognised to be very low but they were nevertheless viewed as a serious social problem in the making.[36] The labour market, seen by liberals to offer the economic opportunities vital to successful assimilation, was shot through with discriminations that restricted choices and chances. Radical academic research into race relations was carried out in ways that fixed negative connections between difference, disorder and delinquency. Solutions to this problem ranged from monitoring and restricting the movements of migrant men to warning white girls to keep to their own communities.[37] These, then, were the politics of prejudice that greeted post-war Commonwealth migrants.[38]

Black Youth

White adults are less tolerant of [youths] than they are of the little children. The round-eyed black baby in a snowy cot, perhaps with an open Bible at his head, is an endearing creature. It is a different matter when he has grown into a reckless schoolboy cyclist or is one of a gaggle of girls who occupy the whole pavement. 'Teenagers are bad enough, but *coloured* ones!'[39]

Pearl Jephcott's picture of race relations in London's Notting Hill in the early 1960s shows just how easily the black child grew from innocent baby into teenage hoodlum within the white public eye and just how little such children would have to do to be cast as trouble.

By 1967 there were approximately 115,000 school age black children in Britain (excluding Northern Ireland). Two thirds of these were under the age of 11 and thus more likely to have been born in Britain, rather than being first generation migrants themselves.[40] The presence of black children and their black mothers opened a new chapter in a history of Commonwealth immigration previously dominated by the movement of male migrant workers. The growth of a community recognised to be permanent rather than transitory began to challenge existing notions of assimilation and differentiation. Although there were obvious legislative attempts to restrict further black immigration, statutory and voluntary agencies clearly began to move towards developing new ways of regulating and managing these permanent black communities.[41] Again, the need to contain future problems which might be presented and encountered by black children was paramount. And diagnoses of these future problems were closely linked to the past problems believed to have been presented and encountered by earlier generations of mixed race children: bad mothering, bad fathering, cultural conflict, social alienation, economic discrimination and lack of discipline.

Concerns about the quality of black mothering and West Indian mothering in particular, were both similar to, yet distinct from, concerns about the quality of white working class mothering. Efforts to limit the ill-effects of illegitimacy were pronounced but complicated by the fact that illegitimacy among West Indians was recognised by many British welfare agencies to be 'part' of Caribbean culture. According to one study, two fifths of all girls in Trinidad, Jamaica and Barbados could 'expect to be a mother in her teens'.[42] Another calculated that 'between 60 and 70 per cent of the children in most West Indian islands are born out of wedlock' and that 'roughly half of these were the product of informal but relatively permanent unions'.[43] Numbers of illegitimate children born to West Indian women in Britain were recognised to be low: though estimates varied these were in the hundreds rather than the thousands.[44] However, welfare workers' observations of mother and baby homes, hospital labour wards and work places suggested that this was a rapidly growing problem which would only be exacerbated by further black immigration. The south London based Southwark Diocesan Association for Moral Welfare, for example, reported that numbers of recorded Southwark cases had more than doubled from 95 in 1955 to 231 in 1957, with up to 25% of these cases involving teenage girls and young women under the age of 21.[45] In response, a number of voluntary sector, church and Colonial Office meetings were held in London and the midlands in the mid-1950s to investigate the 'new problem' of the West Indian unmarried mother.[46]

All these meetings concluded that this young woman was worse off than her white counterpart. She often had more than one child to support, either in Britain or in the Caribbean. Cultural tradition meant that she was less likely to press the father of the child to take any responsibility. She had much worse access to formal adoption networks, as outlined earlier and faced major difficulties finding lodgings. She rarely had relatives to support her and could not rely on extended family child-care networks because these were broken by migration. Further, she apparently had no established community networks in Britain to turn to. Despite the fact that there were over 2,000 West Indians in Nottingham, for example, the Secretary for Moral Welfare in one Nottingham diocese believed (almost certainly wrongly) that there was no West Indian 'community' in the area because they did not 'segregate in language groups or religious groups like Jews, Catholics or Poles'.[47]

The meetings discussed a range of strategies to deal with the problem of the unmarried West Indian mother, many of which were reportedly already in use. These included repatriating the baby to the mother's family in the Caribbean, education in contraception methods, encouraging the mother to marry the putative father, or failing that, to sue him for maintenance. Significantly, they also included plans to set up day nurseries and hostels which would allow these women to go out to work to support their children - an idea which would have been less readily proposed for white women in the same position by the same people. Illegitimacy among white women was still countered by a range of conservative measures, dominated by denial, adoption and marriage where possible. Arguably, white women were still to be saved from the stigmas of illegitimacy, whereas black women - bound by their culture and already bearing other stigmas - were thought by many to be beyond such salvation and were also, in any case, much more readily constructed as workers rather than mothers. As (black) immigrants, they were also expected to support themselves and not expect 'hand-outs' from the (white) 'British' state or (white) 'British' charities. Potentially radical solutions, then, in the form of subsidised housing and child-care for single mothers, were proposed less in the spirit of extending new forms of citizenship to all women than in the spirit of solving what was viewed as a racially distinct social problem.

But black working mothers, whether married or unmarried, 'compromised' their children's development and safety and thereby threatened to raise a generation of delinquents. As contemporary writings on race relations show, this was another widely held and commonly expressed, if contradictory, view. In *Colour and Citizenship*, another text viewed as ground-breaking both at the time of publication in 1969 and subsequently, Eliot Rose gave standard maternal deprivation theory a new racial twist, warning that 'so many West Indian and West African mothers go to work, the shortage of day nurseries and of licensed facilities of any kind may have grave consequences for this generation of coloured children'.[48] He praised Indian mothers to demonstrate the problems posed by others:

> If the West Indian child is more likely to suffer from a sense of rejection, his need for organized social activity is also likely to be greater than that of the Indian school child. The latter returns from school to the warmth of his family and to a mother who is keeping the home, whereas many West Indian children come back to a house that is empty because their mothers are at work. There is also very little room for them in overcrowded lodgings and they have to seek their recreation outside the home.[49]

Those left with child-minders fared no better and faced 'special hazards'. Although many were 'conscientious and affectionate towards their charges', many others badly mistreated them, depriving them of 'stimulation and play' to the extent that they might 'become retarded and handicapped throughout their school career'.[50]

School was indeed another space in which black children were constituted as a problem, often regardless of their personal family circumstances. In the 1960s the notorious use of 'bussing' - transporting black pupils outside their local catchment areas as a means of arresting the de facto development of racially segregated schools -

clearly cast their very presence as a threat to educational standards. The very high proportion of black children, especially 'disruptive' boys, who were diagnosed as ESN (or educationally sub-normal) also testifies to the institutional racism at work in British schools in this period and seriously challenges Ruth Glass' 1961 claim that in 'the sphere of a public institution and particularly in that of education, it is 'not done' to express colour prejudice'.[51]

On leaving school, black teenagers of the post-war period, like their pre-war predecessors, found it difficult to secure good jobs. A consensus emerged within studies undertaken at this time as to why this was: the general prejudice of white society was to blame but that prejudice had to be considered alongside young blacks' often imperfect English (even where English was their first language), their too high expectations and over-estimation of their abilities and their own unwillingness to move outside their own communities. Some of these studies were conducted by national government and can be read as clear attempts to diagnose and deal with the problem of black youth. In 1965 a special committee of the Youth Service Development Council was appointed to consider what part the Service might play 'in meeting the needs of young immigrants'. Its 1967 report, 'Immigrants and the Youth Service', urged local authorities and local youth agencies to improve job-seeking and recreational facilities for this group. These findings were echoed by the 1969 report of the Select Committee on Race Relations and Immigration entitled 'The Problems of Coloured School Leavers', which concluded that young blacks' social disadvantages were caused by four factors: employment discrimination, deficiencies in education, defective social adjustment and personal and psychological stresses arising from the social position of first and second generation migrants.[52]

In addition to these, Leonard Bloom re-visited Cardiff's Bute Town to see what had changed in the quarter century since Kenneth Little's first 1940s investigations. In the 1960s, there was much interest in race relations in Cardiff and Liverpool, with policy-makers and social scientists looking to them, with their second and third generation black communities, for a glimpse of what a future multi-racial Britain might look like. They made depressing crystal balls. Rose summarised Bloom's Bute Town findings:

> We see a second and third generation which lives in a quasi-ghetto, is denied the opportunities available to white English-speaking immigrants, is less ambitious and achieves less than they do. They are not without white friends outside the area and they have a fair amount of social contact with whites, but they fear that they will meet colour prejudice outside Bute Town. They choose to stay in the coloured quarter because it is safer to trust their own kind. Yet no one relishes the prospect of being cut off from the mainstream of Cardiff city life: it is accepted as a regrettable and unhappy consequence of the insecurity of being coloured in a white city.[53]

An investigation by the Liverpool Youth Organisations Committee (prompted by the 1967 Youth Service report) was equally pessimistic. The position of second and third generation black youth here was 'as dismal' as in Cardiff:

> They suffer the same psychological handicaps, they meet discrimination in employment, and when they move outside the coloured quarter they feel very insecure.[54]

The Liverpool investigators confessed to a 'deep sense of unease'. According to Rose, they believed there was 'a danger of conflict unless an active policy of integration [was] urgently adopted'. On Liverpool and Cardiff's evidence, there was 'no room for complacency about the future of the second generation of post-war coloured migrants'.[55]

These fears were not matched in the 1950s and 60s by any marked increase in actual or reported black youth crime but instead seemed to be fixed on more nebulous but more powerful future threats to social order: the spectre of a racially defined underclass, of racially segregated cities and of violent inter-racial tension, as displayed in the Notting Hill riots of 1958. The 'failure', for whatever reason, of black youth to fall into place signalled the wider failure of the assimilationist project and created a deep anxiety about the future face of Britain, a face where sameness looked certain to be scarred by difference. Debates about delinquency did play a part here. Although commentators often stressed the low crime rate among black communities, they did so in a way that suggested that this could not be expected to last forever. John Lambert's important early study of race, crime and policing showed that by the late 1960s, black children had begun to be over-represented in areas of the juvenile justice system, with 11% of Birmingham approved school girls and 5% of approved school boys being of West Indian, Asian and mixed race origin. Katrin Fitzherbert's research into race and child protection showed that significant numbers of mixed race and West Indian children were being placed in care in the 1960s.[56] Regardless of the many routes by which they entered care, the stigma of the experience fell firmly on the children themselves. As outlined earlier, once in care, black children were often marked out as 'difficult', often spent longer in care homes than white children and often found it harder to get work outside.

By the early 1970s, black youth crime was firmly on political and police agenda. The rise in black arrest and prosecution rates at this time was viewed as having numerous causes. Race became consistently visible within criminal statistics for the first time, with the recording of the ethnic group of victims and perpetrators. Outbreaks of 'racial' violence in the inner cities, for example in south London's Brockwell Park in 1974, seemed to suggest a dangerous new urban tension. They also led to more intense policing of the black community and to the notorious over-use of 'sus' laws (stopping a person on suspicion of having committed a crime) by a police force who came to believe that their control of black areas was vital to their wider authority: to control black areas was to control the wider crisis. The high sentences given to young black street robbers (up to 20 years in some cases) created the impression that a new breed of criminal, 'the mugger', was on the streets who required a new level of discipline. All this threw a new spotlight on old ways in black communities, illuminating sites and scenes, or as Hall and his co-writers put it 'that range of informal dealing, semi-legal practices, rackets and small time crime classically known in all ghetto life as *hustling*', which had been present for many years.[57] The streets, cafes and clubs where they took place also appeared to be closely linked to new youth subcultures, which themselves further stirred the emerging moral panic. Black, Chinese and Maltese cafes and clubs had attracted white youths in the port cities from the early twentieth century. From the 1950s, however, they were taken as emblematic of a new (white) youth culture, offering a space for young white (rather than young black) rebellion and, as Dick Hebdige later argued, setting off an enduring process of cultural appropriation in the music scene and beyond.[58] According to Patterson, white teenagers were regulars at Brixton's coloured clubs and shebeens, attracted by the jazz and the 'easy going and uninhibited' atmosphere where they could 'drink, dance or gamble in peace'.[59] Again, white girls were noted clients. But there was another side to this. Other groups of white youths defined their own subcultures in sharp opposition to the black presence. Many Teddy Boys, skinheads and extreme nationalists wore their racism with pride and did much to fuel inner city racial tension. Once again, the question of black youth culture was difficult to discuss in isolation from white.

By the mid-1970s then, the 'social time-bomb' looked set to go off. Serious riots in the early 1980s in London, Bristol, Liverpool and Birmingham confirmed the worst fears of earlier researchers of race relations. Questions of black delinquency became bound up with questions of wider social disorder. Riots were often initially sparked by police investigations of petty crime alleged to have been committed by black youth, or by the alleged mistreatment of black youth in custody. Some saw these events as very much a product of modern times: economic recession; inner city collapse; high unemployment; Conservative government cuts in public spending; hegemonic crises; and a politicisation and militarisation of the police all featured in the blaming and shaming which followed. But as this chapter has shown, these events need to be located within a much longer history.

Conclusions

The construction of late twentieth century black youth as a social problem rested upon earlier negative constructions of young post-war migrants as well as pre-war and even turn-of-the-century mixed race youth. Concerns raised were common to all these groups and revolved chiefly around the character and abilities of their parents, their alienation from mainstream culture, their poor surroundings, their subversive pleasures and their difficulties in integrating into predominantly white schools, white jobs and white housing. In many ways, these same broad fears - about poverty, parenting, education, employment, leisure and subculture - had also shaped diagnoses of delinquency among white working class children from the early nineteenth century onwards as well as among Irish and Jewish migrants. These markers of Otherness have been surprisingly uniform given the range of different groups they have been used to denote. They were certainly not exclusive, either, to any one group at any one time. That adverts for lodgings in post-war London could infamously proclaim 'No dogs, no blacks, no Irish', shows that twentieth century anti-black racism certainly did not displace anti-Irishness (or anti-semitism) even though it may have decentred them in some areas. But these similarities notwithstanding, some markers of difference were applied more exclusively and more enduringly to black and mixed race people, perhaps most particularly ascribed notions of incivility, promiscuity, unruliness and licentiousness. And clearly, it was *black* youth who attracted such concentrated concern and such pronounced hostility in the 1970s and 1980s.

Notably and perhaps uncomfortably many of these negative constructions of black and mixed race children were articulated and circulated by groups who nominally set out to assist them. University social scientists and social anthropologists, urban researchers, voluntary groups and church charities all helped to establish new discourses of race relations in twentieth century Britain. These discourses ended up fixing difference even while, and in some cases, precisely because, they held up universalist ideals of the inclusive society. By using the disadvantages faced by these children to warn of their future exclusion, they reified those disadvantages and transformed them into 'permanent' aspects of black identity, rather than aspects which could be transformed by social action. In short, they helped to create the view that black youth was more than partly responsible for its own oppression. State agencies, too, played a very significant part here. Schools, youth clubs, and employment, health and housing services as well the police, child welfare departments and juvenile justice organisations all had substantial dealings with black children and adolescents. In contrast to the voluntary sector, state agencies' work in this regard was arguably characterised by efforts to avoid formalised racial differentiation and segregation. Yet, as the experience of black and mixed race children has shown, notions of difference were absolutely central to the definition and delivery of social services and social justice.

Endnotes

[1]   H. Mayhew, *London Labour and the London Poor vols 1-4* (London, 1851-1862); C. Booth, *Life and Labour of the People in London vols 1-17* (London, 1889-1903); M. Carpenter,

Reformatory Schools for the Children of the Perishing and Dangerous Classes (London, 1851); H.M. (Dorothy) Stanley, *London Street Arabs* (London, 1890); A. Morrison, *A Child of the Jago* (London, 1896); W. Booth *In Darkest England and the Way Out* (London, 1890) chapter 8; For an overview of this literature, see H. Cunningham, *The Children of the Poor: Representations of Childhood since the Seventeenth Century* (Oxford, 1991).

2 On Irish communities see, J. Feheney, 'Delinquency among Irish Catholic Children in Victorian London', *Irish Historical Studies* 23:92 (1983) 319-29; J. Davis, 'From 'Rookeries' to Communities': Race, Poverty and Policing in London, 1850-1985', *History Workshop* 27 (1989) 66-85; M. Poovey, 'Curing the Social Body': James Phillips Kay and the Irish in Manchester', *Gender and History* 5:2 (1993) 196-211; M. Hickman, *Religion, Class and Identity: The State, the Catholic Church and the Education of the Irish in Britain* (Aldershot, 1995). On Jewish communities see, E. Black, *The Social Politics of Anglo-Jewry 1880-1920* (Oxford, 1988); R. Livshin, 'The Acculturation of the Children of Immigrant Jews in Manchester, 1890-1930', in D. Cesarini ed., *The Making of Modern Anglo-Jewry* (Oxford, 1990); S.L. Tananbaum, 'Making Good Little English Children: Infant Welfare and Anglicization among Jewish Immigrants in London 1880-1939', *Immigrants and Minorities* 12:2 (1993) 176-199; D. Feldman, *Englishmen and Jews Social Relations and Political Culture 1840-1914* (New Haven and London, 1994). On Italian communities see, L. Sponza, *Italian Immigrants in Nineteenth Century Britain: Realities and Images* (Leicester, 1988). For discussion of these and other migrant communities, see, G. Alderman and C. Holmes eds., *Outsiders and Outcasts* (London, 1993); A. Davin, 'Aliens and Little Britons' in her *Growing Up Poor: Home, School and Street in London 1870-1914* (London, 1996).

3 S. Hall et al, *Policing the Crisis: Mugging, the State and Law and Order* (London, 1978).

4 The phrase is taken from J. Solomos, *Black Youth, Racism and the State: The Politics of Ideology and Policy* (Cambridge, 1988). Other key literature here includes: E. Cashmore and E. McLaughlin eds., *Out of Order? Policing Black People* (London, 1991); M. Keith, *Race, Riots and Policing: Law and Disorder in a Multi-Racist Society* (London, 1993); B. Hudson ed., *Race, Crime and Justice* (Aldershot, 1996). For overview of recent work on black British women and criminal justice, see R. Chigwada-Bailey, *Black Women's Experience of Criminal Justice: A Discourse of Disadvantage* (Winchester, 1997).

5 For overview of emerging work on young black and 'mixed race' women in Britain, see H. Mirza, *Young, Female and Black* (London, 1992); J. Ifekwunigwe, 'Diaspora's daughters, Africa's orphans? On lineage, authenticity and 'mixed race' identity', in H. Mirza, ed. *Black British Feminism: A Reader* (London, 1997), pp. 127-152.

6 P. Gilroy, *"There Ain't No Black in the Union Jack": The Cultural Politics of Race and Nation* (London, 1987), p. 76 and especially chapter 3. See also T. Jefferson, 'The Racism of Criminalisation: Policing and the Reproduction of the Criminal Other', in L. Gelsthorpe and W. McWilliam eds., *Minority Ethnic Groups and the Criminal Justice System* (Cambridge, 1993).

7 M.E. Fletcher, *Report on an Investigation into the Colour Problem in Liverpool and Other Ports* (Liverpool: Liverpool Association for the Welfare of Half-Caste Children, 1930).

8 K. Little, *The Negro in Britain: A Study of Race Relations in English Society* (London, 1947); M. Banton, *The Coloured Quarter: Negro Immigrants in an English City* (London, 1955); S. Patterson, *Dark Strangers* (London, 1963); P. Jephcott, *A Troubled Area. Notes on*

Notting Hill (London, 1964).

9 P. Fryer, *Staying Power: The History of Black People in Britain* (London, 1984) p. 327, p. 331, pp. 349-51.

10 See S. Rose, 'Sex, Citizenship and the Nation in World War II Britain', *American Historical Journal* 103:4 (1998) pp. 1147-76.

11 For more detailed discussion of this separate provision, see P. Cox, *Bad Girls: Gender, Justice and Welfare in Britain, 1900-1950* (forthcoming). See also, L. Marks, "The Luckless Waifs and Strays of Humanity': Irish and Jewish Unwed Mothers in London, 1870-1939', *Twentieth Century British History* 3:2 (1992) 113-37; L.A. Jackson, *Child Sexual Abuse in Victorian England* (London, 2000) pp. 144-51.

12 J. Salter, *The East in the West or Work among the Asiatics and Africans in London* (London, 1896) p. 17.

13 Fletcher, p. 22.

14 See Cox, chapter 3; M. Kohn, *Dope Girls: The Birth of the British Drug Underground* (London, 1992).

15 Ibid, p. 34.

16 Banton, p. 168.

17 Ibid, p. 158.

18 Ibid, p. 158.

19 Ibid, p. 156.

20 Ibid, p. 158.

21 Ibid, p. 181 note 10. See also Anon, 'The Prospects for Coloured Children in England', *The Keys* (Journal of the League of Coloured Peoples) Sept (1937).

22 See M. Sherwood, *Pastor Daniels Ekarte and the African Churches Mission, Liverpool 1931-64* (London, 1994), pp. 51-76.

23 Patterson p. 267-8.

24 Ibid, p. 268 note 2, citing *Daily Mirror* 30 Jan 1957.

25 Ibid, p. 266.

26 Ibid, pp. 265-6.

27 Anon, 'Prejudice Getting Worse', *Times Educational Supplement*, 3 June 1960.

28 Fletcher, pp. 19-20.

29 C. King and H. King, *'The Two Nations': The life and work of Liverpool University Settlement and its associated institutions, 1906-37* (Liverpool, 1938) p. 133. See also, P. Rich, 'Philanthropic Racism in Britain: The University Settlement, Anti-Slavery Society and the Issue of Half-Caste Children 1919-1951', *Immigrants and Minorities* 3:1 (1984) 69-88.

30 Little, pp. 175-6.

31 King and King, p. 132.

32 Fletcher, p. 35.

33 Ibid, p. 37.

34 King and King, pp. 128-9.

35 Little, pp. 178-9.

36 In 1940s Cardiff, for example, Kenneth Little found that 'both Police and Probation Officers bear witness to the comparative absence of delinquency in the coloured district', see Little, p.154.

[37] See L. Tabili, *We Ask for British Justice: Workers and Racial Difference in Late Imperial Britain* (Ithaca, 1994).

[38] For recent work on the migration experience and post-war race relations, see K. Paul, *Whitewashing Britain: Race and Citizenship in the Postwar Era* (Ithaca, 1997) and W. Webster, *Imagining Home: Gender, 'Race' and National Identity, 1945-64* (London, 1998).

[39] Jephcott, p. 90.

[40] E. Rose, *Colour and Citizenship: A Report on British Race Relations* (London, 1969), p. 477. It is not clear how these figures were collated.

[41] On immigration policy, see I. Spencer, *British Immigration Policy since 1939: The Making of Multi-Racial Britain* (London, 1997).

[42] P. Jephcott and T. Lynes, *The Needs of Youth in the West Indies: Survey for the Department of Technical Co-operation* (1962), cited in Jephcott, p. 88.

[43] Patterson, p. 223, see also her figures p. 302.

[44] Patterson estimated that there had been between 200 and 300 cases in London over the period 1956-60, see p. 429.

[45] London Metropolitan Archive Acc2201/B5/1/1-22 Welfare of West Indian unmarried mothers, 1955-62. Colonial Office. Advisory Committee on Social Development. Sub-committee on Women's Work, minutes 24 Sept 1957.

[46] London Metropolitan Archive Acc2201/B5/1/1-22 Welfare of West Indian unmarried mothers, 1955-62. 'The West Indian problem in the city of Nottingham' report by the Organising Secretary for Moral Welfare in the Diocese of Southwell, 1956; 'The West Indian migration problem' minutes of meeting chaired by the Bishop of Kingston, 19 April 1956; 'Welfare of West Indian unmarried mothers' report of multi-agency London conference, 28 May 1956; Colonial Office Advisory Committee on Social Development, Sub-Committee on Women's Work, minutes 24 Sept 1957.

[47] LMA Acc2201/B5/1/1-22 'The West Indian problem in the city of Nottingham' report by the Organising Secretary for Moral Welfare in the Diocese of Southwell, 1956.

[48] Rose, p. 479.

[49] Ibid, p. 485.

[50] Ibid, p. 478.

[51] R. Glass, *London's Newcomers: The West Indian Migrants* (Cambridge Mass., 1961) p. 63. For overview, see S. Tomlinson, *Ethnic Minorities in British Schools: A Review of the Literature, 1960-82* (Aldershot, 1987, 2nd edition). For an early study of ethnicity and schooling, see L. Silberman and B. Spice, *Colour and Class in Six Liverpool Schools* (Liverpool, 1950).

[52] Select Committee on Race Relations and Immigration, *The Problems of Coloured School Leavers* (London, 1969). See Solomos, pp. 75-78 for discussion of this.

[53] Rose, pp. 489-90, drawing on L. Bloom, 'Study of Bute Town, Cardiff' (unpublished at time when Rose was writing).

[54] Rose, p. 490, citing Liverpool Youth Organisations Committee, *Special But Not Separate: A Report on the Situation of Young Coloured People in Liverpool* (Liverpool, 1968).

[55] Rose, p. 490.

[56] J. Lambert, *Crime, Police and Race Relations: A Study in Birmingham* (London, 1970); K. Fitzherbert, *West Indian Children in London* (London, 1967).

[57] Hall et al, p. 351.
[58] See D. Hebdige, *Subculture: The Meaning of Style* (London, 1979).
[59] Patterson, pp. 279-80.

Index

Cunningham, Hugh, 12, 25, 59, 63

Dancing, 29, 47, 51, 145, 163, 172
Death penalty, 8, 50
Debauchery, 48, 49
Demographic change/demographic
    concerns, 2, 31, 143, 149
Deportation, *see also* Emigration,
    forced, Transportation, 43, 44, 148
Dice, 46-48, 50-51
Discernment, *see also* Criminal
    responsibility, age of, 7, 94, 110,
    112-16
Divorce, 147, 150, 151, 152
Doctors, 94, 125, 144
Doli Incapax, see also Criminal
    responsibility, age of, 7
Domestic service, *see also* Service, 15,
    127, 128, 133, 166
Donzelot, Jacques, 16
Drinking, *see also* Alcohol, 50, 51, 172
Drugs, 163
Durand, Yves, 141
Dutch East India Company, 43, 44
Dutch Prison Society, 105, 109, 113-
    17
Dutch Republic, *see also* Netherlands,
    3, 41-52
Dutch Revolt, 43

Education, *see also* Schools/Schooling,
    14, 44, 63, 68, 69, 78, 94, 108, 112,
    113, 114, 128, 152, 168, 170, 173
Emigration, forced, *see also*
    Deportation, Transportation, 43-44
Empey, LaMar T., 59
Employment, *see also* Work, 31, 43,
    114, 125, 128, 166, 170, 171, 173
'Endangered child, the', *see also*
    Neglect, 106, 115-17
England, 15, 34, 46, 52, 60, 62, 68,

124, 142, 159, 164
Environmental causes of delinquency,
    15, 99, 102, 135, 144, 145, 146,
    148, 166
Ethnicity, *see also* Race, 2, 159-73

Families, broken, 146, 147, 149, 150,
    151
Families, elite, 43, 52
Families, noble, 64, 65, 69
Families, single parent, 141, 151
Family breakdown, 2, 141, 149, 151,
    152
Family, reputation of, 11, 41, 45, 51,
    61, 65, 151
'Family, the', changing views of, *see
    also* Parents, 14-17, 131-32, 146-52
Fatherhood, concepts of, 146-52, 165
Felony, 32, 33
Feltham reformatory, 111
Femininity, *see also* Gender, 128-31,
    135-36, 162-4
Fighting, 42, 43, 47
Fitzherbert, Katrin, 171
Fletcher, Muriel, 160, 163, 165-66
Formative experiences, 24-25
Fostering, 127-28
Foucault, Michel, 90, 123
France, 2, 3, 5, 7, 8, 9, 12, 77-85, 105,
    108, 110, 111, 141-53
Frankfurt, 105, 107, 108, 109, 115
French Revolution, 24, 79
Fry, Elizabeth, 110

Gall, Franz-Joseph, 82
Gambling/Gaming, 46, 50-51, 172
Gamet, Alfred, 141, 143-45, 147-48,
    150-51
Garland, David, 93
Gender, 4, 17, 113, 123-36, 152, 166
Gent, 89-101

Germany, 8, 13, 17, 50, 105, 142, 147
Gillis, John, 25
Gilroy, Paul, 160
Girls, 3, 4, 7, 10, 12, 15, 42, 68, 69, 80,
    93, 97-98, 110, 113-14, 123-36,
    148, 161-62, 165-68, 171-72
Goffman, Erving, 91

Habermas, Jurgen, 11, 21, 23
Hacsi, Timothy, 69
Hall, Stuart, 160, 172
Hanawalt, Barbara, 9, 52
Hard labour, 65
Harrington, Joel, 7, 52
Hebdige, Dick, 172
Hereditary causes of crime, 28, 149
Holland, *see also* Netherlands, 7, 46,
    48
Home Office, the (Britain), 162, 164
Homosexuality, 97
Honour, 65
Hospitals, 50, 168
Houses of correction, 16, 27, 61
Hudson, A., 134
Humphries, Steve, 124, 130- 131

Idleness, 45, 48, 63
Illegitimacy, 15, 127, 129, 130, 132,
    135, 136, 163, 164, 166, 168, 169
Immigrants/immigration, 159, 160,
    163, 167-70
Immorality, 126, 128, 147, 164
Industrial schools, 12, 110, 111
Industrialisation, 2, 3, 23, 123, 124
Innes, Joanna, 27
Inspectors, 106, 125, 129, 131-33, 136,
    164
International Penitentiary Commission,
    108
Internment, 59, 60, 62-66, 68, 70
Irish, the, 159, 173

Jephcott, Pearl, 161, 167
Jews/Jewish, 159, 161, 162, 173
Juvenile courts, *see also* Courts, 8, 9,
    16, 30, 62, 148, 151-53
'Juvenile delinquent, the', emergence
    of, 6-11, 23, 92-94
Juvenile institutions, development of,
    11-14, 27, 59-60, 67-70, 92-94,
    108-13, 123, 161-62
Juvenile justice systems, emergence of,
    7-14, 116-17, 123, 143-4, 152-3,
    161-2

Kincaid, James, 78
King, Peter, 23, 32, 60

La Petite Roquette (Paris), 108, 114
Lacassagne, Alexandre, 144
Lambert, John, 171
Larceny, 49
Legislation, 7, 8, 10, 12, 13, 15, 27,
    103, 123, 125, 126, 136
Leiden, 43, 46, 49, 50, 51
Leisure, 2, 3, 47, 50, 51, 52, 173
Life-cycle, 14, 27
Lille, 68
Liverpool, 15, 160-61, 163-66, 170-72
Local authorities, *see also* Civil
    authorities, Municipal authorities,
    Town councils, 13, 85, 170
Lombroso, Cesare, 144
London, 7, 9, 11, 12, 15, 16, 26-29, 32-
    33, 52, 68, 107-8, 110-11, 159-60,
    163, 167-68, 171-73

Maginnis, Robert L., 141
Mandler, Peter, 69
Marriage, 32, 128, 130, 135, 169
Masturbation, 24, 85
Mayhew, Henry, 159
Medical discourses, 3, 82, 99, 126, 145